Foucault 2.0

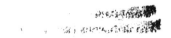

Foucault 2.0

Beyond Power and Knowledge

ERIC PARAS

OTHER PRESS • NEW YORK

Production Editor: Mira S. Park

Text design: Rachel Reiss

This book was set in 10 pt. Palatino by Alpha Graphics in Pittsfield, NH.

10 9 8 7 6 5 4 3 2 1

Library of Congress Cataloging-in-Publication Data
Paras, Eric.
Foucault 2.0 : beyond power and knowledge / Eric Paras.
p. cm.
ISBN: 1-59051-234-0 (978-1-59051-234-0)
Includes bibliographical references and index.
1. Foucault, Michel. I. Title: Foucault two point zero. II. Title.
B2430.F724P35 2006
194—dc22
2005022293

To Edward and Jenifer

Contents

Acknowledgments

This book was not written without the accumulation of a great many debts. The greatest of these have accrued to my mentors at Harvard: David Blackbourn, Peter Gordon, and Charles Maier. Their collective vigilance ensured that no misstep would be fatal. David Blackbourn's timely advice, unwavering support, and manifest concern made everything else possible, and for that I am truly thankful. Peter Gordon provided a model of how intellectual history should be done. He also gave freely and generously of his time to ensure that each and every chapter received critical attention. These pages were invariably written with his sharp eye and discerning ear in mind. Charles Maier was an inspiration from my first arrival at Harvard, and a friend to this project at very critical moments.

I am grateful to the many Harvard faculty who shared their time and lent their guidance during the last seven years. Stephen Greenblatt went out of his way to offer his own reflections, as well as needed background information. Susan Ware provided support and encouragement. Mark Kishlansky gave not only valued advice, but demonstration by example of what it means to be a professional historian. I am particularly grateful to Ann Blair, who made the last years of my graduate school experience the best years. Her genuine interest in my intellectual and professional development, to say nothing of my personal well-being, was more than appreciated. A more dedicated scholar, a kinder individual, and a better mentor could hardly be imagined.

It was among colleagues that many of the book's most pressing questions were first addressed. I owe a large debt to the participants in the Modern European History Workshop at the Minda de Gunzburg Center for European Studies. Its organizers, Katja Zelljadt and Helena Toth, performed a great and selfless service in making available a forum for the presentation of work in progress. Bo-Mi Choi, Deborah Coen, Chris Hilliard, David Meskill, and Sharrona Pearl each provided extremely useful feedback. I would also like to thank Tom Wolf for his insightful comments and thought-provoking conversations.

The helpful and dedicated staff of Harvard's Widener Library was an invaluable aid to my research. So, too, were the staffs of the Fondren Library of Rice University, and of the Bibliothèque Générale of the Collège de France. The Minda de Gunzburg Center for European Studies made the truly innovative aspects of the work possible with a generous research grant. A much-appreciated fellowship from the Mrs. Giles Whiting Foundation enabled me to complete the project with at least a portion of my hair not yet silver.

Finally, I would like to thank my wonderful family. My wife Jenifer shared every moment of this project with me. My son Edward, to my great delight, shared the final ten months. What is good in these pages came from them.

Foucault 2.0

Into the Archive

AFTER MORE THAN FOUR YEARS OF LABOR IN THE FOOTSTEPS OF Michel Foucault, I have developed a tremendous admiration for the man, both as a philosopher and as an individual. Foucault's concern for the preservation and expansion of human freedom was unwavering. In its service, he deployed a critical intellect matched by a writing style of rare sublimity. He had a rich sense of humor, one that perhaps came across most forcefully when he spoke. As I listened in their entirety to twelve of the thirteen semester-length lecture courses that Foucault offered at the Collège de France, Foucault made me gape, reflect, and laugh out loud on a number of occasions, often to my considerable embarrassment. He also taught me more than any other single scholar under whom it has been my privilege to study.

Arnold I. Davidson observed that, with the 1994 publication of the more than three thousand pages of text comprising Foucault's *Dits et écrits*, it had become possible, and even necessary, to undertake a reevaluation of Foucault's place in twentieth-century intellectual life. But, Davidson hastened to add, "We have still not yet reached a firm and stable position, since his courses from the Collège de France, still unpublished, go well beyond anything that can be found in his books or in *Dits et écrits*."[1] Davidson's reflection was, in a way, the starting point for this work.

1

This book represents the first broad-based historical study to make full use of Foucault's lecture courses from the Collège de France. It employs the courses as a complement to publicly available sources, and treats each course as a discrete work with a distinct message. Davidson's contention that access to the course material would have a transformative effect upon our understanding of Foucault's project is, in the event, more than vindicated. Each individual course is a unique and original foray into a research topic that Foucault considered to be of present importance. As distinct from Foucault's major published works, no time lag separated the appearance of these lectures from the spark of interest that prompted them, while three or more years would often elapse between the genesis of one of Foucault's projects and the appearance of a book on the subject. The courses have a stunning immediacy: the lectures are filled with references to current world events, to books that have recently come into print, and even to headlines from the morning's newspaper.

Taken together, the courses represent nearly two hundred hours' worth of speech: a remarkable expansion of the documentation available to us. They reveal a side of Foucault with which many devoted readers of the philosopher would be unfamiliar. Speaking before a large audience week after week on ideas that were typically half-formed and conjectural, the philosopher invariably appeared composed, prepared, and engaged; yet his seriousness of demeanor was a powerful foil for a personality that tended to the playful and irreverent. No transcription of these courses is likely to convey the fact that Foucault's audiences rarely escaped his lectures without laughter—even when the topic of discussion was as grisly as multiple homicide, or as dry as fifth-century baptismal practices.

More significantly, Foucault's courses are dense philosophical explorations. If the French publishing house Le Seuil has begun releasing the course transcriptions as independent books, it is in part because the studies permit that level of scrutiny. *The Punitive Society*, which Foucault taught in early 1973, was a wide-ranging but analytically rigorous investigation of incarceration in the modern world. The philosopher's 1981 offering, *Subjectivity and Truth*, was a textually rich examination of the history of so-called arts of living in the ancient world. Both courses, taken on their own, are valuable works that give insight into the sources that Foucault consulted and the methods that he applied. They are doubly useful to the historian, however, in that each manifestly provides the foundation upon which a book will be constructed: *Discipline and Punish* and *The Use of Pleasure*, respectively.

Perhaps most crucially, the courses show us Foucault's thought at a very high resolution. They allow us to observe an evolution that is taking place at the scale of weeks and months rather than years. In so doing, they eliminate the gaps that had plagued our knowledge of the philosopher, a service that is particularly vital for the early and late 1970s, periods in which Foucault produced no books, but that were nevertheless immensely fruitful for the philosopher. The result is that the courses allow us to ask new questions. The specific question that runs through this work is one that few close readers of Foucault will have escaped asking: namely, *How and why does Foucault go from being a philosopher of the disappearance of the subject to one wholly preoccupied with the subject?*

THE COLLÈGE DE France—the most prestigious institution of learning in France—is today a complex of stately buildings and courtyards spread throughout Paris's fifth arrondissement. Its mission is unusual. Founded by Francis I in 1530, it exists to generate research and to provide instruction to the French public—without charge, without examination, and without diplomas. Professors of the Collège de France, once elected, hold their positions for life. They are required to teach no less than twenty-six hours of each year. The material that they present must at all times be original; it should ideally push the boundaries of existing knowledge.

In 1970, the assembled faculty of the Collège de France voted Michel Foucault to its chair in the history of philosophy. The iconoclastic young author of *Madness and Civilization, Birth of the Clinic, The Order of Things,* and *The Archaeology of Knowledge* would offer instruction to the public at the Collège until his death in 1984 at the age of fifty-seven. As was his right, Foucault gave a name of his own choosing to his chair: he was Professor of the History of Systems of Thought.

No better label could be imagined to describe Foucault's intellectual project as it appeared to him at the end of the 1960s. He would advance the program that he had described in *The Archaeology of Knowledge*: he would study the history of philosophy as the description not of a succession of thinkers, but of the "systematicity" of discourses. He would bring to light the hidden order behind knowledge that gave rise to meaning without the intervention of a subject, an entity that founded the order of representations while remaining outside of it. This was, as Foucault described it in 1968, *the* problem of contemporary philosophy. As he gleefully told an interviewer from *La Quinzaine littéraire*, "Man is disappearing in philosophy, not as an object of knowledge but as a subject of liberty and of existence."[2] This vanishing man-as-subject marked, in Foucault's phrase, the space of an absence in which it had finally become possible to think. He built his own philosophical career upon that cleared space.

In this enterprise, Foucault was joined by a host of others. The notion of the dissolution of the subject—as speaker, as actor, as creator—was the guiding principle of multiple domains of French thought during the 1960s. Its philosophical application was, as Foucault and others recognized, the result of a series of conceptual importations traversing linguistics, anthropology, and finally literature. This phenomenon, which brought together under a single roof researches as diverse as Claude Lévi-Strauss's *The Savage Mind*, Louis Althusser's *For Marx*, and Foucault's *The Order of Things*, has received extensive and exacting treatment by historians. François Dosse's 1991 *History of Structuralism* is the most recent and by far the most wide-ranging contribution to our understanding of this intellectual current; it joins, however, a field already crowded with fine scholarship.[3]

While the emergence of a kind of thinking that forwent a founding subjectivity has received copious attention, far less consideration has been given to the decay and disappearance of this mode.[4] If we know a great deal about the constellation within which Foucault moved when he challenged the hegemony of "man," we are comparatively ignorant of the process by which he abandoned his hard structuralist position and later embraced the ideas that he had labored to undermine: liberty, individualism, "human rights," and even the thinking subject. It is Foucault's migration away from the fire-eating antihumanism of 1968 and his asymptotic approach toward a style of thinking that countenanced a partially autonomous and reflexive subject that form the substance of this study.

What this volume sets out is an intellectual history conducted as a history of *practice*. That is to say, it analyzes Foucault's practice of philosophy—his methods, materials, concepts, and rhetorical strategies—in order to decipher the startling evolution of his understanding of subjectivity. If this is a difficult task, it is because, as will become clear, to confront the trajectory of Foucault's career is to encounter a practice that never stands still, and that scoffs, "No, I am not there where you seek me, but over here, looking on and laughing."[5]

FOUCAULT'S MOST VISIBLE intellectual associates during the early 1960s were members of the French literary avant-garde. It was the small coterie of writers and critics affiliated with the journal *Tel Quel* that gave Foucault his first large-scale public forum, as well as his first stable pool of interlocutors. Founded in 1960 by a committee that included literary wunderkind Philippe Sollers, *Tel Quel* was, in its early years, a site for the presentation of new fiction and poetry, as well as for reflection upon the state of contemporary literature.[6] *Tel Quel*'s proclivities ran in the direction of *nouveau roman*–style experimentation. Two years after its foundation, the journal had already published texts by Artaud, Borges, Bataille, Alain Robbe-Grillet, Francis Ponge, Robert Pinget, Denis Roche, and Umberto Eco. Foucault found in the journal not only an echo of his own long-standing concerns, but a sympathetic audience for a number of his nascent ones.

At a September 1963 conference organized by *Tel Quel* at Cerisy-la-Salle, Foucault described "a kind of extraordinary convergence, isomorphism, resonance" that existed between his explorations and the creative work of the *Tel Quel* authors. He cited Blanchot and Bataille as two figures who had provided a common language for the literary and philosophical explorations occurring under the *Tel Quel* umbrella.[7] What precisely were the interests that Foucault felt he shared with these poets and enthusiasts of the *nouveau roman*? In brief, they were the development of formalism in literature, the disappearance of the writer into the work, and the central position accorded to language. These were, as Foucault saw it, linked themes —or rather, they were three distinct faces of the same theme.

That theme was antisubjectivity. What one saw in the works of the *Tel Quel* writers, Foucault noted, was the "effacement . . . of all proper nouns." They were not interested in creating a literature of the subject, or of the interior, or of imagination; their writing, in fact, served to negate each of these concepts. It was, Foucault wrote, a literature of *aspect*. The language that appeared in books like Sollers's *The Park*:

> is not a language of subjectivity; it opens up and, strictly speaking, "gives place" to something that one might describe with the neutral word *experience*. . . . the separation of distance and the relations of aspect are a matter neither of perception, nor of things, nor of the subject, nor even of what is generally and bizarrely the "world"; they belong to the dispersion of language.[8]

For a writer like Sollers, literature presented not people and things, but rather movements and distances. It offered up a series of relations in which the elements were a matter of indifference. Foucault found this notion of an anonymous discourse extremely thought-provoking. Yet he preferred to treat it less as a stylistic innovation of the *Tel Quel* authors than as their lucid presentation of a general truth about language and being. Language was an inescapable dimension, an exterior of which there was no interior. Meaning, like the subject for whom that meaning existed, was an internal effect of this language, a kind of "folding" within it.

A vision of the auto-creation of meaning-bearing texts is, in fact, at the core of one of Foucault's least-studied books: his 1963 *Raymond Roussel*.[9] The interest that Foucault held in the relatively obscure Roussel was multi-faceted, but centered upon Roussel's creation of a "procedure" for the writing of books. Roussel's works, Foucault wrote, were in appearance elaborate flights of imaginative fancy; in reality, they were the result of a process that was wholly divorced from meaning or intention. Foucault described Roussel's method of composition:

> take a phrase at random—in a song, on a poster, on a visiting card; reduce it to its phonetic elements, and with these reconstruct other words which will serve as the required plotline. All the microscopic miracles [of Roussel's writing] . . . are nothing but the products of the decomposition and recomposition of a verbal material that has been pulverized, tossed up in the air, and allowed to fall in figures that may be called, quite literally, "disparate."[10]

That images as rich and compelling as those in Roussel's *Locus Solus* and *Impressions of Africa* had originated in the arbitrary juxtapositions of phonetic bits—in "the improbable encounter" of meaningless particles of language—was shocking.[11] It was also, Foucault suggested, a kind of lesson. By writing his books in this way, Roussel had installed an image of the functioning of language *within* his own writing. The significance of Roussel's books, that is to say, was that they demonstrated the same phenomenon that Foucault purported to see in the works of the *Tel Quel* authors: a literature that imitated Being itself by generating meaning and subjective voice as an epiphenomenon of the chance foldings of language. This was literature as ontological parable.

Sollers published a complimentary review of *Raymond Roussel* in the summer of 1963, highlighting the affinities between Foucault's critical apparatus and the aims of *Tel Quel*.[12] The philosopher, for his part, continued to hone his ideas on the undoing of the speaker within language. In mid-1963, he expressed—in the literary-philosophical style of *Tel Quel* rather than the "epistemological" style that would characterize his works of the late 1960s—his views on this point: "The collapse of philosophical subjectivity, its dispersion within a language that dispossesses it—but multiplies it in the space of its absence—is probably one of the fundamental structures of contemporary thought."[13] As Foucault's words themselves show, it was possible to overstate the connection. Where Sollers explored the disappearance of characters and Barthes would later write of the death of the author, Foucault tended to transpose the question directly into philosophy and speak of the effacement of the phenomenological subject. Yet *Tel Quel* and the early Foucault manifestly shared a conceptual vocabulary: one in which the work of Blanchot was foundational.[14] While *Tel Quel* would abandon this orientation in the mid-1960s in favor of a thoroughgoing politicization, Blanchot's powerful vision of language as an enveloping totality would continue to inhabit Foucault's thought for a decade and a half to come.

It was the 1966 publication of *The Order of Things* that permitted Foucault to emerge from the specifically literary milieu, and to take his place as one of France's most significant philosophers. Foucault's "book on signs" was a major sensation and a deliberate provocation. With its contentious argument that man was no more than the discursive avatar of a particular historical conjuncture—one fated, moreover, to disappear as suddenly as it had arisen—*The Order of Things* challenged a kind of thought in which man was central. The censured "anthropological" thinking was broad enough to take in the humanism of Pierre Teilhard de Chardin and Antoine Saint-Exupéry, the existentialism of Jean-Paul Sartre and Albert Camus, and the social sciences in their entirety.[15]

As the first chapter of this book will describe, the critical response to Foucault's book was energetic. *The Order of Things* sold well, and Foucault quickly went from a relative unknown to the most identifiable figure of the younger philosophical generation. Existentialist-leaning publications like *Les Temps Modernes* lashed out at Foucault, citing his failed efforts at positivism, his denial of history, and his inability to satisfactorily explain the kinds of cultural changes that his book had described. Yet even the most incensed critics acknowledged the newcomer's brilliance. Michel Amiot wrote:

> Many years have passed since French philosophy has produced a work as magisterial, as striking in its style and erudition, and as apparently original as Michel Foucault's *The Order of Things*. Such compliments as these, it is clear, are often the preface to critique: on this point, we will not buck the trend. But our disagreement, however radical it imagines itself to be, should be taken first of all as a tribute to a monument, the magnitude of which we will attempt to take the measure.[16]

Le Monde Columnist Jean Lacroix added his belief that, "Foucault's work is one of the most important of our times."[17] The recognition that Foucault's presentation of "system" represented a genuine challenge to philosophical orthodoxies was universal.

That challenge was viewed within the context of a vibrant and expanding structuralist movement that, in 1966 and 1967, seemed poised to sweep all before it. Jean-Marie Domenach, the editor of *Esprit*, lamented to his readers that "the fashion is for structuralisms."[18] For Domenach, the essential congruency of Foucault's work with that of avowedly structuralist thinkers operating in other fields was clear. "The three musketeers of structuralism"—Claude Lévi-Strauss, Jacques Lacan, and Louis Althusser —had added a fourth in Michel Foucault. Their shared program, wrote Domenach, was more than apparent:

> A convergent enterprise aims to overturn the order of terms upon which philosophy has lived until now, and to deny the autonomous activity of consciousness: I do not think, *I am thought*; I do not speak, *I am spoken*; I do not act, *I am acted*. It is from language that all departs, and it is to language that all returns. System, which is grasped through it, is proclaimed the master of man.[19]

Domenach had unquestionably put his finger on the point of contention. If the "metaphysics of System" was a kind of "cold, impersonal thought," it was because it was quite literally "built upon the absence of any subject, individual or collective, and ultimately denying the very possibility of a subject capable of autonomous action and expression."[20]

Few experienced the transformative power (or the professional threat) of structuralist modes of thought with the immediacy that Sartre himself did. In a passionate 1966 interview, Sartre castigated his philosophical juniors for their overhasty abandonment of the dialectic and their willingness to suppress serious reflection upon the human condition in the vain pursuit of an intellectual fad. Singled out for special criticism was Foucault, whom Sartre compared to Spengler and branded a writer of "pseudo-histories."[21] Foucault's 1969 *Archaeology of Knowledge* must be understood not only within the context of a structuralist vogue that was already on the wane by 1968, but against the background of a very public intellectual confrontation between Foucault and Sartre. That conflict, which ostensibly pitted history against synchrony and stasis, was ultimately about the relevance of the concept of the subject to contemporary philosophy. However lucid Sartre's arguments, the trend of the times was with Foucault. If *The Archaeology of Knowledge* was not the sensation that its predecessor had been, its reduction of subjectivity from a founding consciousness to a surface effect of anonymous discourse was nevertheless axiomatic by the start of the 1970s.

IT IS ONE of the ironies of Foucault's career that the towering edifice assembled with infinite care and labor in *The Archaeology of Knowledge* was essentially given over to dereliction immediately upon its completion. Foucault never applied the rigorous formal method that he christened "archaeology"; indeed, after 1970, he rarely even used the word. Existing scholarship has explained this phenomenon by highlighting the "methodological failure" of archaeology, or the fact that Foucault's working principles, once transformed from a set of ad hoc imperatives into a formal methodology, revealed themselves to be incoherent and flawed.[22] As the second chapter argues, however, it is less a question of a functional failure than of a shift in the goals toward which Foucault sought to enlist archaeology.

The thorough restructuring that Foucault's thought underwent between 1969 and 1973 was a complex reaction to a very particular set of circumstances. If Foucault was, throughout the early- and mid-1960s, consistently apolitical—even to the point of hostility toward traditional concepts of "engagement"[23]—this ceased after 1968. With his return to France from Tunisia in late 1968, Foucault was pulled into the whirlwind of university politics: a whirlwind that drove him visibly leftward. Surrounded at Vincennes by a faculty that rivaled its students in the stridency of its radical politics, the philosopher entered—first tentatively and later with increasing gusto—into the fray. In 1969, he marched and protested alongside the students of the Latin Quarter. In 1971, he founded a political action group, the Group for Information on Prisons (G.I.P.), meant to highlight conditions within France's prisons.

Foucault's rapid post-1968 politicization provides the essential background against which we must view his desire to reimmerse within the social the very discourses that archaeology had so effectively distilled. In a working atmosphere defined by far-left politics, Foucault increasingly adopted a Marxist rhetoric of class, class-consciousness, repression, and revolution that had been, prior to 1968, notably absent from his work.[24] At the same time, concepts borrowed from his colleague and partner in protest, Gilles Deleuze, allowed Foucault to rethink the relations between discourse and the societies within which they arose. For Foucault was not abandoning a flawed archaeology, but rather integrating it into the study of the social, which had become a far more pressing and immediate-seeming concern to him than the history of the sciences. The method that

Foucault dubbed "genealogy" continued to highlight systematicity, but substituted "power" for "discourse" as the conditioning element within which structured change occurred. From 1973 onward, Foucault possessed a sophisticated new set of concepts with which to analyze social functioning.[25]

Genealogy was developed and tweaked in the confinement-focused courses that Foucault taught at the Collège throughout the early 1970s: *Penal Theories and Institutions*, *The Punitive Society*, and *Psychiatric Power*. It was only with the 1975 publication of *Discipline and Punish*, however, that a broader public became aware of the new direction that Foucault's thought had taken. While the immediate critical reaction to the book unsurprisingly focused on its novel presentation of power—of the phenomena that Foucault labeled "discipline" and "panopticism"—the work's most striking leap forward was arguably in its treatment of the individual social agent. Foucault now offered a vision of the individual as the by-product of the functioning of systems of *power–knowledge*. This "disciplinary hypothesis," which recalled but also visibly departed from the argument of *The Archaeology of Knowledge*, challenged the idea that self-assertion opposed the discourse-driven forms of power at work in modern societies. Rather, Foucault argued, the operation of these discourses "created" the individual subject as the correlate of the case data that they recorded and tracked. Individuality did not preexist a kind of power that tracked and monitored populations at the granular (or "case") level, but rather emerged as the result of that tracking and monitoring.

As the third chapter will demonstrate, Foucault soon questioned the validity of his own analysis. Just as *The Archaeology of Knowledge* had shown itself ill-adapted to the changed political climate in which Foucault was compelled to work after 1968, so did *Discipline and Punish* (and its sister work, the 1976 *History of Sexuality, Volume I*) prove out of step with the philosopher's political engagement of the late 1970s.[26] Foucault's interaction with the so-called *nouveaux philosophes*,[27] a group of young ex-Maoists whose conversion to liberalism marked the first clean break with "the thought of '68," offers a valuable window into the transformation of his own thought during this period. Foucault's public support for the *nouveaux philosophes*, as well as his gradual migration toward their neoliberal, rights-based politics, placed him in opposition not only to his recent work, but to his friend and collaborator Deleuze.

Historians looking at this particular moment in Foucault's career have tended to stress his shift of interest from confinement to sexuality. This volume looks instead to the fourteen important, but largely ignored, articles that Foucault devoted to the Iranian Revolution in 1978 and 1979.[28] The passionate interest that Foucault displayed in the "political spirituality" then rising in Tehran, viewed in conjunction with his changing political affiliations, helps us to understand his emergent interests in religion and ethics. It also elucidates his move away from the "strong" anti-subjectivity position expressed in the disciplinary hypothesis, and his first, tentative moves in the direction of the study of the subject as an independent phenomenon.

THE PERIOD FROM 1979 until Foucault's death witnessed a series of major changes in his practice as a philosopher. He began to spend a significant portion of each year working and teaching in northern California; in the process, he cultivated new acquaintances who would become his most important interlocutors. He turned away from modern forms of power and discourse in order to focus on religious and ethical practices in the ancient world. His genealogical method increasingly gave way to a text-driven hermeneutics that, in a way that recalled the archaeological analyses of the pre-1968 period, deemphasized social and political context. He spoke more openly and with greater frequency about his own homosexuality. Perhaps most interestingly, he shocked many by advocating for human rights—an act that would have been unthinkable for the militant antihumanist of ten years earlier.[29]

The existing historiography has stumbled in treating this part of Foucault's life—and not surprisingly. Foucault published no major works between 1976 and 1984, a fact which has at times forced commentators into speculation about the state of his intellectual project. The fourth chapter of this book will address this lack, examining the transformations in Foucault's practice in dialogue with an exceedingly rich body of evidence: his lecture courses of 1979 and 1980. Those courses, *The Birth of Biopolitics* and *The Government of the Living*, have, owing to their scarcity, been almost wholly absent from the critical literature.[30] Yet they are crucial to understanding the evolution of Foucault's thought—and particularly his understanding of subjectivity—during the final part of his career. *The Birth of Biopolitics* saw the gradual abandonment of genealogy and the initiation of what Foucault student (and eventual editor) Alessandro Fontana called, "a detour . . . to find the individual outside of mechanisms of power."[31] *The Government of the Living*, for its part, showed Foucault for the first time speaking of individuals as independent loci of experience—and as subjects able to *act upon themselves* in the pursuit of certain goals. Autonomy and reflexivity emerged as the characteristics of a subject that could no longer be seen as a mere relay of power.

The consequences of this shift were not long in appearing. One of the most striking aspects of Foucault's thought during these final years was the philosopher's willingness to dissociate himself—sometimes in forceful language—from the style of work that had characterized his entire intellectual career. In an interview conducted shortly before his death, he told his interlocutor:

> In admitting—and I admit it!—that I practiced in *The Order of Things*, *Madness and Civilization*, even in *Discipline and Punish*, a philosophical study essentially founded upon a certain usage of the philosophical vocabulary, rules, and experience, and that I gave myself over to it whole hog, it's certain that, now, I am trying to detach myself from that form of philosophy.[32]

It was the admission of a fairly substantial change of heart. If the works that had brought Foucault to the attention of the world shared an identifiable set of traits—allusiveness, contrarianism, use of visceral imagery, and a willingness (in Edward Said's happy phrase) to draw limitless conclusions from limited French evidence—then all of that was what Foucault sought to slough off in the early 1980s. His published volumes were of a markedly different character—in tone, in pace, in method, and in nearly every other way—than what had come before them. Gary Gutting writes that "Foucault's last writings attain a calm humanity not found in his previous work."[33] Indeed, a mood of placidity pervaded the latter two *History of Sexuality* volumes, just as it did the courses that Foucault taught during these years. The philosopher moved slowly and deliberately in these expositions; he worked from a small pool of texts; he avoided contentiousness; he spoke professorially.

The fifth chapter will look at a number of these stylistic shifts from the vantage point of two of Foucault's most fascinating courses: *Subjectivity and Truth* and *The Hermeneutics of the Subject*. These twin investigations, which together provided the material for the *History of Sexuality* volumes published in 1984, demonstrated not only a new voice, but a new set of commitments as well. Topically, they focused upon so-called "arts of living," or techniques developed in the ancient world that enabled the shaping of one's own existence in line with aesthetic goals. Conceptually, they relied upon the deployment of what might be termed a "prediscursive subject": that is, a subjective nucleus that precedes any practices that might be said to construct it, and indeed one that freely chooses among those practices. Taken together, they offered a vision, unprecedented in Foucault's work, of individual freedom.

Recognizing the role of the arts of living and the prediscursive subject in Foucault's late work helps us to understand several aspects of his post-1980 thought that are difficult to square with a hard constructivist position. These include the tremendous importance attached to creativity and beauty, the resurrection of the notion of "experience," and the latitude granted to the individual subject (as opposed to the determinant "system") in the elaboration of selfhood. It also permits us to see Foucault's extensive late-career commentary upon the Enlightenment as the concomitant of his investigation of subject-formation in antiquity. Finally, it offers insight into the figure who could, by 1984, issue the remarkable statement, "Thought is freedom in relation to what one does, the motion by which *one detaches oneself from it*, establishes it as an object, and reflects on it as a problem."[34]

THERE IS MUCH in Foucault's writings to suggest that he was deeply preoccupied with death. He reflected upon the diversity of rituals with which cultures surrounded the moment of death,[35] and wrote in earnest about his desire to pass out of the world in a kind of painless drug-suicide.[36] He produced no less than two full-length studies—*Birth of the Clinic* and *Raymond Roussel*—that can be considered meditations on death. For all that, he did not believe that writing was a means of conjuring death, nor that what he wrote would in any way preserve him beyond his appointed time.[37]

Foucault, the great reader of Borges, would have appreciated the way his discourse has been preserved in his home institution. The contemporary visitor to the Collège de France discovers a library collection with no centralized catalog—and often, no catalog at all. The auditorium in which Foucault taught has been redone. Any furnishings or mementos that might have recalled his presence are long since vanished. And while Foucault may well have been the greatest philosopher to walk the halls of the Collège in all of the twentieth century, to inquire after the lectures of Foucault is to enter upon a path that has grown quite cold.

Questions beget leads, however, and to ask enough questions is eventually to find oneself in an ill-lit chamber filled with folio volumes and representations of Greek icons. This is the Byzantine Library. And if one follows the librarian there behind the circulation desk to a locked closet in the back room, one comes face to face with a remarkable sight. There among the icons are fourteen years' worth of the collected *énoncés* of philosopher Michel Foucault—ordered just as history would have them.

PART ONE

Discourse

CHAPTER ONE

Surface Effects

Foucault, Sartre, and the Critique of the Subject

The breaking point was reached the day when Lévi-Strauss for societies and Lacan for the unconscious showed us that meaning was in all likelihood nothing but a kind of surface effect, a shimmering, a froth . . .[1]

As best sellers go, Michel Foucault's 1966 The Order of Things was atypical. The four-hundred-page treatise subtitled "An Archaeology of the Human Sciences" was not merely the work of a little-known author. It was also terrifically uncongenial: abstruse in its content, apocalyptic in its tone, laden with footnotes, and overlong. The whole, manifestly intended to give a sense of massive and effortless erudition, succeeded at the expense of rendering itself practically impenetrable to the lay reader. The work's stated aim—to highlight a historically coincident set of discontinuities in the discourses of general grammar, natural history, and analysis of wealth—corresponded to no obvious cultural hunger.

And yet a best seller is just what *The Order of Things* became. It sold through its first print run of 3,000 copies within a week; an additional 5,000 copies were gone inside of two months. Four months after its release, the book registered on the best-seller list of *L'Express*.[2] None of the philosopher's four earlier books had met this kind of public embrace; in a relative sense, none of his subsequent books would be so greeted. Foucault's new volume was a smash success: a must-have book and a topic of conversation.

The enthusiasm generated by *The Order of Things* was, as its author recognized, wholly incommensurate with its subject and intended audience. Yet if the work was consumed far beyond the boundaries of the narrow stratum that might have been expected to appreciate it, that had not a little to do with its character as an intellectual event. Rightly or wrongly, *The Order of Things* was seen and understood within the context of a structuralist wave that swept France in 1966, one that included Jacques Lacan's *Écrits* and Roland Barthes's *Criticism and Truth*.[3] Foucault's work in particular, with its high style and unmistakable swagger, was seen as marking a watershed: it gave substance to the notion that a legitimate challenger-movement to existentialism had at last arrived. *The Order of Things* was the *Being and Nothingness* of a new generation, and Foucault was its Jean-Paul Sartre.

An intellectual *gigantomachia* in the offing: this was the way in which nearly all philosophical journals of the time—and certainly the more mainstream press when it took an interest—chose to cover the publication of *The Order of Things*.[4] Here was a book that did not merely confront but actually scoffed at the Sartrean inheritance: Marxism, meaning, the transcendental, even man himself. How, it was asked, would the venerable king of French philosophy defend his legacy, now that every part of it was under direct attack from a brazen newcomer?

Sartre himself seemed to view the matter in these terms. In the fall of 1966, the elder statesman of French thought lashed out at the new philosophical current. Structuralism, he declared, represented a retrograde movement. It was a denial of history and of the dialectic, a myopic focus on the synchronic and the determinate; it short-circuited the liberatory potential of class struggle, which was an inherently historical process. Sartre singled out Foucault for his most scathing criticisms, calling the younger man the builder of a new ideology, "the last barricade that the bourgeoisie can erect against Marx."[5]

This chapter will lay the groundwork for an analysis of Foucault's later thought by examining his early confrontation with Sartre.[6] It will highlight the philosophical positions that Foucault staked out in the mid- to late-1960s, at the beginning of his rise to intellectual stardom, and argue that his work of this period should be viewed, in large measure, as a response to Sartre's criticisms. The formal "method" of archaeology systematized by Foucault in *The Archaeology of Knowledge* was, as a close analysis of that text reveals, meant as a counterattack: it offered a direct challenge to the ideas that Sartre had set down in his 1960 *Critique of Dialectical Reason* and his 1964 autobiography, *The Words*. This attack was quite successful. If, by the beginning of the 1970s, Foucault no longer targeted Sartre, it was not least because their confrontation had eclipsed the latter thinker. As the decade ended, Foucault's violent rejection of the autonomous subject was *de rigueur*.

How is one to understand *The Order of Things*? Foucault noted in the well-known preface to the work that the book began in response to a passage from Borges.[7] That passage, drawn from an essay entitled "John Wilkins' Analytical Language," sees Borges cite an apocryphal "Chinese encyclopedia." This latter text divides animals into "(a) those that belong to the emperor; (b) embalmed ones; (c) those that are trained; (d) suckling pigs; (e) mermaids; (f) fabulous ones; (g) stray dogs; (h) those that are included in this classification; (i) those that tremble as if they were mad; (j) innumerable ones; (k) those drawn with a very fine camel's-hair brush; (l) etcetera; (m) those that have just broken the flower vase; (n) those that at a distance resemble flies."[8] What is unthinkable for us, Foucault suggested, is not the juxtaposition of these many categories: it is the site in which they would all coexist. The stark impossibility of conceptualizing an order like the one that Borges describes—an order that nevertheless ostensibly possessed value and significance within the confines of a different culture—drove Foucault to pursue the question of the experience of order within Western culture.

While artful, this vignette was misleading. *The Order of Things* was not a playful thought experiment; if its subject was order, its stakes were elsewhere. In the context of French thought in the mid-1960s, *The Order of Things* was a kind of polemic. A strident work, a deliberate and occasionally histrionic effort at idol-shattering, Foucault's book took aim at two targets.

The proximate target was the so-called "sciences humaines," or what in English would be called social sciences, a category that was meant to include psychology, sociology, and economics, but also history and its offshoots, the history of ideas and the history of science.[9] The follow-on target, of far greater importance, was the philosophical movement of existential phenomenology, the kind of thinking introduced into France in the late 1930s by Jean-Paul Sartre.

What both of these styles of thought shared, as Foucault would argue, was a concern with *man*. The human sciences were that set of disciplines "that takes as its object man insofar as he is empirical."[10] Existentialism was likewise focused on the figure of man as heroic agent and meaning-giver to a meaningless world. Foucault's claim was that this shared object was a false one. "Man" was not the oldest and most immediate theme of reflection. On the contrary, he was a new object, one formed in the brief historical interstice between two modes of knowledge rooted in *language*. Let us briefly examine this surprising argument.

Foucault undertook, in *The Order of Things*, a study that had strong surface similarities with his previous major efforts, *Madness and Civilization* and *Birth of the Clinic*. The idea common to all of them was that, through the empirical study of certain historical "discourses"—as, for instance, psychology and medicine—we can discover structural regularities that are of far greater significance than the manifest *content* of those discourses. *Birth of the Clinic*, to take an example, had begun by offering a demonstration of the sharp discontinuity between a medical description written in the 1760s, and another written in the 1820s. It was not simply that the two descriptions used non-overlapping concepts, but that, in a fundamental sense, they were not speaking the same language.[11] Foucault set out to describe the change whereby one kind of medical knowledge—a quasi-zoological discourse based on the classification of illnesses—gave way, within a very short period of time, to a wholly new form of medical knowledge, this one anatomo-clinical and grounded in the observation of damaged tissues. The change was symbolized in the transformation of the eighteenth-century doctor's question, "What do you have?" into that with which his counterpart of the nineteenth century began the clinical dialogue: "Where does it hurt?"[12]

Foucault had styled *Birth of the Clinic* an "archaeology of the medical gaze." In a parallel way, *The Order of Things* was an archaeology of the human sciences.[13] It was an attempt to delineate a massive historical discontinuity in not one, but three discourses: biology, economics, and medicine. But the very nature of that project widened the scope of Foucault's conclusions. For if one discourse completely transformed itself at a given moment in history, that was noteworthy; but if *three* discourses transformed themselves all at the same time, didn't it suggest that something deeper was going on? Foucault sought to isolate and identify that deeper something. He wrote, a propos of economics:

> A monetary reform, a banking custom, a commercial practice can be rationalized, developed, maintained or dissolved each according to its appropriate form; they are always founded upon a certain knowledge: *a dark knowledge that does not appear in itself* in a discourse, but the necessities of which are precisely the same for abstract theories and speculations without any seeming connection to reality.[14]

This "dark knowledge" that stood behind and indeed founded both speculative discourse and everyday practices was what Foucault would come to call the *épistémè*. The sway of this *épistémè* was not to be restrained. "In a culture and at a given moment," he wrote, "there is only one *épistémè* defining the conditions of possibility of all knowledge."[15]

As in previous works, Foucault placed the key moment of change at or around the French Revolution. It was then, he suggested, at the end of the eighteenth century and the beginning of the nineteenth, that what might be called the "classical" *épistémè* gave way to a properly "modern" one. This was not to say that the epistemic shift in question was unique. On the contrary, Foucault implied that revolutions in our knowledge occurred with some regularity. It was only in the mid-seventeenth century, or a mere hundred and fifty years prior to the dawn of modernity, that the "Reniassance" *épistémè* had given way to the classical one. In this case, as in the more recent shift, "the fundamental arrangement of the entire *épistémè* of Western culture [was] modified." In both instances, it was not a matter of a superficial shift in people's opinions and beliefs; it was rather a question of "modifications that altered knowledge itself, at that archaic level that makes possible both knowledge and the mode of being of that which is to be known."[16]

If, Foucault would have suggested, he had foregrounded the circa-1800 transformation, it was because the modern *épistémè*, and it alone, had given rise to man. The "man" with which the human sciences concerned themselves—that is to say, the figure who is both the subject and object of knowledge—was unthinkable within the confines of classical thought. The eighteenth-century *épistémè* was organized around language and representation, and in particular around interlaced representations in the form of the *table*. If adequate representations of all things were possible, it was nevertheless the case that "he for whom the representation exists, and who is himself represented in it," was not on the table: he remained unrepresentable. The figure in which the entire system came together could not himself be represented within the system.[17] This is what Foucault meant when he wrote:

> Before the end of the eighteenth century, *man* did not exist. . . . The Classical *épistémè* was articulated along lines that in no way isolated a domain proper and specific to man. . . . man, as a dense and primary reality, as a complex object and sovereign subject of all possible knowledge, finds no place there.[18]

With the passage to modernity, on the other hand, there emerged the paradoxical figure that, while a finite creature, was yet capable of serving as the foundation of all knowledge. If man was the universal knower, he nevertheless, in the very positivity of his knowledge, encountered his own finitude at every turn: his discourses showed him that he was merely an object of nature to be deployed by systems (of language, of production, of living beings) that manifestly preceded him.[19] Kant's *Critique of Pure Reason* perhaps revealed the birth of an empirical-transcendental "man" most clearly, but it was, Foucault asserted, common to all discourses. Hence, an analysis of wealth focused on exchange-value gave way to an *economics* focused on labor; a general grammar rooted in the representational nature of language saw itself transformed into a *philology* based on the evolution of words; a natural history based on the classification of beings devolved into a biology based on the phenomenon of life. In all cases, phenomena gained a thickness and a historicity that had been absent in classical thought; in all cases, one found man, "a being such that, in him, one gained knowledge of that which made all knowledge possible."[20]

And it was precisely this figure of man, Foucault cryptically asserted, that was now—in the 1960s—poised to disappear. The signs of the appearance of a new *épistémè*, one that replaced and upended the modern, were unmistakable. Foucault found them in the growing importance of *language*. In theoretical discourse, linguistics was emerging as a model for the analysis of formal relationships in other areas; in contemporary literature, there was an ever-increasing and self-referential concern with literature itself as an authorless event, as an effect of language. A nascent *épistémè* thus promised to be, like the classical one that preceded modernity, organized around language. "Is man," he asked, "having formed when language was dispersed, not likely to disperse when language reassembles?" Foucault himself had no doubt that this would be the case, and that man would prove to have been little more than "a figure between two modes of being of language." When the structure that supported the form of modern thought finally gave way, man would disappear, in the philosopher's famous phrase, like a face in the sand at the edge of the sea.[21]

WHAT DID IT mean that Foucault chose to present his argument in this way? It was, first and foremost, an indication of the distance that he had traveled as a thinker since the beginning of the decade. As noted in the introduction, Foucault's perspective through at least 1964 paralleled that of the Blanchot-inspired authors affiliated with the journal *Tel Quel*: human existence was, in this view, a kind of fold in language.[22] After that date, he swung rapidly toward a style of analysis inspired by structuralism and the French history-of-science tradition. In this sense, *The Order of Things* represented a meaningful advance.

Foucault showed himself no longer content to present the transaction in which subjective experience emerged from "the murmur of language" as a simple and ahistorical one; indeed, the notion of experience itself was increasingly suspect in his eyes, and the word appears almost nowhere in *The Order of Things*. What was replacing it was an ontological schema in which *discourse*—now occupying the same position formerly reserved for "language" or Being—modified itself incrementally over time, thereby giving rise to discrete *subjectival positions*.[23] As Foucault noted in 1967:

> For a long time, there was within me a kind of ill-resolved struggle between the passion for Blanchot and Bataille and on the other hand, the interest that I bore in certain positive studies, like those of Dumézil and of Lévi-Strauss, for example. But, ultimately, these two orientations . . . contributed in equal measure to drive me to the theme of the disappearance of the subject.[24]

Viewed from the perspective of the end of the 1960s, *The Order of Things* appears as a kind of hybrid work between Foucault's *Tel Quel* writings and the quasi-positivistic methodology that he would christen "archaeology." From 1966 to 1968, as Foucault labored on *The Archaeology of Knowledge* in Tunisia, any residual language-mysticism would be allowed to wither on the vine.[25]

But Foucault was right to see that both strands of thought had driven him toward the theme of the subject's disappearance. The argument of *The Order of Things*, with its emphatic rejection of the figure of man, was at its heart an attack on the philosophy of the autonomous subject. The denial of man was intended as a challenge to those currents of thought, still flowing in France in the mid-1960s, that invoked a "strong" individual: a coherent, singular Cartesian subject. Foucault's assertion that man was a nineteenth-century invention, and one whose time was all but finished, must be understood as the obverse side of his claim, in an interview conducted shortly after the publication of *The Order of Things*, that Sartre's *Critique of Dialectical Reason* was "the magnificent and pathetic effort of a man of the nineteenth century to think the twentieth century."[26] To say that "man's" time was up was another way of saying that a philosophy grounded in subjectivity had no future—was, in fact, already obsolete; the claim that man was "nineteenth-century" was less a historical description than the deployment of an epithet.

The Order of Things was meant to be an open challenge to these schools of thought. Foucault proclaimed the need to overcome "the stubborn obstacle that is obstinately opposed to future thought," and vowed opposition

to all those who still wish to speak of man, of his reign or of his liberation; to all those who still pose questions as to what man is in his essence; to all those who wish to start with man in order to have access to
the truth. . . . who do not wish to think without first thinking that it is
man who thinks.[27]

In this struggle against a retrograde existentialism, Foucault presented
structuralism as an antidote, even as the manifestation of the nascent
épistémè. The unsubtle praise, in the book's penultimate section, of the
"counter-sciences" of psychoanalysis and ethnology was both a doff of the
cap to Foucault's (then) more prominent colleagues Jacques Lacan and
Claude Lévi-Strauss, and an implicit declaration that only structuralism
was equal to the task of contemporary philosophical reflection.[28]

The critique of the autonomous subject that Foucault launched in *The
Order of Things*—and the concomitant attack on existentialism and phenomenology—was repeated and amplified in a crucial interview that Foucault
gave in the spring of 1966. He told interviewer Madeleine Chapsal that his
philosophical generation had come to the realization, as early as 1950, that,
"we were very, very far from the preceding generation, from the generation of Sartre, of Merleau-Ponty."[29] His generation—the cohort that had
been too young to take an active role in the war—respected but could not
share the passion of its predecessors for life, politics, and existence. "We,"
he observed, "we have discovered something else, a different passion: the
passion for the concept and for what I would call 'system.'"[30]

A "passion for system" was a remarkably honest and concise description of French structuralism. Across a broad spectrum of activities, self-
styled structuralists were—in 1966 as in no year before or since—looking
to understand the ways in which systematicity and not intent determined
sense. Roland Barthes, having just completed his seminal structuralist
manual *Elements of Semiology*, was at work upon *The Fashion System*, a
semiotic interpretation of dress and style.[31] Jean Baudrillard, a student of
Barthes, was already at work on *The System of Objects*, a structural interpretation of modern consumption and collecting.[32]

All of these efforts were ways of thinking through the coherence of ordered cultural phenomena without having recourse to a transcendental
subject that would be *responsible* for that order. Foucault's book did just
this. In contrast to the philosopher's prior works, which had nibbled around
the edges of the question of subjectivity, *The Order of Things*, as Domenach
noted, directly challenged the "modern" conception of subjectivity: the
freestanding, thinking, speaking subject that encounters the world and
creates meaning therein. The clarity of this challenge was intimately related
to Foucault's departure from the *Tel Quel* orbit. As long as archaeological
thought was permeated with Blanchot's notion of "experience," it was
impossible for him to make a radical break with the philosophy of the subject; as *Madness and Civilization* demonstrated, the ontological centrality of
language continually collided with the manifest importance attributed to
the lived experience of individuals. With *The Order of Things*, Foucault began
to purge his work of its Blanchot-inspired elements. Words like *noise* (*bruit*),
monotone, *murmur*, *frothing* (*moutonnement*), and *bleating* (*bêlant*), all of which
had been used to describe the disquieting awareness that an endless and
indifferent language speaks through us, vanished utterly from Foucault's
working vocabulary. So, too, did the notion of experience.

The "systemic" thought that Foucault increasingly advanced was, as its
opponents had been correct to recognize, in synchronicity with other challenges to the subject launched during these years. To pronounce the names
of Barthes, Lévi-Strauss, Derrida, Althusser, and Lacan is to capture but
the smallest fraction of the structuralist or structuralist-inspired research
taking place in the second half of the 1960s. But the recourse to formalism—
in France particularly—was a pervasive phenomenon that extended far
beyond the boundaries of philosophy and the social sciences. In the visual
arts, the figures affiliated with the Supports/Surfaces group attempted, from
1966 onward, to dispense with the notion of artistic subjectivity, and to create a minimalist vocabulary at once raw and "structured." The theme of the
matrix—the woven net, the grid, the pattern—is a constant in the work of
Claude Viallat, Patrick Saytour, Daniel Dezeuze, and Marc Devade.[33] Likewise, the inroads of formalism into French letters is nowhere clearer than
in the case of Philippe Sollers, whose 1968 *Nombres* and 1971 "Lois" presented readers with a kind of literary machine; or as Sollers himself described them, "a square matrix engendering narration and reflection."[34]

What did Foucault in particular mean when he invoked the idea of system? Sartre, Foucault explained, had responded to the temptation of the absurd by asserting that *meaning* was all around, that the individual subject was a maker of meaning. For a number of reasons, Foucault said, his own generation could no longer accept this response. It had come to see meaning itself as a matter for interrogation. Asked by Chapsal when the change had occurred, he responded:

> The breaking point was reached the day when Lévi-Strauss for societies and Lacan for the unconscious showed as that *meaning* was in all likelihood nothing but a kind of surface effect, a shimmering, a froth, and that which traversed us deeply, that which was before us, that which upheld us in time and space, was *system*.[35]

Meaning was not the sovereign creation of autonomous subjects. It was the surface effect of a "system" that preceded human existence. This system was to be understood as a set of relations that obtained, and underwent transformation, independently of the elements that it linked. "Before all human existence, all human thought," Foucault said, "there must already be a knowledge, a system, that we are rediscovering."[36]

Paul Ricoeur, looking on unmoved at the structuralist vogue, argued that "the type of intelligibility that is expressed in structuralisms" triumphed wherever one worked upon a closed system or completed corpus, established an inventory of elements, placed the elements in relations of opposition, and established an algebra or "combinatory" of these elements and oppositional pairs.[37] While Foucault would perhaps have found Ricoeur's language reductive, on the whole he would have been in agreement. Structural linguistics, Foucault noted in 1968, had pioneered the idea of transformational—that is, combinatorial—grammar. "It is something like this method," he noted, "that I try to introduce into the history of ideas, of sciences, and of thought in general."[38]

SARTRE'S LACK OF regard for structuralist analyses—throughout the early 1960s, he sparred with Lévi-Strauss over the limits of the structuralist enterprise—was well-known and surprised no one. What did give surprise was the virulence of the response that *The Order of Things* stirred up in Sartre. The work was undoubtedly a provocation. But Sartre treated Foucault's brand of structuralism as a unique evil: a tangible menace that philosophy ignored at its mortal peril.

In October of 1966, the French philosophical journal *L'Arc* published an issue focused on the theme of "Sartre Today." A number of prominent thinkers offered their reflections on the impact and significance of Sartre's work almost a quarter of a century after the appearance of his seminal *Being and Nothingness*. Sartre himself then responded to an interviewer's questions. *L'Arc* was not an existentialist enclave like *Les Temps Modernes* or *Esprit*: only six months before, it had published a lengthy piece by Foucault on the literary voice of Jules Verne.[39] Nevertheless, Sartre used the opportunity represented by the interview to lambaste Foucault and other front-rank structuralists in exceedingly direct language.

What the young generation of French thinkers had in common, Sartre claimed, was a disturbing tendency to deny history. The success of Foucault's book was proof of this. Foucault offered, to speak properly, not an archaeology but a geology: a series of layers, each defining the conditions of possibility of a type of thought that was once dominant, forming the subsoil of the present. But, Sartre continued:

> Foucault doesn't tell us what would be the most interesting thing: namely, how each kind of thought is constructed starting from these conditions, or how men pass from one thought to another. For that, he would have had to interpose praxis—thus history—and it is precisely this that he refuses to do.

Certainly, Sartre said, Foucault's perspective remained more or less historical, in the sense that it distinguished epochs, and looked to the before and after—"But he replaces the motion picture with the magic lantern, movement with a succession of immobilities."[40] Foucault's magic lantern was a stack of synchronic snapshots. Movement was absent and unexplained. So-called archaeology was unable to engage with, unable even to acknowledge, the living flow of history and its actors.

Sartre revisited the fact that *The Order of Things* had enjoyed a great commercial success. This, he argued, was the clearest demonstration that its author had nothing new to offer. Foucault's treatise was a book that people had been waiting for; "Now a truly original thought is never expected." Rather than offering a genuinely new way of understanding the world, Sartre said, Foucault had simply served up a fashionable hodgepodge: "an eclectic synthesis in which Robbe-Grillet, structuralism, linguistics, Lacan, and *Tel Quel* are utilized each in turn to demonstrate the impossibility of historical reflection."[41]

But if Foucault lacked precision and originality, he could not even claim the merit of good intentions. Sartre was nowhere more scathing than in his attack on the political motivations that underlay *The Order of Things*. Behind the veil of a critique of history, he asserted, Foucault was manifestly targeting the entire political project of the progressive left. "It's about creating a new ideology," he explained, "the last barricade that the bourgeoisie can erect against Marx." It was possible for a serious historian not to be a communist; but it was not possible for serious history to be written without placing material life, relations of production, and praxis at the center of the analysis. Foucault, unable to surpass Marxism, had thus attempted to suppress it. His system-building represented a most reactionary brand of hubris.[42]

Foucault, like so many other would-be Lévi-Strausses, had failed to recognize that there were limits to the applicability of structural analysis. The structural—that is to say, nondialectical—perspective was, by itself, simply incapable of explaining historical phenomena. It was not that "structures" didn't exist; it was rather that their existence was merely "a moment of the practico-inert." The essential point, which structuralists were invariably unwilling to admit, was that all human creation was a matter of seizing and overturning these structures. Auguste Comte's expression, "Progress is the development of order," was, Sartre commented, relevant in this context:

> It applies perfectly to the idea that the structuralists have of diachrony: man is in some way developed by the very development of structure. For my part, I don't believe that history can be reduced to an internal process. History is not order. It is disorder. Let us say, it is a rational disorder. At the very moment in which it maintains order, which is to say structure, history has already begun to undo it.[43]

History was a teeming disorder in which, if men encountered structures that preceded them, it was nevertheless their place to take them in hand and overturn them through action. The structuralists' abjuration of the thinking, acting individual was thus philosophically indefensible and politically repugnant at the same time.

The *L'Arc* interview enjoyed a wide diffusion. As Foucault's own notoriety continued to grow throughout late 1966 and into 1967, it was rare that his interviewers did not, at some point, reference Sartre's critical comments. The challenge to Foucault was direct and personal. The response would be in kind.

THROUGHOUT HIS CAREER, Foucault's preferred method of intellectual confrontation was to initiate conflict with his books, but do the actual ground fighting in journals and the mainstream press. Rather than reinforcing his established works with responses to critics, he waited for the smoke to clear, then engaged his individual opponents in highly visible media debates. This would be his *modus operandi* in dealing with George Steiner in 1971,[44] and with Jacques Derrida in 1972.[45] His encounter with Sartre stood as a noteworthy exception to this practice.

For Foucault showed himself determined to have the final word in this conflict. While he did not resist the temptation to lash out in print when the opportunity presented itself, his strategy throughout 1967 and 1968 was essentially a long-term one. He plotted a massive counterattack in the form of a methodological treatise—the only such book he would ever write. *The Archeology of Knowledge* was more than a codification of the philosophical principles that underlay Foucault's empirical works. It was a pointed response to the criticisms that Sartre had launched in the *L'Arc* interview; a lampooning of core Sartrean ideas as voiced in the latter's autobiography, *The Words*; and an attempt to outgun Sartre's *summa*, the *Critique of Dialectical Reason*, with a magnum opus of the subject's dissolution.

From 1966 through the end of 1968, Foucault worked on the draft of *The Archaeology of Knowledge* in the relative seclusion of Sidi-Bou-Saïd in Tunisia. He manifestly understood the work to be a response to his critics, with Sartre first among them. For this reason, he was greatly displeased by the decision of *La quinzaine littéraire* to publish in March 1968 an interview in which he expressed strong criticism of Sartre. His words, Foucault felt, had been spoken off the record, and presented to the public without his permission. But more importantly, as he angrily informed the review's editors: "For eighteen months, I have held back from any kind of reply, because I am working to give a response to questions which have been posed to me, to difficulties that I have encountered, to objections that have been formulated—and among others, those of Sartre."[46] This reply, Foucault affirmed, would be published shortly. It would provide a rebuttal far more faithful to his actual opinions than decontextualized comments elicited in private conversation.

The Archaeology of Knowledge appeared precisely one year later, in March of 1969. It was a work of immense ambition. In just under three hundred pages, Foucault attempted to found a new discipline, one that would be organized not around the study of the history of *ideas* (in the sense of opinions and beliefs, or what Foucault called "doxology"), but rather the study of the history of the conditions of possibility of ideas. This discipline, which Foucault had ostensibly practiced without having yet formalized it, in *Madness and Civilization* and *Birth of the Clinic*, was *archaeology*.

Archaeology, Foucault wrote, was not—as its use of the Greek *arche* might suggest—an exploration of origins. It was, rather, a descriptive enterprise: a description of the *archive*. This last was itself a term of art for Foucault. It referred not to the sum of texts produced and conserved by a culture; rather, the archive was "the law of what can be said, the system that fixes the appearance of statements as singular events."[47] The description of the archive was meant to elucidate regularities within the seemingly fortuitous irruption of discourse; those regularities, in turn, would allow one to discern the governing principles that gave bodies of knowledge their particular form. Archaeology, that is to say, was the attempt to ascertain the rules governing the production of discourse for a given culture at a given time.

Its practice entailed both a negative and positive component. The negative aspect was a radical critique of the concepts and methods of the history of ideas as traditionally practiced. This meant calling into question the utility of analytical categories that the history of ideas deemed natural and necessary: influence, evolution, and "mentality" or "spirit of the age." It also meant abandoning all the too-familiar subdivisions of discourse: the work, the genre, and the author.[48] The positive aspect involved the construction of an alternative set of categories within which one might think the history of knowledge. This latter task yielded a basket of counterintuitive and often-neologistic concepts: statement, discursive formation, positivity, archive, and several dozen others.[49]

What was the point of this hard labor of substitution, whereby timetested (and seemingly incontestable) categories like author and work were jettisoned in favor of new and dubious successors? It was to reconfigure the history of knowledge in such a way as to elide the notion of the thinking, speaking subject. It was to demonstrate, as Foucault wrote with characteristic brio, that:

> so many things said, by so many men, for so many millennia, did not surge forth according to the laws of thought alone, or on account of the mere play of circumstance; that they are not simply the signaling, at the level of verbal performances, of that which had developed in the order of the spirit or in the order of things; but that they appeared thanks to an entire set of relations that are the proper characteristics of the discursive level; that rather than chance figures grafted somewhat arbitrarily onto mute processes, they are born according to specific regularities; in short, that if there are things said—and those things only—we need not seek explanation from the things that get said or from the men who say them, but from the system of discursivity, from the enunciative possibilities and impossibilities that it establishes.[50]

The archaeologist prided himself on his commitment to a rigorous neutrality where discourse was concerned. His concern was not to interrogate texts so as to ascertain their true meaning: meaning at no point entered the picture. Still less was it to detect the subjective intentions that revealed themselves in discourse. The essential was to observe and weigh the statements themselves, and to discover the structural similarities that made a given kind of statement possible at one time and not at another.

The history of knowledge, as observed by the archaeologist, was not the story of the progress of reason; it was certainly not the recounting of a narrative wherein men's thoughts arose and made their impact in the world. The history of knowledge was the unfolding of an anonymous process: a process of the formation and transformation of bodies of *statements* according to isolable rules. Foucault could not emphasize enough that his intended domain was this raw and apparently undifferentiated mass of statements. Attribution was irrelevant. Proper nouns were almost entirely excluded from *The Archaeology of Knowledge*.

For what needed to be dispensed with was the notion that men's thought was their property, an object of their own creation. The painful truth that needed to be embraced was that men were the wholly interchangeable speakers of *systems of thought* that transcended them. Archaeology did not exist to exalt the voices of those who speak, but to demonstrate that every speaker is a ventriloquist's dummy.

FOR ALL THAT *The Archaeology of Knowledge* might have seemed an internal affair for historians of science, its sights were trained directly on Sartre. If there was an unusually sharp and defensive tone to the work, it was because a negative task—the refutation of Sartre's criticisms—was one of its essential organizing principles. It not only acknowledged and countered every one of the arguments raised by Sartre against Foucault in his interview with *L'Arc*, but ultimately took the offensive and challenged several of the elder philosopher's core beliefs. Let us first examine the defensive elements.

Foucault's introductory essay was written almost entirely in the reactive mode. Sartre, it will be remembered, had labeled Foucault's work a synthesis of structuralism and other fashionable literary movements. Foucault refused to allow Sartre to so define his archaeological project, writing in his introductory essay, "It is not a matter of transferring to the domain of history—and particularly the history of knowledge—a structuralist method that has proved itself in other fields of analysis." The refusal of the structuralist label was clear. It was also disingenuous. Foucault himself, as noted earlier, had said in 1967, "What I attempted to do was to introduce structuralist-style analyses into domains where they had not to this point penetrated: that is to say, into the domain of the history of ideas, the history of knowledge, the history of theory."[51]

Foucault also struck back at Sartre for his assertion that archaeology "replaces the motion picture with the magic lantern," and that it merely presented a succession of immobile scenes, or tableaux.[52] In a piquant foot-note—one of only seven in the entire work—he spewed: "To the last stroll-ers, must we explain that a 'table' . . . is formally a 'series of series'? In any case, it is not a little fixed image that one sets in front of a lantern for the greater deception of children—who, at their age, certainly prefer the vivacity of motion pictures."[53]

Foucault thus offered two criticisms. Firstly, he suggested—again, some-what disingenuously—that Sartre had misunderstood his employment of the term "tableaux," thinking it to mean "two-dimensional images." Sec-ondly, he parried the accusation of puerility, implying that motion pictures (and, implicitly, an understanding of history as essentially linear and cin-ematic) were the real province of children.

More elaborate was the response to Sartre's accusation that Foucault's critique of history was, in reality, a targeting of Marx and Marxism. Marx, Foucault argued, had been responsible for a great and liberating act of "decentering" in historical discourse: he had moved historical analysis away from a unified subject of history (of the Hegelian variety) to focus instead on relations of production, economic determinations, and class struggle. What was *against* Marx, Foucault wrote, was the persistent effort to reinstate that sovereign subject in the name of humanism. Sartre had written, in the *Critique of Dialectical Reason*, "if culture is more than an ac-cumulation of heteroclite knowledge and dates . . . , then what I know ex-ists both within me and outside me as a field of particular tensions; bodies of knowledge, however disparate their content or the dates of their appear-ance . . . , are linked by *relations of interiority*."[54]

Sartre suggested in this passage that all knowledge—however seem-ingly limited and fractured—derived from participation in a "diachronic process of totalization": that is, a singular historical process of develop-ment. Foucault argued that this kind of thinking, not his own, represented a betrayal of the Marxian tradition. Marx had anticipated the structural-ists in dispersing the subject of history. "Continuous history," on the other hand, "is the indispensable correlate of the founding function of the sub-ject."[55] To posit a coherent and unified subject—a subject who imbued his world with meaning, and who was the sovereign creator of his own knowl-edge—was likewise to posit a kind of linear, teleological narrative in which the march of history was also the story of the progress of reason.

This line of argument continued when Foucault confronted Sartre's claim that, insofar as history was structured, this structuration was merely "a moment of the practico-inert": an objective constraint to be overcome through essential human freedom. Such an assertion, Foucault implied, represented a misunderstanding of the nature of the regularities that archaeology observed. The "system" that archaeology discerned was not an object to be spontaneously deployed (or overcome) by a subjectivity that ran still deeper; it was, on the contrary, that which rendered the *apparent* spontaneity of actors possible. He wrote: "Behind the finished system, what the analysis of formations discovers is not life itself, boiling up and still uncaptured; it is an immense thickness of systematicities, a dense set of multiple relations."[56] The attempt to seize discursive regularities after the fact and reinsert them into the "lived experience" of actors—actors who were nothing but points *within* that network of discursive regularity—was destined to fail. There was no freer reality outside of discourse, no primal prediscursive state from which the latter might be taken in hand and mastered by consciousness. Prefiguring an argument that he would employ later in respect to power, Foucault wrote, "The dimension of discourse is all there is."[57]

Finally, Foucault attempted to reclaim the terms of the argument from Sartre. The latter had painted Foucault as the paragon of structuralism, and therefore as the arch-denier of history. This, Foucault countered, had simply been a form of misdirection, for what was at issue in *The Archaeology of Knowledge*, as in *The Order of Things*, was neither structure nor history. He explained:

> this work, like those that have preceded it, is not inscribed—at least not directly or in the first instance—in the debate over structure (as opposed to genesis, to history, to becoming); but in the field where . . . questions of human being, consciousness, origin, and the subject make their appearance.[58]

While the immediate matter of discussion was history (and the structure of history), Foucault explained, the stakes of the argument were elsewhere. The reason that the structuralists' approach to the past had aroused such vociferous dissent in certain philosophical quarters was that it appeared to undermine the autonomy, or even the existence, of the human subject.[59]

Sartre's description of Foucault's work as antihistorical was thus a kind of stalking-horse; the real danger of structuralism was not that it would cripple history, but that it would dissolve the *subject* as conscious creator of history.

THE MOST INCANDESCENT moments of *The Archaeology of Knowledge* were reserved for its final section. The book's sixteen-page conclusion was written as a kind of drama: an extended encounter between a figure who is clearly Foucault, and a hostile interlocutor.[60] The interlocutor bore many of the characteristics of Sartre, as would have been evident to readers: he reiterated the arguments of the *L'Arc* interview, admonished Foucault for failing to recognize the limits of the structuralist enterprise, and affirmed the central existentialist line that all knowledge derived from the constituent activity of conscious subjects. A virtual Sartre and Foucault thus collided on terms dictated by Foucault. Their choreographed verbal confrontation over what had or had not been achieved in the preceding chapters gave Foucault the opportunity to move beyond reaction, and to take his attack directly to Sartre.

In his opening salvo, the interlocutor blasted Foucault for the temerity that had allowed him to carry structural analysis into the history of ideas, where it manifestly had no place. He charged:

> In the manner of a certain form of linguistics, you've attempted to dispense with the speaking subject; you believed that it was possible to scour discourse of all its anthropological references, and treat it as if it was never formulated by anyone, as if it was not born under particular circumstances, as if it was addressed to no one.[61]

Foucault opted not to counter this criticism, but to accept it with a grin. "You are right," he replied, "I misunderstood the transcendence of discourse; I refused, in describing it, to refer it to a subjectivity."[62] He gave no ground, accepted that his analysis had sidestepped the notion of a speaking and thinking subject, and lamented only the persistence of sterile polemics around the word "structuralism."

The interlocutor then redoubled his efforts, noting that structuralism may have had its local successes: in the formal study of language, in the study of myth, and even perhaps in the study of the unconscious mind. It was one thing to play with elements and relations and discontinuities when one was analyzing Indo-European legends or the tragedies of Racine;[63] it was quite another thing to do it when what was at stake was the very form of knowledge that allowed one to speak here and now. The latter, in its historical thickness, was irreducible.

Foucault, at his most cruel, absorbed this argument, and then parroted it back to his adversary in mocking echo. He responded:

> Allow me . . . to tell you how I understood your comments just now. "Sure," you said through closed teeth, "we have been constrained, in spite of all the rearguard battles in which we have engaged, to accept the formalization of deductive discourses; . . . Sure, we've had to abandon all these discourses that, formerly, we brought back to the sovereignty of consciousness."[64]

But these losses were acceptable, the parroting Foucault continued, because they would be recuperated in the second degree. Structural analyses themselves, that is to say, would be from this point forward submitted to fundamental interrogation and asked to specify from what point they spoke. The reason that inhabited them would be brought into the open and questioned in proper transcendental fashion: in terms of its origins, its teleological horizon, and its temporal continuity. The history of thought would thus become the last refuge of "historico-transcendental dominance": a fortress to be defended at all costs.

Switching back into his own voice, Foucault said that this strategy— the use of the history of thought as a fortress from within which one might safely rain arrows on the invading structuralist armies below—had been more than apparent to him in the crafting of *The Archaeology of Knowledge*; hence the choice of topic. The essential was "to free the history of thought from transcendental subjection." By analyzing the history of knowledge as a discontinuity that no teleology could reduce in advance, as a dispersion that no horizon could gather up, and as the deployment of "an anonymity upon which no transcendental constitution would impose the form of the subject," Foucault declared, he had thrown open the gates of this fortress and denied sanctuary to that which it was intended to protect: the constituent powers of consciousness.[65]

Seemingly shocked by the audacity of Foucault's claims, his interlocutor turned upon him the charge of intellectual hypocrisy. "You yourself make strange use," he declared, "of this liberty that you challenge in others." How could Foucault justify, he asked, the position from which he at that moment spoke? How could he, in good conscience, speak of the strategies that he had employed and the intentions that he had executed in the crafting of archaeology? The interlocutor probed:

> have you forgotten the care that you took to lock up the discourse of others within systems of rules? Have you forgotten all these constraints that you so meticulously describe? Have you not taken from individuals the right to intervene personally in the positivities within which their discourses are situated?[66]

Foucault responded that his interlocutor had committed a grave error. The archaeological description of discursive formations was not to be understood as a set of constraints operating upon an otherwise-free speaker. These formations were a literal positivity: the site, the rules, and the relations that made meaningful speech possible in the first place. Discursive practices, Foucault said, were just that: *practices*. To elucidate them in their thickness and complexity was a way of showing that to speak was to *do* something, and something quite other than to express what one thought.

While it might have been interesting to know how the interlocutor would have responded to this claim, Foucault did not give him the opportunity; he reserved the final word for himself.

FOUCAULT'S CLOSING STATEMENT, while only two pages in length, was an essay in itself.[67] It began with a faux apology. Foucault said that he fully understood what an ungrateful labor he had been engaged in for ten years. He acknowledged that it was both unpleasant and provocative to reveal the limits and necessities of a practice where one had been accustomed to seeing the play of genius and liberty. He admitted that it was nearly intolerable to watch texts dismembered, analyzed, and recombined without once encountering the face of the author—when manifestly what each wanted most was to place "himself" into his discourse.

Having said these things, Foucault let the other voice—now sounding thoroughly desperate—reenter for a final plea. The entreaty merits quotation at length:

> What! So many words piled up, so many marks deposited on so much paper and offered to innumerable gazes, . . . such a profound piety attached to conserving them and inscribing them in the memory of men, —all this so that nothing might remain of the poor hand that traced them, of this inquietude that sought to tranquilize itself in them, and of this completed life that no longer has anything but them in order to live on? . . . . Must we admit that the time of discourse is not the time of consciousness carried into the dimensions of history, or the time of history present in the form of consciousness? Must I suppose that my discourse does not betoken my survival?[68]

How could it be, the voice wished to know, that discourse was not the record of a consciousness? What hope of salvation—even the modest earthly salvation of textual immortality—could there be if one's written legacy was not even one's own?

The acerbity of this passage is difficult to overstate. For the two ideas expressed within it—namely, that discourse is the time of consciousness carried into the dimensions of history, and that discourse allows one to speak beyond one's death—were the unmistakable property of Sartre. Both ideas were expressed throughout his oeuvre, and both were prominent within his works of the 1960s.

In *Search for a Method*, the introduction to the *Critique of Dialectical Reason*, Sartre had repeatedly stressed that works were the works of men. They were, as such, the expression of the specific projects of their creators: they revealed the work of consciousness. To forget this was to reify cultural products. As Sartre noted in regard to *Madame Bovary*:

> if in the course of reading the book, we do not constantly go back . . . to the desires and ends—that is, the total enterprise—of Flaubert, we

simply make a fetish out of the book (which often happens) just as one
may do with a piece of merchandise by considering it as a thing that
speaks for itself and not as the reality of a man objectified through his
work.[69]

Madame Bovary showed us Flaubert's thought, and directly translated a
project that he had conceived and carried out. Moreover, Sartre wrote, we
may say that from December 1851 through April 1856, the novel had formed
the unity of Flaubert's existence. Discourse formed the connection between
historical time and the time of consciousness.

As to the argument that works offered a kind of immortality, this was a
major—and highly personal—theme for Sartre. In *Nausea*, he had broached
the possibility that one might live on in the art-objects that one had freely
created. A book, a record, or any other physical thing that captured and held
the human voice carried the promise of restoring that voice to future listeners, long after its bearer had departed.[70] In his autobiography *The Words*,
Sartre described the realization that he had come to while still a young man:
"I discovered that in belles-lettres the Giver can be transformed into his own
Gift, that is, into a pure object. Chance had made me a man, generosity would
make me a book. I could cast my missive, my consciousness, in letters of
bronze; I could replace the stirrings of my life by indelible inscriptions, my
flesh by a style, the faint spirals of time by eternity."[71] Viewed from the height
of his tomb, Sartre wrote, his birth seemed to him as a necessary evil: one
required for his transfiguration through the word. "In order to be reborn, I
had to write." Sometime around 1955, he imagined, a larva would burst open
revealing twenty-five folio butterflies, each of which would fly to its place
on the shelves of the Bibliothèque Nationale. "I am reborn," he imagined, "I
become at last a whole man, thinking, talking, singing, thundering, a man
who asserts himself with the peremptory inertia of matter."[72]

If, as Sartre suggested, he had ultimately freed himself of this vision and
recognized that there would be no genuine conjuring of death, he continued to believe that his books were his legacy and the truest representation
of himself. "I write," he asserted, "and will keep writing books." It might
be the case that culture could neither save nor justify man, but it remained
his truest product. "[H]e projects himself into it, he recognizes himself in
it," wrote Sartre; "that critical mirror alone offers him his image."[73]

Such were the views that Foucault pilloried when he had his broken-sounding interlocutor ask, "Must I suppose that my discourse does not betoken my survival?" To such a question—and to the existential angst that animated it—Foucault offered neither remedy nor consolation. He could only respond that he understood the malaise of those who were gripped by it. Bad enough, he said, that they had already discovered rules that had no place in consciousness inhabiting their history, their economy, their social practices, their language, the myths of their ancestors and "the very fables that were told to them in childhood."[74] That they should have to give over the very words that come from their lips—"this discourse in which they wish to be able to say immediately, without distance, what they think, believe, or imagine"—was too much.[75] Naturally, Foucault sneered, they preferred to deny that discourse was a rule-governed practice. With so many things having already escaped them, these unfortunates could not bear to lose that frail fragment of discourse that would carry their life a bit further.

The closing lines of Sartre's autobiography, unsurprisingly, affirmed his determination to continue making himself through writing. They read:

> Without equipment, without tools, I put all of me to work in order to save all of me. If I consign an impossible Salvation to the proproom, what's left? *A whole man, composed of all men* and as good as all of them and as good as any.[76]

The closing lines of *The Archaeology of Knowledge* gave the cold-blooded response:

> Discourse is not life: its time is not yours; in it, you will not be reconciled with death; it may be that you have killed God under the weight of all that you've said; but don't imagine that you will make, out of all that you've said, a man who will live longer.[77]

THE ARCHAEOLOGY OF KNOWLEDGE was without doubt the magmum opus that Foucault had hoped to create. As deft in construction as it was rich in content, the book performed the valuable service of inscribing Foucault's previous studies within a methodological framework that was unified and clearly defined. At the same time, it revealed the philosopher's almost limitless capacity to manufacture concepts: a trait for which Gilles Deleuze admired him greatly. Deleuze would write many years later that Foucault was "[a] new archivist": *new* in the sense that he ordered knowledge like no archivist before him. Neither formalization nor interpretation, but *description* was the essence of archaeology.[78]

For Foucault had put his own stamp on the notion of "archive." He had defined a new domain, which was that of discourse. Formalizing the insights gained in his prior works and at the same time lending them a more recognizably structuralist cast, Foucault had offered a way of practicing the history of knowledge that was purged of the intervention of consciousness. As the philosopher explained in a 1968 article, "one can say that knowledge, as a field of historicity in which the sciences appear—is free of all constituent activity, freed of all reference to an origin or a historico-transcendental teleology, detached from all reliance upon a founding subjectivity."[79] Knowledge, that is to say, was wholly immanent. In describing the appearance and development of different forms of knowledge, there was no need of recourse to depth. There was no need to move to *another* level in order to explain the level of discourse, or things said. Discourse contained within itself its own principle of order. It was a plane or a surface—with nothing beneath.

If meaning appeared to arise within discourse, that was, as Foucault had suggested in 1966, a kind of "surface effect." The phrase itself was meant half in jest. A surface effect demands hidden depths that would have produced the effect; Foucault's dark humor is that he posits no such depths. Even the "immense thickness of systematicities" that Foucault placed "behind the finished system" was not meant to be taken literally in a spatial sense.[80] Rather, it was a way of describing relations that were internal to the system—that, whatever their density, existed within the plane that revealed their silent operation.[81]

To make these arguments explicitly in 1969 was to undo the ambiguity that came with the name "archaeology." More centrally, it was to publicly combat Sartre's claim that Foucault was a sifter and a digger of the "subsoils" of Western culture. Archaeology was not, the younger man now replied, a failed effort to unearth the traces of human practice. It was the triumphant demonstration that man's footprints were absent from the paths of knowledge.

For all that it achieved, *The Archaeology of Knowledge* was not a "successful" work in the way that *The Order of Things* had been. Readers found it arid and schematic. Critics passed over the book in a fashion reminiscent of the author's early works. From the perspective of the Sartre–Foucault conflict, none of this mattered. By the beginning of the new decade, Foucault was not an intellectual upstart, but rather the newly minted Professor of the History of Systems of Thought at the Collège de France; he was, as one critic noted, France's "mandarin of the hour."[82] The anti-subjectivity position that Foucault had defiantly championed in 1966 was, by 1970, absolutely dominant. Whether archaeology had been instrumental in bringing a close to the Sartrean philosophical era was a matter for speculation. The evident fact was that man was dead. Foucault would not mourn his passing.

CHAPTER TWO

Restructuring

Foucault and the Genealogical Turn

*The fundamental notions that confront us now are no longer con-
sciousness and continuity . . . nor are they sign and structure. They
are event and series, with the whole set of associated notions: regularity, chance, discontinuity, dependence, transformation.*[1]

IN FOUCAULT'S WORK, THE PERIOD FROM 1969 TO 1973 MARKED A
transition. An increasing concern with the role of nondiscursive practices
led the philosopher away from an "archaeological" focus on historical
épistémès—and away from the history of science generally—in the direction
of "genealogical" analyses that owed more to Nietzsche than to Canguilhem.
Works like *The Order of Things* and *The Archaeology of Knowledge*, in which
the transformation of systems of knowledge was the central concern, gave
way to *Discipline and Punish*, in which the driving concern was *power*.

As this turn from archaeology to genealogy represents a defining moment in Foucault's intellectual career, it is a matter of some consequence
how we understand it. Why did Foucault stop using the word "archaeology" to describe his researches? Why did he turn his attention to the social
context of knowledge?

The traditional answer to these questions has come not from historians, but from philosophers: Foucault, it is said, *did* not pursue further work under the banner of archaeology because he *could* not. The project of archaeology was to treat the historical transformation of discourse as a rule-governed phenomenon—one that could be meaningfully studied in isolation from its "nondiscursive" context. This project, once it was rigorously and systematically developed, showed itself to be irretrievably flawed. It suffered from internal contradictions that could be neither tolerated nor resolved. Faced with this failure, the interpretation runs, Foucault searched for a way to recast the archaeological question. He found it in the genealogical approach of Nietzsche, with the result that his analyses moved definitively toward society and power.

This text-driven and internalist approach to Foucault's career is illuminating, and unquestionably helps us to see a number of conceptual flaws to which he himself was inattentive. As an explanation for the change in his practice of philosophy, however, it is inadequate. Foucault's altered trajectory cannot be wholly derived from his reasonings; nor can it be understood without once raising our eyes from his writings. The "methodological failure of archaeology" was a necessary, but not sufficient, cause of the so-called genealogical turn.

While the method that Foucault formalized in *The Archaeology of Knowledge* had logical holes in it, so, it must be said, had each of his prior studies. Far from considering this an indictment of his work, Foucault felt (and repeatedly said) that inconsistency was the natural concomitant of his style of work: by the time he finished a book, he was invariably asking different questions than when he began it. Some questions were simply left in abeyance; some problems could not but receive unsatisfactory solutions. The essential point was to maintain a vigorous questioning. Hence, the fact that archaeology as a doctrine proved less than perfectly coherent, while interesting, tells us nothing about why Foucault turned to genealogy. Conversely, a close look at Foucault's *practice* of philosophy—his situated deployment of concepts—promises to tell us a great deal.

On the strength of a wealth of evidence, including books, treatises, essays, talks, lecture courses and interviews, this chapter will offer an alternative account of the genealogical turn. It will argue that, rather than viewing the transition from archaeology to genealogy as a *problem-driven* event, we should see it as a *concept-driven* one. In Foucault's thought, the period after 1968 was characterized by the large-scale importation of concepts. Specifically, Foucault grafted onto archaeology, sometimes well, sometimes clumsily, categories derived from Marxism and from the thought of his philosophical associate Gilles Deleuze. It is a fact that many of these transplanted categories withered on the vine after several years (with the result that their irruption has been largely ignored in the critical literature). But as this chapter will show, it was the use of an essentially alien vocabulary that *allowed* Foucault to restructure his thought; and it is impossible to follow the path that leads from *The Archaeology of Knowledge* to *Discipline and Punish* without recognizing an intervening period of restructuring.

As THE FOREGOING chapter showed, *The Archaeology of Knowledge* offered a summation and elaboration of the method Foucault believed he had created, and responded to prior philosophical currents as well as to particular disciplinary questions in the history of ideas. Archaeology was meant to be a descriptive enterprise: a way of investigating historical texts making claims to scientificity. The essence of the method—which Foucault felt he had applied, with varying degrees of self-consciousness, in *Madness and Civilization*, *The Birth of the Clinic*, and *The Order of Things*—was the bracketing of textual meaning in favor of an exclusive focus on description. In a 1969 interview, Foucault called archaeology "the description of this set, this extraordinarily vast, massive and complex mass of things that have been said in a culture—as it happens, in our own culture . . . that is what, in the large, I understand by archaeology."[2] Archaeological description set itself apart from traditional analyses in the history of science by isolating an original domain. That domain was the totality of discursive *statements*, as distinguished from (logical) propositions and (grammatical) sentences. Rather than tracing the development of scientific disciplines in the familiar terms of influence, tradition, and genius, the archaeologist voluntarily confined himself to evaluating raw statements within so-called "discursive formations."

No consideration was to be given to statements' significance or truth-value. They were to be evaluated solely in terms of the objects they deployed,

the concepts they utilized, the theoretical strategies in which they partici-
pated, and the subjective positions that they allowed. Unlike the historian
of science, the archaeologist did not attempt to read the progressive unveil-
ing of truth in the sciences he examined; instead, he sought to establish the
conditions that had rendered a given statement, at a given time, scientifi-
cally *acceptable*. This was Foucault's meaning when he said, as early as 1966,
that archaeology's concern was with "the limits of enunciability."[3]

The Order of Discourse, which was published as a stand-alone volume in
1971, differed markedly in form from its predecessor. It was not a treatise
but a speech: Foucault's inaugural oration at the Collège de France. Unlike *The Archaeology of Knowledge*, which was massive in scope, specific in
its aims, and addressed to a narrow professional audience for whom the
relevant debates were clear, this work was small in scale, exceedingly broad
in its aims, and addressed to a large audience of nonspecialists. Small as it
was, however, *The Order of Discourse* allowed Foucault to make three important moves in relation to his prior work. Let us briefly examine each of
them in turn.

Firstly, Foucault expressed his supposition that "in every society the
production of discourse is at once controlled, selected, organized and re-
distributed by a certain number of procedures, the role of which is to con-
jure its powers and dangers."[4] Examples of such procedures included acts
of exclusion (like forbidding a subject), acts of classification (like attribution to an author), and acts aimed at limiting acceptable speakers (like li-
censing). These procedures had not played any significant role in *The Archaeology
of Knowledge*, where the emphasis was placed on discursive systems in
themselves and not the relationship of society *to* those systems. Now, however, Foucault implied that only by looking at society's wish to banish certain dangers could one understand the order of discourse.

Secondly, Foucault made an announcement that would have come as a
surprise to even his most devoted readers. He declared his intention to
examine the "will to truth" that had dominated the history of the West since
ancient Greece. Never, in any of his prior writings, had Foucault shown
the slightest inclination to embrace this Nietzschean–Heideggerian notion.[5]
Suddenly, he seemed to suggest, our attention was owed to particular
events at the dawn of Western history: these events—this "historical break"
between Hesiod and Plato—*initiated* the discursive paradigm described in

The Archaeology of Knowledge. The epistemic transformations that had come under scrutiny in *The Order of Things* were, by this logic, simply moments in the 2500-year evolution of a Western will to truth. Foucault wrote:

> Everything happens as if, starting from the great Platonic break, the will to truth had its own history, which is not that of constraining truths; a history of objects to know, a history of functions and positions of the knowing subject, a history of material, technical and instrumental embodiments of knowledge.[6]

This move engendered two deformations in the archaeological perspective. It placed historical and geographical limits on what had seemed to be a metahistorical—and hence universally applicable—approach to knowledge. And as the reference to "material, technical and instrumental embodiments," showed, it put the nondiscursive aspects of knowledge production—that is, the outside world—squarely on the research agenda. Discourse was no longer to be treated, even provisionally, in its autonomy.

Finally, Foucault offered a harsh critique of the history of ideas. He challenged the historiographical tradition that recounted, in the sciences or elsewhere, "the continuous unfolding of an ideal necessity." The corrective that he proposed demanded that the historian "treat not the representations that might exist behind discourses, but rather the discourses themselves as regular and distinct series of events."[7] Such a critique, as we have seen, was already central to *The Archaeology of Knowledge.* This was still visibly the same argument: traditional history *interprets* the representations behind texts, while archaeology seeks to *analyze* component statements in their coexistence and succession.[8] Where the argument differed was in its concepts. Archaeology had put great emphasis upon the ideas of *systems* (systèmes), *discontinuities* (discontinuités), *series* (séries), *transformations* (transformations), and *thresholds* (seuils).[9] Foucault now shifted the focus to "chance, the discontinuous, and materiality."[10]

IT IS QUESTIONABLE whether Foucault's audience on December 2, 1970, the day he gave the lecture entitled "The Order of Discourse," would have been attuned to these subtle changes of position. Many were undoubtedly seeing and hearing the philosopher for the first time. Most would have come to the lecture with a simple and pragmatic goal: to discover the topic that Foucault had chosen to teach during his first year as a professor of the Collège de France. Much of the difficulty that critics have experienced in deciphering *The Order of Discourse* stems from the fact that it has not been read for what it is: the oral prologue to a course. The title of that course was *The Will to Knowledge*.

The course summary that Foucault wrote for the 1970–1971 annual catalog of the Collège de France provides a sense of how he imagined the decade unfolding. He foresaw a series of explorations devoted to the question of the "will to know." Some of these investigations would be regional, involving particular historical researches. Others would be global, treating the will to know in itself and in its theoretical implications. *The Will to Knowledge* belonged to the latter variety.

What precisely did Foucault study in order to provide a general framework for a question as large as this one? His words deserve to be quoted at length:

> The transformation of a discursive practice is linked to a whole set of modifications, often quite complex, that can be produced either outside of it . . . or within it . . . or alongside them [sic]. . . . These principles of exclusion and of choice . . . do not point back to a subject of knowledge (whether historical or transcendental) that would successively invent them or found them at a primary level; they instead designate an anonymous and polymorphous will to knowledge, susceptible to regular transformations.[11]

It is a remarkably dense passage, but one that reveals the fundamental orientation of the course. Let us examine it piece by piece.

Foucault starts from the standpoint of "[t]he transformation of a discursive practice," which is to say that he positions himself as an archaeologist examining the fluctuation of discursive formations. He then links this fluctuation to "a whole set of modifications, often quite complex," and suggests that there are three kinds of these. Modifications that occur inside or alongside a discursive formation (as, for instance, the refinement of concepts within a discipline, or the migration of concepts from one discipline to an adjacent one) are the traditional domain of archaeology. Modifications that occur *outside* of the discursive formation (including economic, social, and political changes) were purposely bracketed in *The Archaeology of Knowledge*, but seem now to be matters of active concern. The joint effect of all three kinds of modifications is described by Foucault as yielding a "[principle] of exclusion and of choice."

Recapping, we can say that every such modification—whether it takes place within discourse or in the world surrounding it—is treated by Foucault as a limiting factor. Every change is a choice, and excludes other choices. The totality of these exclusions narrows the range of allowable discourse to that with which any given era is actually confronted. These choices, however, do not point back to a chooser. There is no "subject of knowledge" controlling the trajectory of choices and exclusions, no guiding mind "who would invent them or found them at a primary level." As the foregoing discussion suggested, there is simply an aggregate of events.

The heightened interest in sociopolitical context apart, this is a straight description of the archaeological method. It would be nothing more than that if Foucault did not go on to characterize the aggregate of choices and exclusions as "an anonymous and polymorphous will to knowledge." This surprising move, which sets *The Will to Knowledge* apart from all of Foucault's pre-1970 work, radically alters the archaeological equation. For a "will to know," even one that wells up anonymously from countless material events, remains a *will* (i.e., a drive) and a will *to know* (i.e., there is direction to the drive). To say that this will is "susceptible to regular transformations" is to beg the question. Where knowledge is concerned, susceptibility to transformation was the acknowledged starting-point: underlying will is the novelty. Foucault introduces momentum into his system at the expense of an inexplicable teleology.

HUBERT DREYFUS AND Paul Rabinow, who worked closely with Foucault during the latter's California sojourns of the late 1970s and early 1980s, provided the first rigorous analysis of the archaeological method in their 1983 *Michel Foucault: Beyond Structuralism and Hermeneutics*. Their argument, which has continued to dominate the historiography of Foucault's early work, was that archaeology represented a valiant effort to transport phenomenological detachment into the study of knowledge; that it had failed, however, to achieve coherence; and that this failure had directly induced the turn to Nietzschean genealogy.[12] This argument was fleshed out with ample citation from Foucault's major works. The authors made no pretense of looking beyond the texts.

The fatal flaw that Dreyfus and Rabinow observed in archaeology was its unwillingness to maintain phenomenological restraint. Originally committed to a task of pure description, Foucault, they argued, came to conflate the *regularities* that he observed in statements with *rules*; the difference, of course, is that the former may merely be said to be observable, while the latter govern. "The peculiarity of this strange alliance between rules as *descriptive regularities* and as *prescriptive operative forces*," they wrote, "becomes obvious when Foucault is led to speak of 'locating the various *regularities* that [statements] *obey*.'"[13] In addressing the causal power of the rules, Dreyfus and Rabinow continued, Foucault "illegitimately hypostasized the observed formal irregularities which described discursive formations into conditions of these formations' existence."[14]

The seriousness of this error was compounded by Foucault's determination to treat discourse as essentially autonomous and undetermined. Since he could not provide a contextual response to the question of what force regulates discursive practices, he was thrown back upon "the strange notion of regularities which regulate themselves." "[T]he archaeologist," the authors concluded, "must attribute causal efficacy to the very rules which describe these practices' systematicity."[15]

In the "self-imposed silence" that followed *The Archaeology of Knowledge* and lasted until 1975, Dreyfus and Rabinow saw circumstantial evidence for their assertion that the failure of archaeology was apparent to Foucault. The philosopher subsequently showed himself to be, as they put it, "one of those rare thinkers, like Wittgenstein and Heidegger, whose work shows both underlying continuity and an important reversal not because their early efforts were useless, but because in pushing one way of thinking to its limits they both recognized and overcame those limitations.[16]

Specifically, Foucault extricated himself from the illusion of autonomous discourse by immersing himself in Nietzschean genealogy. The genealogical imperative—to confront the past in the full knowledge that every "eternal truth" is a violently imposed interpretation—allowed Foucault to situate his formerly free-floating discourses within a conditioning structure of practices. Moreover, they argued, his 1971 essay, "Nietzsche, Genealogy, History," presented the thinker's first halting steps toward a theory of power. Dreyfus and Rabinow were not modest in the value they attached to this piece. "[I]t would be hard to overestimate the importance of the essay for understanding the progression of the work which followed," they wrote; "all of the seeds of Foucault's work in the 1970s can be found in this discussion of Nietzsche."[17]

DREYFUS AND RABINOW did not linger over *The Order of Discourse*, Foucault's follow-up to *The Archaeology of Knowledge*. With only one page devoted to it, it received the most cursory treatment of any of Foucault's books. This is perhaps unsurprising. The argument of *Beyond Structuralism and Hermeneutics* stressed Foucault's self-imposed silence in the wake of archaeology's failure. *The Order of Discourse*, which achieved broad circulation and showed clear ongoing commitment to archaeological categories, was a singularly inconvenient piece of evidence.

Critics who have engaged with *The Order of Discourse*, on the other hand, have tended to view it as fundamentally a programmatic statement—a discourse on method highlighting changes in Foucault's theoretical apparatus and offering the key to his genealogical works of the 1970s. Its unique place in his oeuvre encourages this interpretation. It was the philosopher's first publication as a professor of the Collège; his first major work to employ the term "genealogy"; and his first major work *not* to employ the term "archaeology." Moreover, inaugural lectures at the Collège de France have the express aim of laying out the method and substance of the investigations that a chairholder intends to undertake in the years to come.

Béatrice Han, one of the most insightful contemporary readers of Foucault, used *The Order of Discourse* as a road map to Foucault's later writings. In this, she departed from Dreyfus and Rabinow, whose interpretation she otherwise scrupulously followed. Han argued, like her predecessors and with explicit reference to them, that archaeology rendered itself incoherent by positing self-regulating discursive regularities.[18] She hesitated, however, to attribute Foucault's genealogical turn simply to Nietzschean thought, noting that Nietzsche played a privileged role in *all* of Foucault's work, from start to finish. She wrote: "How, then, can the transition from archaeology to genealogy be understood? *The Order of Discourse* shows that this Foucauldian 'turn' is due to the importation of a specific Nietzschean concept, the 'will to truth.'"[19]

Han argued that the concept of the "will to truth" was doubly useful to Foucault. It enabled him to use Nietzsche's own method for confronting the will to truth—namely, genealogy—and thereby "to escape the impasses of archaeology by shifting from the study of the discursive to a contextual analysis of *all* practices." At the same time, it allowed him, by questioning the historicity of will to truth, to conceptualize the relationship between knowledge and power in a new way. Rather than seeing the two as distinct and isolable, or even seeing one as the instrument of the other, Foucault moved toward a vision of power and knowledge as linked and reciprocal. "Henceforth, to respond to the question of the conditions of possible knowledge," wrote Han, "will involve, not only an archaeology of knowledge, but also the genealogy of this 'power–knowledge nexus,' which remains to be defined."[20]

For Han, then, the notion of the will to truth was vitally important. It provided the framework for all of Foucault's genealogical analyses of the mid-1970s. It stood implicitly behind *Discipline and Punish*, and explicitly behind the first volume of *The History of Sexuality*, the French subtitle of which was *The Will to Knowledge*. Most importantly, it made sense of the radical and abrupt changes that Foucault's work underwent around 1970.

IT WILL HELP to look briefly at the nature of those changes. There is no clearer way to observe the metamorphosis of Foucault's thought during this period than to watch the shift in meaning that one of his key concepts undergoes. "Exteriority," an idea that plays a critical role in the thinker's works throughout his career, provides an excellent barometer for the change that is taking place in his philosophy as a whole. Let us examine the distinctive meanings that this single word takes on over the course of three years.

In *The Archaeology of Knowledge*, we find the following description of the archaeological method:

> Another characteristic trait: the analysis of statements treats them in the systematic form of *exteriority*. . . . In order to restore the statements to their pure dispersion. In order to analyze them in an exteriority that is unquestionably paradoxical inasmuch as it points back to no opposing form of interiority.[21]

In using the word "exteriority" here, Foucault's object is to demonstrate that statements can be analyzed as a field without reference to a subject or consciousness that would have produced them. To view statements in their exteriority is to treat them as a system of dispersion. As Foucault himself suggests a few sentences later, "neutrality" would capture just as well the meaning that he wants to convey. Going outside is simply a way of saying that statements have no inside.

The Order of Discourse seems, on the surface, to maintain this concern. Foucault declares that his method is defined by a "rule of exteriority," and defines that as a commitment not to search for hidden meaning within discourse. This is consistent with the earlier usage. But the relevant section reads:

> Fourth rule: that of *exteriority*: to not go from discourse toward its interior and hidden nucleus, toward the heart of a thought or of a signification that would have manifested itself in it; rather, starting from discourse itself, from its appearance and its regularity, to go toward its external conditions of possibility, toward that which gives rise to the chance series of these events and fixes its boundaries.[22]

The first thing to notice is that exteriority is no longer a seen as a position vis-à-vis "statements"; the relevant domain is now the more all-encompassing "discourse." The concern in this passage is to describe a kind of analysis that would move from the observed regularities of discourse to the extrinsic phenomena that have rendered that particular kind of discourse possible. While the meaning of "external conditions" is ambiguous, it is evident that "exteriority" has lost its status as a synonym of "neutrality": going outside is now, quite literally, the act of looking outside of discourse for the factors that condition it.

The meaning-shift reaches its conclusion in the final lecture of *The Will to Knowledge*. Foucault finishes the course with a retrospective glance at the principles that have guided his investigation of the will to know. He tells his listeners:

> As to the principle of *exteriority*: I have never tried to do the analysis of the text starting from the text itself. . . . I have attempted to dispense with the principle of textuality by placing myself in a dimension which was that of history . . . I have tried to mark the discursive events that have their place not in the selfsame interior of the text or of many texts, but which have their place in the fact of the functions or roles that are given to different discourses in the interior of a society. To pass outside of the text in order to rediscover the function of discourse in the interior of a society—that is what I call the principle of exteriority.[23]

What do we observe in this passage? Foucault continues to use the word "exteriority," but now gives it a meaning that is frankly functionalist: to go outside of the text is to find the societal function of the discourse that it represents. Lest he be thought unclear on this point, Foucault says moments later, "I have tried to show how [the] knowledge of the order of things and of the order of man . . . arose only as a pretext in the wake of an economic and political caesura."[24] Economics and politics take the front seat. There is no conception of the "power–knowledge nexus" here; there is, instead, the frank subordination of knowledge to a power understood in wholly sociopolitical terms.

How ARE WE to understand this migration of meaning? Why did Foucault begin—suddenly and quite without precedent—to treat knowledge as that which serves a social function? Why, to be clear, did he broaden his archaeological inquiry to include nondiscursive practices, and begin to speak what sounds disturbingly like the Marxist language of ideology?

Throughout the decade of the 1960s, Foucault's radical opposition to the Marxist conceptualization of knowledge—and to Marxist analysis in general—could not have been more evident. For years after the publication of *The Order of Things*, he drew the fire of the left for having written that "Marxism resides in the thought of the nineteenth century like a fish in water: which is to say, anywhere else it stops breathing."[25] So far from repudiating the claim, Foucault self-consciously (and biliously) echoed it in his 1966 attack on Sartre: "The critique of dialectical reason is the magnificent and pathetic effort of a man of the nineteenth century to think the twentieth. In this sense, Sartre is the last Hegelian, and I would even say the last Marxist."[26]

Foucault repeatedly opposed the structuralist communists grouped around his former teacher Louis Althusser, telling them flatly that "Marx does not represent an epistemological break."[27] At the same time, he distanced himself from nonstructuralist communists, calling their thought "a soft, insipid, humanist Marxism."[28] At all times, he refused the expedient of class analysis. The extent to which this was the case is manifest when we scan Foucault's *Dits et écrits*: the words "capitalism" and "proletariat" do not appear in *any* work by Foucault prior to 1970.

In September of 1968, Foucault returned to Paris after two years in Tunisia. He submitted the manuscript of *The Archaeology of Knowledge* in November. In January of 1969, he began his tenure as director of the philosophy department at the newly created Centre universitaire expérimental de Vincennes.[29] Vincennes was a highly unusual institution. The brainchild of Minister of Education Edgar Faure, it represented a considerable departure in French higher education. An attentive response to the events and demands of May 1968, the university had been built from the ground up, was largely interdisciplinary, and offered courses in nontraditional fields like psychoanalysis and semiotics.[30]

Upon his return to France, Foucault had been nominated by the steering committee of Vincennes—a prestigious group which counted among its members Jacques Derrida, Roland Barthes, and Georges Canguilhem— to a panel that would make hiring decisions for departmental chairs. Foucault and his colleagues did their work, and then took the unusual step of allowing Foucault to resign his seat on the panel in order to himself stand for the position of chair of the philosophy department. He was elected without dissent.[31]

Faced with the task of creating an entire philosophy department from scratch, Foucault chose to surround himself with individuals whom he knew personally. David Macey cites Foucault's partner Daniel Defert to the effect that the philosophers's recruits were alike in "having difficulties of one kind or another with the educational establishment." It is certainly not surprising that Foucault would have felt an affinity for academic outsiders: he had been one for practically the whole of his professional career. It is striking, however, that Foucault chose to surround himself with colleagues who, taken as a whole, were far more politically radical than he himself was. "Whatever his precise motives," writes Macey, "Foucault had succeeded in creating a political hornets' nest."[32]

When teaching began in January of 1969, the atmosphere of the new university was, like its faculty, pervaded by the spirit of May 1968. Didier Eribon offers a sense of the prevailing mood with an itemization of philosophy courses on offer during 1969 and 1970: Jacques Rancière's "revisionism-leftism" and "theory of the second stage of Marxism-Leninism: Stalinism"; Etienne Balibar's "sciences of social formations and Marxist philosophy"; Judith Miller's "cultural revolutions" and "third stage of Marxism-Leninism: Maoism"; Alain Badiou's "ideological struggle" and "Marxist dialectics"; and Henry Weber's "introduction to twentieth-century Marxism-Leninism: Lenin, Trotsky, and the Bolshevik movement."[33] More than five thousand students entered the "experimental center" ready to imbibe these subjects. A great many were equally ready to continue the university uprising of the preceding spring.

Foucault, who was initially considered a rightist by students because of his earlier writings (and who had, in fact, been out of the country during the May events), was thus operating in an immensely politicized environment. Professionally, he was surrounded by committed Marxists. He taught at a university that would, within a year, be shut down by minister of education Olivier Guichard for the Marxist–Leninist content of its courses. And he quickly found himself in the midst of a social struggle that seemed to vindicate the most hysterical Marxist prophecies.

Outsider status did not keep him from being swept into the political maelstrom. In late January, a mass of students and professors occupied Vincennes in solidarity with struggles then taking place in the Latin Quarter. Foucault was among the two hundred and twenty participants gassed and then apprehended for questioning. In the aftermath, thirty-four students were expelled. In February of 1969, Foucault spoke at a large Latin Quarter rally protesting the authorities' response and deploring its "calculated repression."[34]

Foucault's status increased within nonestablishment leftist circles, as the philosopher was increasingly seen not as the author of *The Order of Things*, but as a fellow fighter who had faced arrest.[35] At the same time, his contacts within the left multiplied rapidly. In a remarkable shift, Foucault spoke on the same stage, and for the same cause, as Jean-Paul Sartre. Defert became a member of the Maoist-inspired Gauche Prolétarienne, creating thereby a direct channel of communication between Foucault and one of the most extreme leftist groups then in existence.

The upsurge of a Marxist vocabulary within Foucault's work, just at this particular moment, was swift and unmistakable. It began in February 1969, when Foucault, in a seeming reversal, called Marx a "founder of discursivity": that is, an individual who had established the possibility of a limitless discourse.[36] In an article published at the same time, Foucault wrote of "the civil consciousness of the parliamentary bourgeoisie" in the seventeenth century.[37] This nonironic reference to a class actor, and to the notion of class consciousness, was literally without precedent in Foucault's oeuvre.

Over the ensuing three years, the trend broadened and intensified. A February 1970 interview saw Foucault implicitly link reflection on the Vincennes experience with a newly functionalist perspective on knowledge:

> Now note how recent developments have caused new problems to appear: it is no longer what are the limits of knowledge (or its foundations), but who are those who know? How is the appropriation and distribution of knowledge achieved? *How can a form of knowledge take its place in a society*, develop there, mobilize resources, *and put itself in the service of an economy*?[38]

In an autumn interview in Japan, Foucault told his interlocutor that the university students of the West had thus far missed the major lesson of May 1986, namely, that "[their] instruction was ultimately nothing other that the renovation and reproduction of the values and forms of knowledge of bourgeois society." He warned that "the bourgeoisie is a system that has an enormous capacity for adaptation," and lamented that "capitalist society has totally dispossessed literature" of its subversive function. Pointing directly to the Chinese cultural revolution and other revolutionary movements worldwide, he asked, "Is it not now time to move on to truly revolutionary actions?"[39]

Foucault's synchronization of his own project with that of the French far left had serious consequences. His presentation of his work, both past and present, changed dramatically. In a 1971 interview in Brazil, he hinted at theoretical inadequacies in his *Archaeology of Knowledge,* saying: "I did not systematize the relations between discursive formations and economic and social formations, the importance of which has been incontestably established by Marxism."[40]

At the same time, Foucault revisited older works in order to present them in a way that was consistent with a thoroughgoing Marxist perspective. The complex theses of *Madness and Civilization* were distilled, in a talk he gave in late 1970, to the notion that the medicalization of madness was brought about for economic and social reasons. If so-called madmen were locked up in 1665, it was because "capitalist industrial society could not tolerate the existence of groups of vagabonds." If so-called madmen were released in 1793, it was because they were deemed "a reserve army of labor power." The madman, rather than a marker for successive eras' confrontation with unreason, was "an avatar of our capitalist societies."[41]

How fully did Marxist categories infiltrate Foucault's thinking? We can glean the extent from his comments in a February 1972 debate. On the subject of penal justice—of which he would later provide such nuanced and multilayered critique—he proclaimed, "Penal justice was not produced by the plebs, nor by the peasantry, nor by the proletariat, but well and truly by the bourgeoisie."[42] The intellectual coherence of the statement is undeniable: the bourgeoisie creates knowledge to serve a sociopolitical function. What is remarkable is its stark simplicity. Foucault's traditional epistemological concerns are wholly absent; his determination to treat knowledge as something more than a stick that authority wields is not yet present.

This, however, was to be the high tide of Marxism in Foucault's work. Over the next three years, it would progressively ebb. By the time *Discipline and Punish* appeared in 1975, the language of class and repression would have vanished entirely; so, too, would the reductionist desire to look at knowledge in terms of its function.

MARXISM, THEN, PROVIDED a ready-made and highly productive framework within which Foucault could discuss the relation between knowledge and sociopolitical forces. It also allowed him, just as crucially during the heady

days following May 1968, to participate in the shared idiom of social protest within the French left. What it did *not* provide, as we have already seen,
was any sophisticated way to conceptualize what Han called the "power–
knowledge nexus." Inasmuch as Marxism gave grounds to speak of power
at all, it was by treating it as a quasi-object possessed by the ruling class:
power and the state were synonymous.

Perhaps unsurprisingly, this is the way Foucault employed the word
power when, in mid-1971, it first appeared in his conceptual arsenal. Speaking on the subject of the prison, he told the readers of *Combat* that "It is one
of the instruments of power, and one of the most excessive. By what right
does power keep it secret?"[43] The meaning of these sentences is unchanged
if we replace the word power (*le pouvoir*) with state (*l'état*). Likewise, in a
discussion later in the year, Foucault equated the conflicts engendered by
power with "the political struggle understood as class war."[44] Yet the philosopher was struggling, even as he made these statements, toward a more
inclusive understanding of the exterior forces that acted upon discourse.
From his first empirical studies of the early 1960s, he had demonstrated a
sensitivity to the existence of power centers that were irreducible to the
state and its extremities. Consistent Marxist critique, however, demanded
that such institutions—hospitals, asylums, schools, courts, and others—be
recognized as instruments of political oppression and class justice.[45]

It has been noted that the high-water mark of Marxism in Foucault's
work came in February of 1972, and that after that date its vocabulary and
conceptual apparatus entered into retreat. It is no coincidence that March
of 1972 saw the publication of *Anti-Oedipus: Capitalism and Schizophrenia*,
the landmark text by psychoanalyst Félix Guattari and Foucault's longtime
philosophical collaborator, Gilles Deleuze. The emergence of a recognizably "Foucauldean" model of power was not only contemporaneous with
that book's publication, but was voiced in explicit reference to it.

Anti-Oedipus was an original work, and on many levels a shocking one.
Stylistically, it was like nothing before it: giddy, fragmented, frequently
obscene, and given to tangents. Thematically, it made the revolutionary
leap of suggesting that the major problem confronting modern Western
culture was not the one identified by Freud, but rather Freudianism itself.[46]
Conceptually, it offered a (nonmetaphorical) vision of the world as an
aggregation of interconnected machines. "What a mistake," wrote the au-

thors, "to have ever said *the* id"; "Everywhere *it* is machines—real ones, not figurative ones: machines driving other machines, with all the necessary couplings and connections."[47]

To mark the arrival of *Anti-Oedipus*, the journal *L'Arc* organized a session during which Foucault would interview Deleuze. The two were a natural pairing. Deleuze and Foucault had united as early as 1966 on a revision of Nietzsche's works. In 1972, they worked together still as social activists. Foucault and Defert had, in 1971, founded the Group for Information on Prisons, or G.I.P. Headquartered in Foucault's apartment at 285 Rue Vaugirard, the G.I.P. had as its mission to raise public awareness about what was going on inside France's prisons, and to provide a forum in which prisoners and ex-prisoners could themselves speak about what they had experienced. Deleuze was immediately attracted to the group's program, and joined Foucault and Defert in their labors. "I was convinced beforehand," Deleuze remarked years later, "that [Foucault] was right, that he had indeed created a group of a wholly new type."[48] Throughout the early 1970s, Deleuze and Foucault operated in close proximity, both as activists and as thinkers.

In the course of the *L'Arc* interview, the two thinkers appeared closely aligned on major theoretical points and intimately familiar with each other's ongoing work. Deleuze remarked, for instance, upon Foucault's use of prison-reform texts by Jeremy Bentham, although Foucault was fully three years away from publishing his findings on that topic.[49] Foucault, for his part, attributed his very ability to confront the question of power to the work of Deleuze:

> If the reading of your books (from the *Nietzsche* all the way up to what I've gleaned of *Capitalism and Schizophrenia*) has been so essential for me, it's because they seem to me to go very far in posing this problem: Beneath this old theme of meaning, signified, signifier, etc., finally the question of power, of the inequality of powers, of their struggles. Each struggle develops around a particular site of power.[50]

Suddenly, "power" was not merely one concern among many for Foucault, but the very nucleus of his concerns as a philosopher. And the idea of searching beneath the "old theme" of meaning, of signified and signifier, and getting to the question of power: this Foucault attributed to Deleuze. Deleuze had seen that there exist multiple centers of power around which struggles develop, and this was a major breakthrough. It was upon this notion that *Discipline and Punish* and *The History of Sexuality* would be built.

Existing frameworks of thought were useless in dealing with the question of power, Foucault suggested, because they failed to recognize it as such. "We still don't know," he told Deleuze, "what power is." Foucault continued:

> And Marx and Freud are perhaps insufficient to help us to know this deeply enigmatic thing, at once visible and invisible, present and hidden, invested everywhere, that is called power. The theory of the State and the traditional analysis of the State apparatus do not, undoubtedly, exhaust the field of exercise of power's functioning.[51]

These two sentences contained no fewer than three innovations, each one of tremendous import. Firstly, Marxism's position as a comprehensive critical theory was called into question. Secondly, analysis in terms of the state and the state apparatus was pronounced unequal to the task of comprehending power in its functioning. Finally, power was described as an enigmatic entity that was visible and invisible, present and hidden, but most importantly, "invested everywhere." Foucault now spoke of power not in the singular, but in terms of "systems of power" that could be found deeply and subtly interwoven "throughout the network of society."[52] Power was distributed, dynamic, and nodal.

FOUCAULT'S HOMAGE TO his interlocutor was more than lip service. This conceptualization of power, which represented a radical innovation for Foucault, owed much to Deleuze. As Foucault himself suggested, it relied upon an image of power not as the indivisible possession of a ruling group, but rather as a centerless network of points.[53] *Anti-Oedipus*, like many of Deleuze's shorter essays, offered just this. It also demanded, as Foucault's use of the expression "functioning of power" hints, a conception of the social field as machinelike in nature. Again, Deleuze had written: "There is no such thing as either man or nature now, only the process that pro-

duces the one within the other and couples the machines together. Produc-
ing-machines, desiring-machines everywhere, schizophrenic machines, all
of species life."[54]

From 1972 onward, Foucault visibly liquidated the anthropological
vocabulary that, for more than a decade, had served him so well. Whereas
for years he had spoken in terms of *culture*, *exclusion*, and *transgression*, he
now spoke of *society*, *mechanisms*, *devices* (*dispositifs*), and *relays*.[55]

If Foucault was able to make such effective use of the ideas in *Anti-
Oedipus*, it was because Deleuzian concepts had, in fact, progressively colo-
nized Foucault's thought since 1970. Daniel Defert notes that, in the autumn
of 1970, Foucault made a study of Deleuze's work.[56] At that time, Deleuze
had just published the two most important books of his career to date: *The
Logic of Sense* and *Difference and Repetition*. Foucault's reading went into a
laudatory review piece entitled "Theatrum philosophicum," which *Critique*
printed in November of 1970. Foucault praised the two books as "great
among the great," and speculated, in words that have since become famous,
that "one day, perhaps, the century will be Deleuzian."[57]

Difference and Repetition was a frontal attack on the Hegelian dialectic,
an effort to found an ontology rooted in the concept of difference. The crucial element for Deleuze was to think difference in itself—that is, not as an
element of negativity to be opposed to identity and sameness, but rather
as an element that is already contained in each and every thing. Difference,
Deleuze affirmed, is *what we are*; repetition—the complex and dynamic
repetition of that difference—is Being. In *The Logic of Sense*, Deleuze crafted
a logic appropriate to a thinking grounded in difference. The aim was to
go to the very origin-point of philosophy's intoxication with identity, to
Platonism, and to overturn it. Overturning Platonism meant, first of all,
recognizing the gravity of Plato's decision to depict Being in terms of the
true and the false, the original and the simulacrum.[58] This founding act had
infected all subsequent Western thought.

Claire Colebrook observes that Deleuze's critique of Platonic simulacra
must be seen simultaneously as an effort to radicalize phenomenology. The
phenomenologists had bypassed any formal attempt to conceptualize the
"subject," preferring to leap "to the things themselves," the *phenomena*.
Their efforts would be directed at comprehending the flux of experience.
Deleuze carried this imperative a step further. Rather than treating the

onrushing stream of phenomena as appearances *of* something (i.e., with something else behind them), Deleuze impishly substituted the Platonic concept of the *simulacrum*, or the appearance as appearance and nothing more.[59] He asked, in essence, that we take only the part of Plato's system that he would have wished us to throw away. This permitted the thinking of a thoroughgoing world-as-appearance, which was crucial to Deleuze's larger project of banishing dualism. A world constructed entirely of simulacra was wholly immanent. Its appearances hid no truer world; it was as it seemed.

Few ideas in *The Logic of Sense* resonated more strongly with Foucault than this one. His review piece lingered over the exploration of simulacra, and held that through this concept new life had been given to metaphysics. Deleuze, wrote Foucault, had not treated metaphysics as an illusion, but instead treated illusion as a metaphysics. That is to say, Deleuze had presented the very idea of "illusion"—of the surface appearance *as opposed to* the real—as the concomitant of a particular Western metaphysics.[60] "Instead of once again denouncing metaphysics as the forgetting of being," he wrote, Deleuze had reinvented it as the "discourse of the materiality of incorporeals."[61] In *The Order of Discourse*, written the following month, Foucault made this expression a personal rallying cry, advocating that philosophy advance "in the direction, paradoxical at first glance, of a *materialism of the incorporeal*."[62]

It is worth asking what "materialism of the incorporeal" meant. For Deleuze, this was a description of Stoic logic. Unlike most of their philosophical contemporaries—and more importantly, unlike Plato—Stoic thinkers had separated causes from effects, on the principle that the two were incommensurable. Only bodies (like rocks and trees) could be causes; effects (like crushing and flowering), which took place *because* of bodies, were a distinct class of entities. Effects were thus *events* that took place at the surface of bodies. They were incorporeal entities that nevertheless manifested themselves in the realm of bodies.[63]

For a number of reasons, Foucault found this problem—that of the interrelation of corporeal and incorporeal entities—to be exceedingly productive. He wrote that Deleuze had discovered, through his interaction with Stoic logic, a new way to "think the pure event." Rather than positing a substance that sustains the accidents of events, Deleuze had worked from the event outward: "The event—the wound, the victory-defeat, death—is always an effect: produced, we may be sure, by bodies that collide, intermingle, or separate. But this effect is itself never a kind of body."[64]

The concept of the "pure event" had transformative power. Inserted into Foucault's own line of questioning, which was archaeological, it yielded a new way of thinking about the relationship between discourse and external world. This is what Foucault was driving at in his inaugural address when he said, with a clear nod to Deleuze, that, "The fundamental notions that confront us now are no longer consciousness and continuity . . . nor are they signs and structure. They are *event and series*."[65]

Foucault here summarized two different ways that contemporary philosophy had attempted to think the history of knowledge. Conscience and continuity were the core concepts of the existentialists and phenomenologists, sign and structure the core concepts of the structuralists. The first group had turned to the idea of a founding subject, while the second had sought to isolate cultural practices that gave rise to meaning. But *event* and *series*—the third set of terms—belonged to Deleuze: they were the key concepts of *The Logic of Sense*. The older ways of linking knowledge to the external world, Foucault implied, could be superseded by a kind of analysis that derived from Deleuzian questioning. The essential point was to treat discourse as a series of events. The discourse-event was incorporeal, but had its impact in the realm of bodies. To advance in the direction of a "materialism of the incorporeal" was thus to grapple with the kind of causality appropriate to the interaction between discourse-as-event and the world.[66]

THE PERIOD FROM 1969 to 1972 was critical in the shaping of the ideas for which Foucault would be best remembered. If his major published works were few, what works there were nevertheless revealed great upheavals within his thought. It was in this stretch of years that the philosopher first turned his attention explicitly to the problem of prisons, first analyzed social and historical questions through the lens of power, and first formulated the outlines of genealogy as a critical program. *Discipline and Punish* and *The History of Sexuality, Volume I*, the thinker's two most forthright works of social criticism, both derived from a thought process that was initiated during this particular moment.

Yet this period that followed so closely in the wake of the events of May 1968 was, viewed from the perspective of his career as a whole, also highly anomalous. During this time, Foucault engaged in a series of openly political activities. He threw himself into the inflamed university situation that, by the end of the decade, would make the names of Vincennes and Nanterre famous beyond France. His work with the G.I.P., his participation in highly visible protests and marches, his occupation alongside colleagues of state facilities, and his adoption of a Marxist-inflected rhetoric of class war and revolution: all of this was uniquely tied to the historical conjuncture of post-1968 France, all of it inseparable from the leftist politics that flourished within the Parisian universities.

For Foucault, this kind of engagement had no clear precedent. While the philosopher always acknowledged that he had, very briefly, been a member of the Communist Party in his youth, he had distanced himself from it in short order. His rise to intellectual prominence had been singularly lacking in the political partisanship that accounted for half the reputation of figures like Althusser and Sartre. Foucault had, with great consistency, shunned group action; he had written not to place himself at the head of movements, but in order, as he noted in *The Archaeology of Knowledge*, "no longer to have a face."[67]

Yet from 1969 onward, Foucault's face would become iconic within the action committees and groupuscules of the French left. The philosopher transitioned, with great rapidity, from the sun-drenched isolation of Tunisia to the politically charged visibility of the Latin Quarter. He made common cause with his longtime nemesis Sartre. He utilized his notoriety to support and defend the causes of the left. He toiled alongside Deleuze to improve the status of prisoners. At the Collège de France, he taught courses on punishment and penal institutions that meshed seamlessly with his political activity, courses that would provide the essential material for *Discipline and Punish*.

These facts have, for the most part, not been considered critical to the understanding of the emergence of the genealogical method. The primary reason for this, again, is that Foucault's development of genealogy has been treated almost exclusively as an intellectual event—an internal affair of philosophy in which historical conditions were at best ancillary, and at worst irrelevant. Yet Foucault's genealogical turn should be seen neither as the result of the methodological failure of archaeology, nor as the result of a sudden interest in Nietzsche. These elements, while present, were not decisive. What *was* decisive was Foucault's concrete situation as a practicing philosopher and social activist in post-1968 France. As this chapter has suggested, the elaboration of the concepts that comprise genealogy is unthinkable absent the specific circumstances in which the philosopher worked. Those circumstances included participation in a philosophical community in which the dominance of Marxist categories was unchallenged, as well as collaboration with no less a thinker than Gilles Deleuze.

Engagement with the French far left and its causes provided an opening for the remarkable, if temporary, upsurge of Marxist concepts within Foucault's thought. It also created the conditions in which, far more so than in the past, it was necessary to situate knowledge in terms of its social function—this being viewed, at first, in class terms. At the same time, a close and mutually productive relationship with Deleuze catalyzed Foucault's unprecedented deployment—always phased in synchronicity with Deleuze's works—of concepts that allowed knowledge to be interlaced with the exterior world: power, machines, incorporeals.

These two philosophical streams together provided a conceptual language in which it was not merely possible but necessary to speak about discourse in a way that showed it to be situated, purposeful, and machine-like. In the years that followed, Foucault would do just that—casually jettisoning much that was integral to his earlier thought in the process.

In this regard, no bit of evidence is more telling than the opening lecture of *The Punitive Society*, Foucault's 1973 course at the Collège de France. Foucault began this course, as was his wont, with a textual citation. Rather than choosing a shocking excerpt from a properly historical work, however, he quoted a passage from Claude Lévi-Strauss's 1955 *Tristes tropiques*. There is a moment, Foucault declared, late in this work, when Lévi-Strauss playfully suggests that societies have but two solutions for dealing with the hostile force of the criminal:

> that is the anthropophagic solution, where absorption permits the simultaneous assimilation and neutralization of this force. The other solution consists of attempting to conquer the hostility of this force. . . . This practice of exclusion, he calls anthropoemia (from the Greek *emein*,

to vomit): mastering the dangerous forces of our society means not assimilating them, but excluding them.[68]

Assimilation or exclusion: here were the two fundamental ways to dispose of the dangerous individual.

For a number of reasons, Foucault continued, this was not the way that he himself would approach the problem of criminality in *The Punitive Society*. The point of contention was *exclusion*. "This notion of exclusion," Foucault said, "seems to me, first of all, a notion that is too 'large,' and more importantly, too composite and artificial." To speak about the punishment of criminals in terms of exclusion was to make a double error. Firstly, it was to treat the sequestration of the criminal individual as if it were a simple and transparent event; the idea of exclusion necessarily ignored "the aims, the relations, and the specific operations of power through which exclusion occurs." Secondly, and perhaps more crucially:

> in this notion, society in general is made to bear the responsibility for the mechanism by which the excluded individual finds himself excluded. In other words, . . . exclusion has the appearance of referring to something like a social consensus that rejects; while behind that there are perhaps a certain number of perfectly specific (and consequently definable) instances of power that are responsible for the mechanism of exclusion.[69]

The notion of exclusion, that is to say, was too imprecise to permit the fine resolution of social analysis that Foucault hoped to achieve. It ignored the specific processes through which punishment occurred, just as it ignored the specific agencies and institutions that drove the "mechanism of exclusion."

What was his audience to think? For "exclusion" was not simply Lévi-Strauss's term: it was a foundational concept in Foucault's own work. *Madness and Civilization* was nothing if not an attempt to explain the exclusion of particular persons from society. *The Order of Discourse* had, as recently as 1970, affirmed the continuing importance of the term. But of course, this was the very point that Foucault wanted to confront. Exclusion *had been* an integral part of his thought, but it would be so no longer.

It was an inadequate concept, unequal to the tasks of genealogy. "I say it all the more," Foucault confessed, "in that I myself have made use, and perhaps abuse, of it."[70]

The notion of exclusion, and the related notion of transgression, should be thought of, Foucault now argued, "as instruments that had their historical importance." For a time, that is to say, they had allowed us to think differently. But it was increasingly evident that these terms themselves had become a hindrance. Analyses that had been conducted in terms of exclusion and transgression—and here, Foucault was pointing directly at himself—should, in the future, pose the question "of power rather than law, of knowledge rather than representation."[71] Lévi-Strauss thus appeared as the representative of an entire conceptual apparatus with which Foucault sought to part. Foucault raised his idol before the crowd only to shatter it in pieces.

The inaugural lecture of the 1973 course explicitly dramatized the transition from one conceptual apparatus to another. Exclusion, trangression, even "culture": these concepts were no longer congruent with the objects of Foucault's analyses. What were those new objects? As Foucault's explanation itself revealed, they were *societies*: societies imagined as machines, performing "functions," carrying out particular "processes" and "operations," generating "mechanisms of exclusion." It was upon the foundation of these latter concepts that Foucault would build *The Punitive Society*, and later *Discipline and Punish*. The restructuring was complete.

PART TWO

Power

CHAPTER THREE

Planetary Forces

Foucault, Iran, and the Nouveaux Philosophes

The age of Candide has returned, in which we can no longer listen to the sweet universal song that makes sense of everything. . . . The morality of knowledge, today, is perhaps to render the real acute, harsh, angular, unacceptable.[1]

ON SEPTEMBER 8, 1978, ARMED FORCES LOYAL TO THE SHAH OF IRAN opened fire on massed demonstrators in Tehran's Jaleh Square, killing hundreds. While the government declared martial law, the enormity of the "Black Friday" massacre quickly became known to the world, and the Iranian political situation seized the attention of Western media. The response of Michel Foucault to the events that followed, the Iranian Revolution of 1978–79, stands, on the surface, as one of the most indecipherable moments in his long trajectory as a public intellectual.

While a number of political events in the 1970s drove Foucault to take a public stand—the condemnation of militants in Spain, the extradition to West Germany of lawyer Klaus Croissant, the state visit of Leonid Brezhnev—none seems to have stirred him so deeply as this Islam-inspired "earthquake" in the Middle East.[2] Ultimately he devoted fourteen published pieces to Iran.

75

Foucault's observations were not those of a disinterested spectator, nor were they made from a comfortable distance. A great deal of his time in the autumn of 1978 was spent in ferrying back and forth between Paris and Tehran, even as the latter city slid toward anarchy. That the force of new ideas was manifesting itself in the Iranian revolution—and that the stakes were significant—was evident to Foucault from the first rumblings.[3]

As critics at the time and since have noted, Foucault's positions were unequivocal. He expressed the belief that detestation of the ruling dynasty was universal, and showed admiration for the courage of the forces opposed to it. In early November, he recorded that "for ten months, the population has opposed a regime that is among the best-armed in the world, and a police that is among the most redoubtable. This they have done barehanded, without recourse to armed struggle, with an obstinacy and a courage that freeze the army in its tracks."[4]

At the same time, Foucault expressed skepticism that the opposition movement was primarily religious in its orientation or in its goals. Behind the Islamist rhetoric of the mullahs, he detected "a movement traversed by the breath of a religion that speaks less of the beyond than of the transfiguration of *this* world."[5] Even as the Ayatollah Khomeini rallied dissident elements from his haven in France, Foucault was writing, "One fact should be clear: by 'Islamic government,' no one in Iran means a political regime in which the clergy would play a role of direction or leadership."[6]

But more centrally, Foucault saw in the Iranian Revolution—in the sermons passed from hand to hand on cassettes, in the monumental prestige of Khomeini, and in the silent unanimity of a people menaced on all sides by guns and tanks—the first spasmodic steps of a new kind of political creature. He saw, or believed he saw, a force that had at last identified the real enemy:

> When I left for Iran, the question that people asked me constantly was, to be sure, 'Is it revolution?'. . . . I didn't respond. But I wanted to say: it's not a revolution in the literal sense of the term . . . It is the insurrection of barehanded men who want to lift the formidable weight that hangs heavy on each of us, but more particularly, on them, these oil workers, these peasants at the frontiers of empires: the weight of the

entire world order. *It is perhaps the first great insurrection against the planetary systems*, the most modern form of the maddest revolt.[7]

The Iranians, Foucault wrote, were akin to the European students of the 1960s in one way: they wanted it all. But the Iranians' "all" was not, he quickly added, the familiar one of a "liberation of desires"; it was, rather, "that of a freeing in regard to everything that marks, in their country and in their daily lives, the presence of the planetary hegemonies."[8]

Where Foucault's eyes were set when he spoke, mysteriously, of a revolt against planetary forces is a question to which we must return. For the time being, it should be said that the events of the winter of 1978–79 went far toward suppressing his early enthusiasm for the Iranian experiment. On February 1, 1979, Khomeini returned to Iran in triumph and established a theocracy that promptly and bloodily settled accounts with its opponents. Attacked in the French press for his support of the revolution, Foucault told the readers of *Le Monde*, "There is, certainly, no shame in changing one's opinion; but there is no reason to say that one has changed it when one is today against the cutting-off of hands, after being yesterday against the tortures of the Savak." Elsewhere in the same piece, he argued that "[t]he spirituality to which those who rose up and died referred is in no way comparable to the bloody government of a fundamentalist clergy."[9] More interesting than this distancing from the excesses of the revolution, however, were the conclusions that Foucault drew from the revolution's outcome. Power is not by nature an evil, he observed, but it is, in its functioning, infinite. "To power," he reflected, "one must always oppose unbreakable laws and rights without restriction."[10]

From the perspective of Foucault's philosophical evolution, a statement like this one raises very serious questions. How, we might ask, had the defiant antihumanist author of *Discipline and Punish* come, in just four years, to formulate a critique of revolutionary violence in the language of political liberalism?

The present chapter represents an effort to address this difficult question. Employing a range of sources, from essays and interviews to Foucault's lecture courses of 1978 and 1979, it argues that the philosopher's position on Iran must be viewed in the context of larger changes in his thought in the late 1970s. The analytical model that Foucault developed and deployed in *Discipline and Punish* (1975) was broadly reconsidered—and ultimately disassembled—in the ensuing half-decade. That reconsideration had its impetus in the work of the so-called *nouveaux philosophes*, with whom Foucault closely aligned himself. By tracing the stages of that transformation, this chapter will attempt to render comprehensible what, at first glance, is mystifying: Foucault's simultaneous embrace of the Iranian Revolution and of the liberal categories that would critique it.

FOUCAULT'S POSITION THROUGHOUT the mid-1970s was that human individuality, far from being a weapon with which to oppose oppression and domination, is in reality a tactic *of* oppression and domination. Foucault explained his view during a 1974 conference:

> I think that individuality is today completely controlled by power, and that we are individualized, at bottom, by power itself. In other words, I do not believe in the least that individualization is opposed to power, but on the contrary, I would say that our individuality—the obligatory identity of each of us—is the effect and instrument of power.[11]

Discipline is the name that Foucault gave to "the set of techniques in virtue of which systems of power have as their goal and result the singularization of individuals."[12]

The concept of discipline allowed Foucault to oppose at once two ideas that he found misleading. The first was the notion that power is exercised massively and negatively, that it is essentially domination.[13] No, Foucault countered, power is not essentially the action of a master upon a slave; it is positive, it *produces* things. Disciplinary systems of power—like hospitals, schools, armies—function effectively by making each person within them an object of study, by testing capacities and comparing against norms, and by deploying the people thus surveyed in a way consistent with their known aptitudes. Individualizing is a means within an economy of power: a way of making delimited populations more effective at some particular task. This is what Foucault meant when he claimed in *Discipline and Pun-*

ish that, "[t]he individual is . . . a reality fabricated by this specific technology of power known as 'discipline.'"[14]

The second notion that Foucault was able to combat was that which located in human individuality a site of resistance to normalization. Psychoanalyzed, liberated selves are not bastions of freedom from a power that stands outside and against them; rather, the very idea that we have a true self, an identity that persists, is evidence of the continual action upon us of a kind of power that works by documenting, by following longitudinally, by individualizing. "Each of us," Foucault wrote, "has a biography, a past that is continually documented someplace or other. . . . There is always an administrative organism capable of saying at any moment who each of us is."[15] Individuality is imposed. Nothing would be more foolish than the attempt to free ourselves by asserting our individuality—by brandishing, as it were, our identity cards.

Within such a philosophical schema, the place assigned to an independent subjectivity appears small or nonexistent.[16] For Foucault's audience in 1975, this was neither unexpected nor extraordinary. If *Discipline and Punish* was novel, it is because, as Gilles Deleuze recognized, it formulated an idea of power that broke completely with "a certain number of postulates that have marked the traditional leftist position."[17] By presenting power as something exercised rather than possessed, by refusing to view the state as the privileged site of power, by denying the primacy of the mode of production in the emergence of power, and by abandoning the concept of ideology as an explanation of power's functioning, Foucault separated himself from Marxist critique in dramatic fashion.

The year 1975 marked, in other ways as well, a major turning-point in Foucault's connection with Marxism. In an unambiguous and public way, Foucault began to detach himself from Marxist categories and methods. A March 1975 interview saw him lambaste Marxism and Freudianism as "the two great failures of these last fifteen years."[18] In a May discussion with students in California, he denied the utility of the concept of the dialectic, and added:

Marx thought—and he wrote it—that labor constituted the concrete essence of man. I think that this is a typically Hegelian idea. Labor is not the concrete essence of man. If man works, if the human body is a productive force, it's because man is obliged to work. And he is so obliged because he is invested by political forces, because he is caught in mechanisms of power.[19]

Claude Mauriac records Foucault's encounter, in September 1975, with a Spanish student who asked him to organize a conference on Marx. He responded, "Don't talk to me about Marx! . . . I'm totally through with Marx!"[20] In this revolt against Marx, Foucault appeared firmly anchored at the side of Deleuze. He told an interviewer that it was Deleuze who had developed the concepts that enabled a ten-year struggle against Marx and Freud.[21] Deleuze, for his part, wrote of Foucault's book that "[i]t is as if, at last, something new surged up since Marx."[22]

FOR MANY BESIDES Foucault at this juncture in French history, a new kind of thinking had become not only possible, but necessary. As Marxism ceased to be the dominant intellectual force in France—the unsurpassable horizon of modernity that confronted Sartre in 1960—it was the most deeply committed of the generation of 1968 who found themselves without a guiding star. That nothing was to be expected from the French Communist Party was a fact long known to the radicals of May; their rhetoric attested to an abiding hatred of its quietism and sclerosis. But that China, too, should be a failure, and that the great project of the Cultural Revolution should take its place alongside dekulakization as a massive and irremediable atrocity—this proved too much for some on the far left.[23] For these "fallen" Maoists and *tiers-mondistes*, many of whom were still in their twenties, there could be no easy leap from Marx to Freud, or to Nietzsche, or to a contemporary variant of desire-liberation: the shattering of idols was total. It was to this category of repentant and masterless leftists that André Glucksmann, the first and most original of the group that came to be known as the *nouveaux philosophes*, belonged.

Glucksmann's *The Cook and the Man-Eater* caused a sensation in 1975. Its subtitle told the whole story: it was an "essay on the relations between the State, Marxism, and the concentration camps." The ingredients of Glucksmann's volume were, in principle, well-known in France: Alexander

Solzhenitsyn's three-volume *Gulag Archipelago* had provoked intense soul-searching on the left from the time of its first appearance in French translation in 1974. If Glucksmann transformed the terms of the discussion about Marxism and the gulag, it was by refusing to understand the enormities committed in the name of Marx as *errors*. This, Glucksmann suggested, had been the role of Marxist theory for forty years: to explain and to explain away. Glucksmann wrote:

> After the reading of *The Gulag Archipelago*, we chalk up all the doctrines coming out of a more-or-less socialist Russia to the *theoretical cretinism* proper to our century. How does the sensible experience of a fascism become the intellectual meditation of socialism? How does the head listen in seriousness to the Kremlin philosophers when before the eyes the camps are uncovered? How can one speak at once of forced labor and of the collective ownership of the means of production? How does slavery lead to a classless society? Just add a sprig of theory![24]

Glucksmann's contention that Stalinism was not a deviation or a mistake, but that its large-scale centralization, its incarcerations and liquidations merely carried out imperatives that were already present in Marx, was profoundly unsettling to large segments of the French left. So, too, was the claim that Stalinism and fascism were morally equivalent phenomena. But Glucksmann took a further step to argue that the nightmare-worlds built by Hitler and Stalin must not be seen as fundamentally different from contemporary *Western* societies; if the former were hypertrophied forms, they nevertheless belonged to the same intellectual horizon and accepted, in Colony, Order, and Work, the same set of imperatives. "On different scales, in line with historical circumstances and local customs," wrote Glucksmann, "our century produces and reproduces this invention which is proper to it: the concentration camp."[25]

That Glucksmann's thesis owed as much to Foucault as to Solzhenitsyn was evident to the critical public. Glucksmann cited *Madness and Civilization* and *Birth of the Clinic*, while referencing Jeremy Bentham's *Panopticon* as a crucial model. More centrally, he adapted long passages in which Foucault treated of "ideal houses of correction" and "ideal fortresses" to his own argumentative ends, seeing in these carceral utopias the eighteenth century's blueprint for the gulag.[26] In its focus on practices of exclusionary isolation as the key to the history of the West, *The Cook and the Man-Eater* appeared to some as a hysterical expansion of Foucault's major themes. "Poor Foucault," wrote François Furet, "become the Bossuet of this universal history!" Reasoning by analogy from the confinement of madmen to the creation of Buchenwald and Kolyma required, as Furet saw it, disingenuousness or flippancy.[27]

Yet the view that Glucksmann presented already found echoes. In early 1976, Guy Lardreau and Christian Jambet, both former militants in the Maoist Gauche Prolétarienne, published *The Angel*, a self-styled "ontology of the revolution." Frankly confessional in tone, the work adopted a Christian vocabulary and a first-person plural voice to describe a political experience of fall, of conversion, and of renewal of hope: "We have taken the test of a conversion, of a cultural revolution from which the lesson has not yet been drawn—its rudiments will be found here. We left it broken by a failure that, in truth, trying still to think it with the thoughts that we had lost, we did not understand."[28] Retiring to the desert, pursued by demons who repeat the wisdom of Ecclesiastes that *nil novi sub sole*, Jambet and Lardreau concluded that they must not apostatize, but rather travel farther along the road of their imperfect conversion. Against all the powers and dominations of the world, they clung to the hope that "another world is, in spite of it all, possible." This possibility they designated the *Angel*.[29]

One of the most notable aspects of the text, apart from the hair shirt that its author–narrators wore, was the modesty of the "provisional" political goals that it pointed toward. While constantly holding forth the possibility of radical change (the Angel), Jambet and Lardreau acknowledged that this change could not be forced, and that militants, "specialists of the revolution," failed to understand this. In our own present it must be a matter of choosing "the best among the masters."[30] The authors, it is certain, resonated with no one so much as Heidegger ("only a God can save us") when they declared that "[t]he Angel must come."[31] Politically, however, their sympathies were for no less a liberal than Raymond Aron, who, as they noted in a 1976 interview, "chooses the best master by the smallest lot of torture, which has the dignity to weigh the master by the size of the oppression that he promises us."[32]

Jambet and Lardreau reached a larger public thanks, in large part, to the efforts of Bernard-Henri Lévy, their editor and publicist at Éditions Grasset. As manager of two new collections in philosophy and human sciences—the "Figures" series and the "Theoreticians" series—the twenty-seven-year-old Lévy worked to bring the authors of *The Angel*, as well as the other writers under his supervision, into the public eye. In the June 1976 issue of the review *Les nouvelles littéraires*, Lévy contributed a "dossier" feature that highlighted the emergence of a new wave in French philosophy, one that returned to "the most ancient questions of the most ancient tradition."[33] In reality, the heterogeneous body of writers that Lévy assembled—Jambet and Lardreau, Jean-Marie Benoist, Jean-Paul Dollé, Michel Guérin, Annie Leclerc, Philippe Nemo, Michel Serres, and Gilles Susong—had little uniting it apart from its members' common affiliation with Grasset. Lévy also suggested that André Glucksmann and Michel Foucault were among these "nouveaux philosophes." As a promotional strategy, this was extremely effective. The term *nouveaux philosophes* became common coin, and Glucksmann in particular, despite his objections, was increasingly identified as a key figure in this emergent iconoclastic movement.

The near-simultaneous publication in May 1977 of two major works—Glucksmann's *The Master Thinkers* and *Barbarism with a Human Face* by Lévy himself—compounded the sense that a new and vigorous school of thought existed. Glucksmann's book was generally praised, Lévy's criticized; both, however, received the tribute of reaction and discussion. *The Master Thinkers* enlarged on the antitheoretical theme broached in *The Cook and the Man-Eater*. The modern West, Glucksmann argued, had trod the paths marked out for it by German philosophy—by Fichte, by Hegel, by Marx, and Nietzsche. Glucksmann's interest was not to once again convict Germany of original sin in relation to the atrocities of the twentieth century.[34] It was rather to suggest that these "master-thinkers,"[35] despite the diversity of their political commitments, partook jointly in a mode of thinking. This philosophical style, born from the experience of conceptualizing and of *thinking through* the French Revolution under conditions that made it impossible to *replicate*, had as its most salient characteristic the prominent role that it assigned to the thinker himself in legislating the development of the state and society. Glucksmann wrote, by way of example, "You can see that

Marx lives in a world where the history of each country is 'incomplete.' The history of Germany is not at all unique in this, seeing as Marx finds the only 'complete works' of history in his head and on the shelves of the libraries where they all finish."[36]

The subsumption of reality into a philosophical discourse that grants itself predictive (or transformative) power is, Glucksmann argued, dangerous. To differentiate the progeny of these thinkers by the observation that some seek to build a rational society from above, others from below, was, for Glucksmann, to miss the essential. "In fact," he wrote, "the master thinkers speak neither of low nor high, but of themselves and their science." Their only aim: "to be listened to."[37] Left and right, we are heirs to this thinking. Glucksmann was looking not to Hegel but to twentieth-century dystopias when he observed that "we dream a unity the perfection of which feeds on German imperfection."[38]

Barbarism with a Human Face was, for its part, as Lévy wrote, an attempt "to think through to the end the idea of pessimism in history."[39] With its pronounced first-person voice, its tone of resigned confrontation with a bitter reality, and its mistrust of all proposed paths to freedom, Lévy's confessional text magnified elements present in *The Angel* and *The Cook and the Man-Eater*:

> I will soon be thirty and I have betrayed the dream of my youth at least a hundred times. Like everyone else, I believed in a new and joyful "liberation": now, without hope, I live with the shadows of my past hopes. I believed in revolution, a faith that came from books, no doubt. . . . Now, feeling the ground give way and the future disintegrate, I wonder not if it is possible but if it is even desirable.[40]

Lévy presented himself as a witness, "writing in an age of barbarism which is already, silently, remaking the world."[41]

What Lévy called barbarism has at its core the Heideggerian notion of technology—that is, the deployment of all beings as standing reserve, and the relentless and goalless will to power on a global scale. The technological understanding of the world accompanies capitalism, and socialism marks not a departure from this understanding but an intensification and a refinement; "It is as though," wrote Lévy, "to the old question of being, socialism answered with an apology for *work*."[42] Barbarism is the natural concomitant of both liberal and socialist societies, Lévy claimed, because capitalism (understood as technology) is insurmountable and has "no womb out of which its future may come." There is no next stage, no *beyond* of capitalism; it is a limitless "plain of ashes" upon which we and our descendants are destined to see out our time.[43]

There is no dialectic to this enlightenment. For Lévy, these are the last days, even if they are bound to go on forever. The only task that remains is to think through the consequences of our time and protest against them. Pessimism yields a provisional morality, which is "No matter where it may come from, resist the barbarian threat."[44] Hence the importance of witnessing, which seems to stand as the last possible meaningful action of what Lévy called the antibarbarian intellectual: "I will do no more than speak of the massacres, the camps, and the processions of death, the ones I have seen and the others, which I also wish to recall."[45] If protest cannot go further than witnessing, it is because the twentieth century has revealed the dangers of theorizing solutions. Lévy admitted not without some shame that he found himself thrown back onto "vulgar" pragmatism: theories must be judged above all by the concrete consequences that they provoke in reality.[46]

IN APRIL 1976, two months before Lévy brought the *nouveaux philosophes* to the attention of the French public, Foucault addressed the question of revolution and the role of the intellectual. He told an interviewer that one of the legacies of Stalinism was that the masses did not desire the revolution in the twentieth century with the ardor that had characterized the nineteenth century. To the extent that revolution was still desired in Europe, it was by an elitist and increasingly terroristic minority. The lessons that Foucault drew from these contemporary truths were straightforward:

> As I see it, the role of the intellectual today should be to reestablish for the image of the revolution the same level of desirability that existed in the nineteenth century. And it is urgent for the intellectuals—supposing, of course, that revolutionaries and a vaster popular stratum lend

them an ear—to restore to the revolution all the charm that it held for them in the nineteenth century.[47]

Implicit in these statements was, firstly, the idea that the revolution, in spite of its tarnished reputation, was a good and praiseworthy thing; secondly, the idea that revolution was a phenomenon that could be and should be urged on by intellectuals; and finally, the idea that intellectuals worked upon the masses either directly or through the intermediary of revolutionaries.

In the year that followed these statements, Foucault's position modified noticeably. The first sign of this came in a March 1977 interview. The interviewer, Bernard-Henri Lévy, pursued Foucault's assertion that all of modern thought had been commanded by the question of the revolution, inquiring whether or not Foucault himself continued to find this *the* question. Foucault responded noncommittally that "[t]he return of the revolution is indeed our problem. . . . You know it well: it's the very desirability of the revolution that is today a problem." When Lévy pressed the point to ask whether Foucault himself desired revolution, the latter said, "I have no response." He suggested that contemporary politics must be about the effort to ascertain, with as much honesty as possible, whether or not the revolution was desirable.[48]

Alongside this softening on the question of revolution, Foucault began to evince skepticism toward all professedly revolutionary regimes worldwide. In an October 1977 interview, he declared that, looking around at the contemporary world, one could say that for the first time since 1917, perhaps since 1848, "there is no longer a single spot on Earth where the light of a hope could burst forth"—not in the Soviet Union or its satellites, manifestly; but neither in Cuba, nor in China, nor in Vietnam, Cambodia, or Palestine. He announced:

> For the first time, the left, faced with what has just happened in China, this entire body of thought of the European left, this revolutionary European thought which had its points of reference in the entire world and elaborated them in a determinate fashion, thus a thought that was oriented toward things that were situated outside of itself, this thought has lost the historical reference-points that it previously found in other parts of the world. It has lost its concrete points of support.[49]

Not just Marxist theory but the entire socialist tradition was to be called into question, because "everything that this socialist tradition has produced in history is to be condemned."[50]

The link between the worldwide political failures of revolutionary socialism ("what has just happened in China") and the disorientation of the European left was evident to Foucault. But so, too, was the connection between those failures and the paths of contemporary European critical thought, his own included. In November 1977 Foucault observed that, for a century, political analysis had found itself commanded by "important and somewhat solemn theoretical edifices"—by economic theories or by philosophies of history—of which Marxism was the prime example. Today, he suggested, this relationship was coming apart. The experiences of the preceding thirty years, "with Stalinism for example, China equally," had revealed traditional Marxist analysis to be unusable. "I think that it is the failure of the great theoretical systems to produce present-day political analysis," he said, "that now throws us back upon a kind of empiricism which is none too glorious, the empiricism of the historians."[51] Lest there be confusion about his own position, Foucault called himself in a separate interview "a blind empiricist."[52]

Foucault's research from this period bore out this self-assessment. His essay of early 1977, "Vie des hommes infâmes," introduced a collection of "lives": the terse biographies of eighteenth-century delinquents committed to prison by *lettre de cachet*.[53] There was no concern on Foucault's part to narrate or to interpret these fragments of existence, still less to present them as case studies in the functioning of a certain kind of power. It was simply to transcribe them as they stood recorded in the archives of their jailers. Any analysis of the political significance of these lives would have to come after and not before a study of the evidence; even then, it would receive no prompting from Foucault, no afterword explaining the schema and categories that would allow us to see the big picture. The same may be said of Foucault's document-driven 1978 study *Herculine Barbin*. Here, Foucault so foregrounded the evidence that, in these "memoirs of a nineteenth-century French hermaphrodite," there was nothing that might be classed as interpretation at all, save the initial selection of the topic and documents.[54]

Empiricism had its corollary in, firstly, thematic unity, and secondly, a certain intellectual ethic. By focusing on the documentary evidence generated in practices that isolate and observe people, Foucault stayed ever close to the theme of social subjugation. By privileging concrete evidence and testimony over any explanatory system that would offer to make sense of them, Foucault carried out the ethical imperative of "letting suppressed voices speak."[55] He carried it out, however, in the new sense of refusing to reduce the individual human experience to an epiphenomenon of a narrative taking place on a higher level, and of ceasing to see in the historically situated existence a manifestation of a universal like class—or *épistémè*. Foucault affirmed that lives never *represent*, they simply *are*. Gently as the shift may have occurred, this is a view that placed Foucault in opposition to his own positions of ten years earlier.

THE MAGNITUDE OF this change became visible at the point where Foucault's work converged, briefly, with the thought of the *nouveaux philosophes*. In May 1977 Foucault reviewed Glucksmann's *The Master Thinkers* for *Le Nouvel Observateur*. The short piece that resulted, "La grande colère des faits," read like a manifesto for a new philosophical humility.

Glucksmann, wrote Foucault, had produced a "treatise of despair" by turning around Kant's question of what it is permitted to hope, and asking instead in what we must abandon hope. The answer: "the discourses that hold us still under the weight of their promises."[56] Grand theory of the kind that exculpates history by revealing its pattern is what we can no longer accept today, Foucault argued. We have met too many twentieth-century Candides, survivors of massacres and slaughterhouses—Czechs, Greeks, Chileans, Ukrainians—to be able to tolerate the whispering that says: "*It matters little, a fact will never be anything by itself; listen, read, wait; it will be explained farther along, later, at a higher level.*'"[57] If the mission of so much of philosophy since Hegel had been to render the real rational, then the morality of knowledge today must be to do the opposite. Foucault joked darkly: "The decisive test for the philosophers of Antiquity was their capacity to produce sages. . . . in the modern era, it is their aptitude to make sense of massacres. The first helped men to support their own death, the second, to accept that of others."[58]

The Cook and the Man-Eater marked a major step, claimed Foucault, because it revealed the gulag as the consequence not of an unfortunate error, but precisely of theories that were "true" in the order of politics. *The Master Thinkers* allowed a further step forward in that rather than refuting thought by thought, or challenging "wrong" interpretations with "right" ones, it instead placed thought face to face with the reality that mimics it: "For [Glucksmann] it's about plating ideas with the death's-heads that resemble them."[59] It confronted philosophy with the killing fields and asked it to recognize itself.

Foucault saw in Glucksmann's work a resonance with his own: master-narratives of liberation through sacrifice, replaced by unsystematic and empirical solicitude for the imprisoned and the silenced. But he also seemed to acknowledge with admiration those places where Glucksmann had surpassed him and now lighted the way. Glucksmann's profound and almost visceral anti-Hegelianism was a revelation because, in asking how we might become post-Hegelian, it didn't turn Hegel on his head, or reverse him, or humanize him, or free him of his idealism: it wondered instead how we might be "*not at all Hegelian.*" Likewise, Glucksmann's deft mise-en-scène placed *The Master Thinkers*, for Foucault, alongside the great books of philosophy: it was a theater-piece that "raises up, at the heart of the highest philosophical discourse, these fugitives, these victims, these irreducibles . . . . in brief, these 'bloodied heads' and other white forms, that Hegel wished to efface from the night of the world."[60]

This public position-taking on a major and controversial work revealed incompatibilities with Foucault's former views. The author of *The Archaeology of Knowledge*, cocking an ear toward the "white forms," now seemed to put the individual speaker ahead of the determinant system. Perhaps more importantly, he said "no" to the very idea of bloodshed in the name of progress. In this, he may have been calling to account the Foucault of 1971, whose debate on the subject of popular justice had seen him uphold the sound instincts of the people in carrying out the September massacres of 1792.[61] Finally, he now took the line, with Glucksmann (as well as Lévy and others), that the pivotal event of the twentieth century was not an epistemological one but a political one: not the death of man but the birth of the gulag. Each of these changes was in itself substantial.

Yet if, in the last years of the 1970s, Foucault departed from philosophical positions that he had previously discovered and occupied, he also, as his contemporaries noted, departed from the company of those philosophical comrades who occupied them still.

THE RESPONSE OF Foucault to *The Master Thinkers* must be viewed in the context of the reception in France of the *nouveaux philosophes* as a whole. For again, by May 1977 Glucksmann's work *was* seen, correctly or incorrectly, as part of a larger current of thought—one that included Lévy, Jambet, Lardreau, and a number of other lesser-known writers. The general contemporary impression of this movement was that it was youthful; that it was anti-Marxist and even anti-leftist without quite being of the right; and that it was the first serious challenge to the post-1968 configuration in philosophy. Weighing in on Glucksmann at this particular moment, Foucault offered an eagerly anticipated opinion of the value of this ascendant current of thought.

Many others agreed with Foucault that there was substance to the arguments of the *nouveaux philosophes*. Philippe Sollers called Lévy's appeal for an antibarbarian intelligentsia "the dissidence of our time," carried out in "[t]he first great romantic style since 68."[62] Alain Touraine asked what would endure of the crisis that the new current had provoked, and responded:

> This, which is important, that intellectuals who wish above all to combat the State power will do it from now on in the appropriate language: that of liberalism. The confusion of the anarchistic spirit and the Bolshevik spirit, which defined Sartrian thought and its almost uninterrupted train of errors, is from here on impossible.[63]

Jean Daniel declared that while he remained a Marxist, he conceded the *nouveaux philosophes* "the subversive merit of precipitating our rejection of the dogmas of the religion of history."[64]

A very considerable group of French intellectuals found the new movement to be, on the contrary, an amalgam of political reaction and philosophical retrogression. Jean-Marie Vincent, a committed Trotskyist, labeled

Glucksmann a "punk intellectual," accused him of having composed in *The Master Thinkers* an apology for quietism, and blasted his leftism as a "grimacing caricature" of a genuine and ongoing struggle for liberation.[65] Cornelius Castoriadis denounced in the *nouveaux philosophes* "the cluttering of markets with the collages of a plastic *pop*-philosophy."[66] Xavier Aubral and François Delcourt spoke for many of these detractors when they published, late in 1977, *Against the New Philosophy*, a book-length indictment of what the authors viewed as a nascent orthodoxy.[67]

But unquestionably the most important and far-reaching of these responses was that of Gilles Deleuze. Harshly criticized in *Barbarism with a Human Face*—both for espousing a crypto-Marxist philosophy and for contributing, with his *Anti-Oedipus*, to a generalized spirit of cultural decadence—Deleuze struck back in a June interview. He said flatly of his antagonists that "their thought is null." Purveyors of great and empty concepts like "THE master, THE world, THE rebellion, THE faith, etc.," they offered only one novelty, which was to have "introduced into France literary or philosophical marketing." Their articles, interviews and television broadcasts, Deleuze argued, were richer in content than the works that they purported to discuss—and this by design. With the *nouveaux philosophes* and their disc-jockey-impresario Bernard-Henri Lévy, "*journalism discovered in itself an autonomous and sufficient thought*"; their enterprise taken as a whole represented "the submission of all thought to the media." Finally, Deleuze said, it was a matter for him of moral revulsion: "What disgusts me is very simple: the nouveaux philosophes make a martyrology: the Gulag and the victims of history. They live on cadavers."[68]

Lévy and his associates had discovered the witness-function, which they united with other obsolete philosophical attitudes: the "author" and the "thinker." If a concept as reactionary as the thinking Subject had returned to the philosophical scene, declared Deleuze, it could only be a reflection of the awesome intellectual narcissism of the *nouveaux philosophes*, for whom reality resided in the pure act of the thinker.[69]

Foucault's review and Deleuze's interview, for all that they did not directly address each other, placed the two philosophers on opposite sides of a yawning divide. Implicitly or explicitly, Foucault gave his approval to philosophical tactics—the witness-function, journalism–philosophy, the employment of the authorial "I"—that Deleuze could not accept. Deleuze, for his part, publicly denounced in emotional language a type of thought with which Foucault had professed an affinity. It was around this time that the two men, close associates and friends for a decade and a half, ceased to see one another.[70] Of these two thinkers whose ideas were so closely aligned in 1975, it is Deleuze who had arguably held the course. It was Foucault who would have to find a language and a set of concepts consistent with his transformed perspective.

IN THE REVAMPING of concepts that followed upon these months of debate, Foucault turned increasingly, as Touraine had suggested would be the case for the descendants of the *nouveaux philosophes*, to an exploration of liberalism. The topic itself, not simply liberalism in general but, eventually, mid-twentieth-century neoliberalism as it developed in Germany and in the United States, represents such a departure from everything that Foucault had treated previously in his courses that it will be worthwhile to trace the path by which Foucault came to it.

In his 1978 course at the Collège de France, entitled *Security, Territory, and Population*, Foucault studied the emergence of what he called reason of state in early modern Europe. This project seemed to relate to prior investigations: in tracing the rise of state power and extrajudicial forms of authority in the seventeenth century, he was on terrain already scouted in *Madness and Civilization* and *Discipline and Punish*. Examining the texts of, among others, Philipp von Chemnitz, Giovanni Antonio Palazzo, Louis Turquet de Mayenne, and Nicolas de La Mare, Foucault explored the development and transformation of doctrines that sought to provide a specific rationality of governance.[71] One of his determinations was that the *police* is the apparatus put in place to make reason of state function, and that the notion of *réglementation* is the concomitant of administering one's territory according to the principles of reason of state.[72] The goal of the police, Foucault argued, is the oversight and control of the activity of the citizenry to the extent that such activity represents a differential element in the internal development and external power of the state.[73] The "police state," in the specific sense that Foucault gave to that term, is the state that is interested in its subjects in their capacity as *doers*; insofar as this kind of state comes to interject itself into every aspect of its people's lives, it is precisely in order to rationalize and maximize activity to the benefit of the state.

The great project of the police, Foucault argued in the final lecture of the course, is to "make of the town a sort of quasi-convent, and of the kingdom a sort of quasi-town." That is to say, the early modern "police state" is a utopia at the national scale, a "disciplinary dream" with permanent observation and control as its aim.[74] Again, such an argument could only seem a subtle variant on a familiar theme. What made this course a departure is that Foucault did not end the story at this point. Rather, he put forward the surprising claim that it is not this "art of government" whose heirs we are today. We are instead the heirs of the form of governmental rationality that arose to *criticize* it: of a principle of rationality which held, against reason of state as previously defined, that many processes within the order of human cohabitation have their own regularity, and should be allowed to run their course. For this new, economics-inspired art of governance, the well-being of all would no longer depend on the authoritarian intervention of the state in the form of *réglementation* by the police. Instead, the good of all would be assured by the individual behaviors of each, outside of the state.[75]

The first lecture of the 1979 course, *The Birth of Biopolitics*, called this new governmental rationality by its name: liberalism. Liberalism recognizes that there are certain "naturalities" within the order of things, and that one governs better, even according to the power-based standard of reason of state, when, rather than attempting to override these regularities, one conforms to them. Thus, said Foucault, through political economy we see enter into the art of government the possibility of autolimitation (in function of "naturalities") and the question of truth (in the sense that government needs objective knowledge in order to govern properly). These two points are critical, in that their absorption into the art of government overturns a rationality which was predicated on seeing and controlling everything from the center. "Such is, I think, in this question of autolimitation by the principle of truth," Foucault asserted, "the key point that political economy introduced into the limitless presumption of the police state."[76]

There are a number of ways to understand Foucault's attention to liberalism during 1978 and 1979. It may be that it is a natural outgrowth of the multi-century survey of arts of government conducted in the courses. If we heed Foucault's statement in a 1978 interview that *Discipline and Punish* was intended as a study of the links between the exercise of a certain kind of power over individuals on one hand, and the birth of liberal regimes on the other, it may be that he wanted, by 1978, to hone and refine his views on this point.[77] It may even be, as Foucault noted in *The Birth of Biopolitics*, that in the wake of contemporary French debates on law and liberties, of the economic principles of Helmut Schmidt, and of the paths trod by dissidents from the East, the problem of liberalism "finds itself effectively posed for us currently in our immediate and concrete actuality."[78] It may be all of these things, or none.

But viewed from another angle, the attention Foucault gave to the specific question that is liberalism fulfills a vital role in the evolution of his thought. In a 1980 lecture delivered at Berkeley, Foucault told his audience that, in trying to explain the processes through which the self is constructed, he feared that he may have, in the past, "insisted maybe too much on the techniques of domination."[79] In reality, he continued, he had come to see the formation of the self as the result of a dynamic tension between techniques of coercion and techniques in which the individual acts upon himself. "The contact point at which the way individuals are driven and known by others is tied to the way they conduct themselves and know themselves," said Foucault; "This can be called *government*."[80] Government is a difficult and never-static equilibrium.

Connections between this notion and Foucault's course of the previous year are apparent. In *The Birth of Biopolitics*, Foucault announced that what he wished to study was not the actual practice of government (in the sense of its decisions), but rather its reflective manner—its reflection on the best way of governing. He would examine "the self-consciousness of government."[81] It is in this context that Foucault, as noted above, observed that liberal political economy is the force that introduces the question of "autolimitation by the principle of truth" into the "limitless presumption of the police state."

In other words, in the period from 1978 to 1980, Foucault's model of power and his model of the individual underwent transformations that are precisely analogous. The *individual*, no longer seen as the pure product of mechanisms of domination, appears as the complex result of an interaction between outside coercion and techniques of the self. *Mechanisms of power* (like schools and factories, but also states), no longer seen as agents of invasive observation and control, appear as chastened overseers regulating their territory and population, at least in part, according to the dictates of objective knowledge.

At the most basic level, Foucault's model of the individual changed from "determined" to "partially self-constituting," while his model of the exercise of power changed from absolutism to liberalism.

WHEN THE FIRST shock of the Iranian Revolution hit Europe, Foucault was in between teaching *Security, Territory, and Population* and *The Birth of Biopolitics*—that is, in between his courses on absolutist and liberal reason of state. For a number of reasons, and as his journalistic observations make clear, it appeared to Foucault that what the Iranians were confronting in the repressive, Western-backed regime of the Shah was itself something on this order: a brutal combination of police-state absolutism and modernization in the best liberal tradition.

The "hard" portion of the Iranian state power was visible everywhere: "[i]n the Iran of oil and poverty, the army occupies a very important place." Four million people, or one in six Iranians, lived off of it. It was, according to Foucault, not one army but four: a traditional army installed on the land and given tasks of surveillance, an elite guard for the Shah, a sophisticated combat army, and a body of thirty to forty thousand American advisers.[82] With its far-flung network of prisons, its torture chambers and its terror-inspiring secret police, Iran was "the most heavily policed monarchy in the world."[83]

This superpower-backed network of steel, however, captured only half of the "planetary systems" that Foucault saw weighing upon the people of Iran. The other half, it would seem, was the silent penetration, as "modernization," of social, economic, and even spiritual forces that were truly global—as Foucault put it, "the weight that hangs heavy on each of us." These two sets of forces, hard and soft, undergirded a world order that existed essentially at the expense of "these oil workers, peasants at the frontiers of empires."

Foucault described the experience of walking into an Iranian bazaar, just reopened after a strike of eight days. What he found was row upon row of massive sewing machines, of the kind advertised in nineteenth-century European newspapers; each was elaborately decorated with fine filigree designs of old Persian motifs. These obsolete western goods, marked with the sign of a long-expired orient, all bore the inscription "Made in South Korea." Foucault commented: "I had then the feeling of understanding that recent events did not signify the retreat of the most backward groups before a too-brutal modernity; but the rejection, by an entire culture and an entire people, of a *modernization* that is in itself an *archaism*.[84] Modernization in Iran was a dead weight, Foucault emphasized. It was a thing of the past, a political project and a schema of social transformation that was rejected not because of the checks that it had suffered, but "on account of its very principle."[85]

"Planetary" is not a word that Foucault employed with any frequency, either in speeches or in print. He did, however, use it in a lecture on February 14, 1979, two weeks after the triumph of Khomeini. The expression that he employed is "Solzhenitsyn on a planetary scale," which he specified to mean "concentrationary universe," or the gulag at the insidious scale of capitalism.[86] This phrase, which was not used à propos of Iran, nevertheless seems to sum up nicely what it was that Foucault saw himself opposing in the regime of the Shah. The kingdom of the Pahlavi dynasty was a contemporary dystopia, a gulag of millions; its drive to modernity was a sham—that is, it was more visibly so than everyone else's.

The support that Foucault lent to the Iranian Revolution was predicated on the fact that he never viewed it as one. The word "revolution," prior to the actual seizure of power by Khomeini, was almost completely absent from his reports: it was a "revolt," an "uprising," a "movement." This is fundamental. For Foucault, what took place in Iran in the waning months of 1978 was not an organized political event in any traditional sense; it was certainly not part of the West's "gigantic effort," already two centuries old, "to capture the uprising in the interior of a rational and masterable history."[87] Foucault was expressing enthusiasm and not trepidation when he wrote, in November 1978, "What is happening in Iran has that within it to trouble today's observers. They can find neither China, nor Cuba, nor Vietnam, but rather a tidal wave without military equipment, without an avant-garde, without a party."[88]

Iran was the light of hope of which Foucault had despaired in 1977. Its legitimacy as a force for liberation was established, in Foucault's eyes, by the fact that it was *not* Marxist, *not* revolutionary, *not* political, *not even* philosophical. It was a Sobibor—a collective uprising from within the walls of the concentration camp—and Foucault was determined to stand with it.

The path that events took in Tehran was a turning point for the philosopher. After mid-1979, he never wrote or spoke publicly about Iran again. Prior to that, however, he did make a last impassioned plea to Mehdi Bazargan, the Khomeini-appointed prime minister of the new Islamic state, to bring a halt to summary trials and hasty executions. In the course of the brief open letter, published in *Le Nouvel Observateur*, Foucault made reference to "human rights" four times, and to the concept of "rights" seven additional times.[89] "One must—and it's imperative—give to the prosecuted," Foucault wrote, "as many means of defense and as many rights as possible." Is public opinion against the defendant? Is he hated by his people? This itself confers upon him rights all the more intangible. "For a government, there must not be any 'last of men.'"[90] Foucault had chosen a path. One wonders if Lévy's words pursued him:

> I don't believe in man either, and I am quite willing to agree with my worthy teachers that he is in the process of disappearing from the stage of thought; but I simply believe that without a certain idea of man the State soon surrenders to the whirlpool of fascism. I do not grant the slightest theoretical value to what Marxists call formal freedoms, but practically, here and now, I do not see how we can deny their fabulous power to establish and preserve the division of society, and consequently to form a rampart against the barbarian temptation. In other words, we are now in the disturbing position of having nothing left with which to decide political questions but the most fragile and uncertain tools. It is time, perhaps, to write treatises on ethics.[91]

PART THREE

Subjects

CHAPTER FOUR

Deep Subjects

Foucault and the Return of the Individual

The subjectivation of Western man is not Greco-Roman, but Christian.[1]

THE FINAL STAGE OF MICHEL FOUCAULT'S CAREER WAS MARKED BY A number of highly visible departures. He increasingly avoided his native soil, opting to spend an ever-greater share of each year in California. For the first time, he turned away from the study of the modern world in order to interrogate the distant past: hellenistic Greece, imperial Rome, the first centuries of Christianity. He abandoned his sharp focus on the societal functioning of power in order to grapple with—of all things—religion and philosophy. And he found a new set of interlocutors in parallel with his new itinerary: historians of the antique world like Paul Veyne, Pierre Hadot, Peter Brown; Berkeley academics like Paul Rabinow and Hubert Dreyfus; liberal philosophers like Jürgen Habermas.

The greatest departure, however, was that which saw Foucault embrace the concept of subjectivity. The notion of the independent and freestanding subject was simply inadmissible within the framework of Foucault's thought in the 1960s and 1970s. The "speaking subject" had, in some sense, formed the negative of his entire intellectual career. From *Raymond Roussel* to *The Archaeology of Knowledge* to the first volume of *The History of Sexuality*, the effort to *chasser le sujet*—to tear the cloak of self-evidence from the autonomous individual and replace it with the dispersion of language, of discourse, and of power—was central to Foucault's philosophical project. As the 1980s began, this guiding star went into eclipse.

As the foregoing chapter demonstrated, Foucault's interaction with the *nouveaux philosophes*, as well as his abortive engagement with the Iranian Revolution, profoundly affected his work. His migration away from the concept of discipline—even before the ink on American copies of *Discipline and Punish* was fully dry—and toward an understanding of individualization that was rooted less in practices of domination than in auto-initiated practices of limiting and restraint was, to say the least, a paradigm shift. From 1980 on, subjectivity took center stage in his work in a way that was without precedent. The scare quotes were sliding off of the word "subject."

This chapter will examine the rise of the subjectivity theme in Foucault's thought during the last years of his life. Making use of articles, major works, interviews both published and unpublished, but most crucially of the lecture courses that Foucault delivered at the Collège de France in 1979 and 1980, it will argue that the philosopher, as the new decade began, was moving toward a "strong" vision of the subject. Far more than his collaborators were willing to recognize at the time, or historians to recognize since, the late Foucault took individuals seriously.

THE FOREGOING CHAPTER recounted, within the context of Foucault's writings on the Iranian Revolution, some of the basic themes of *The Birth of Biopolitics*, his 1979 course at the Collège de France. As Foucault's most advanced students understood almost immediately, *The Birth of Biopolitics* marked a conceptual evolution of no mean importance. The quotation with which Foucault began the course—Robert Walpole's dictum that whatever stood still should be left to itself—should have been sufficient warning of the change.[2] For the stated aim of the lecture series, as the title indicated, was to gain clarity on the question of biopolitics, a topic with which Foucault had wrestled since 1975. The philosopher hoped to demonstrate, he told his audience during the opening lecture, that the manifold problems that he grouped under the label *biopolitics* "have as their central link what is called population." He asked his listeners' pardon for what he imagined would be a brief digression, as he hoped to preface the discussion of biopolitics with a description of the rise of political liberalism. "Once we know what the governmental regime called liberal was, it seems to me, we will be able to grasp what biopolitics is."[3]

In fact, biopolitics never returned to the table. Whatever its title, *The Birth of Biopolitics* became an investigation of liberal political theory. The central theme of the course was the emergence and transformation of a kind of "governmentality" that ruled not by top-down intervention but rather by a calculated leaving-alone: a *laissez-faire* state. The contrast with prior studies of the functioning of power was stark. The time frame—the end of the eighteenth century and the beginning of the nineteenth—was identical to that of *Discipline and Punish*, *Birth of the Clinic*, *The Order of Things*, and any of a number of Foucault's shorter works; the argument, however, ran in the opposite direction. Rather than a tightening of the reins of social control, Foucault described a kind of slackening: a power that functioned with precision inasmuch as it let natural processes pursue their course, inasmuch as it let individuals follow their inclinations.

But of which individuals was one speaking? As the previous chapter noted, one of Foucault's greatest contributions to post-1968 social critique had been a radical questioning of the very concept of the modern individual. In *Discipline and Punish*, *The History of Sexuality, Volume 1*, and elsewhere, he challenged the self-evidence of the individual, and flatly denied that individuality could be opposed to authority as if the two were somehow antithetical. Rather, he argued, individuals were the *product* of highly rationalized discursive systems; they were the effect of a modern configuration of power. Foucault called this power-configuration "discipline."[4] Discipline—or the society-wide emergence of institutions like schools, factories, and prisons—created the conditions in which populations could be monitored, assessed, and acted upon with such a degree of refinement that power would be brought to bear upon each subcomponent of the group *separately*. In a development without direct historical precedent, masses of information would be assembled and recorded about each and every person within a population. Thus would "individuals" emerge in history. On this point, Foucault's antirealism was absolute. No discipline, no individuals. Prior to the appearance of disciplinary institutions and their associated discourses of psychiatry, clinical medicine, and criminology, "individuals" did not exist. No more, Foucault would have argued, than astronauts existed prior to the discourse of aeronautics.

It was in this sense that Foucault's interest in the liberal discourse of individuals was surprising. Alessandro Fontana, a Foucault disciple who worked closely with the philosopher throughout the late 1970s, recalled this time in a 1984 interview: "We said to ourselves then: through a reflection on liberalism, Foucault is going to give us a book on politics. Liberalism seemed to also be a detour to rediscover the individual outside of the mechanisms of power."[5] To study the doctrines of "liberal governmentality," whether those of the Physiocrats or of the Chicago School, was, as Foucault was well aware, to immerse oneself in a discourse that treated individuals as primary and foundational—as the atoms of the social structure. It was to bracket, however temporarily, the circa-1975 theoretical structure that saw in the rhetoric of individuals little more than the mask of a power that surveys and commands. Such a move was not in itself a declaration of faith. But it was startling.

The argument that Foucault presented in *The Birth of Biopolitics* was a relatively straightforward one. Drawing in copious detail from the texts of Scottish Enlightenment thinkers like Adam Smith and Adam Ferguson, as well as Physiocrats like François Quesnay, Foucault made the case to his audience that liberalism represented the colonization of reason of state by the discourse of economics. Liberalism, that is to say, was an economically inspired critique of a the administrative state as it arose in the seventeenth century—a critique that would ultimately prove quite successful. Far more than a mere demonstration of the errors of mercantilist politics, the political economy of an author like Smith constituted, as Foucault saw it, a disqualification of a political reason indexed to the state and sovereignty.[6]

To govern according to the dictates of liberalism required a number of changes in perspective. It demanded that one think not in terms of state and sovereign, but of civil society. In parallel with this, it demanded that a nation's territory and resources be managed not in the interest of the ruler, but rather in the collective interest of the ruled. Finally, and most importantly, it demanded the recognition of a new kind of political subjectivity.

The "juridical subject"—the *sujet de droit* as he had emerged in the administrative state—was not merely distinct from the "economic subject" who acted within the civil society; the two obeyed rigorously different logics.[7]

The subject of law—or *homo juridicus*—is characterized by acceptance of renunciation: renunciation of natural rights in exchange for limited positive rights. The economic subject—*homo oeconomicus*—is, in contrast, a subject of *interest*. He acts in accordance with his needs and wants. Not only can he not be asked to renounce his interests, but he must pursue them to the fullest if the interests of all are to be served. The market and contract function in exactly opposite ways. "They are," Foucault declared, "two heterogeneous structures."[8]

In relation to juridical will, interest thus constituted an irreconcilable element. *Homo oeconomicus* and *homo juridicus* represented distinct forms of political subjectivity; that is to say, they posed wholly different questions to the power that would govern them. These two kinds of "subjects"— the double entendre was essential to the argument—experienced power through different grids. The subject of interest did not respect contracts because they were contracts; he respected them because it was in his interest to do so. This, Foucault explained, was what Hume was driving at when he argued (against Blackstone) that the existence of a juridical structure did not negate the subject of interest: the latter continued to exist and overflow the subject of law.

WHAT WAS SIGNIFICANT in all this? Firstly, Foucault had described a moment in the history of thought in a profoundly ungenealogical way. Genealogy would have required that he seek out a historical discontinuity in the configuration of power in order to examine the associated transformation in knowledge. This had not been his approach. Rather, he had analyzed the discourse of political theory over time in order to highlight what he viewed as a massive strategic shift. Methodologically, this was far closer to what he had attempted in the proto-archaeology of *The Birth of the Clinic* than to, say, the first volume of *The History of Sexuality*.

Secondly, and perhaps more centrally, Foucault had placed the emphasis of the study on changes in so-called political subjectivity. This ran against the grain of all of his previous studies, which, as has been shown, continually reaffirmed the derivative nature of subjectivity, and shied away from any perspective that smacked of "lived experience." The innovation was not lost on Foucault's students. In a 1984 interview, Fontana observed to Foucault that: "Your impatience for the phenomenological subject was well-known. At that moment, one was beginning to speak about a subject of practices, and the rereading of liberalism was undertaken somewhat in that spirit." That the analysis of political subjectivity was a first and tentative step toward a reappraisal of subjectivity in general was also apparent. Liberalism appeared to Fontana, again, as "a detour to rediscover the individual outside of the mechanisms of power."[9]

All three parts of Fontana's appraisal were essentially correct. Liberalism was a "detour," a path that would open up new vistas for Foucault, but that he would not follow to its end. It would allow him to "rediscover the individual," inasmuch as it would free him to think and speak openly, for the first time in his career, about subjects who possessed liberty of action. Finally, liberalism would place him "outside of the mechanisms of power," offering (in itself) a model of a power-configuration that bore little resemblance to the "society of surveillance" as it appeared in *Discipline and Punish*.

Liberalism, as Foucault presented it, was precisely that kind of power within which the center comes to recognize that it cannot control all of the nodes, and that, in fact, the life of the nation is made up of a number of processes that are not only independent of the central authority, but which augment the force of the nation only to the extent that they are left alone to run their course. The infiltration of political discourse by economics was, Foucault argued, the theoretical admission of the futility of absolutist interventionism. The world, as the economists saw it, was not a transparent system to be manipulated and fine-tuned. It was, on the contrary, opaque and nontotalizable. Foucault intoned:

> Economics is an atheist discipline, economics is a discipline without God, economics is a discipline without totality, economics is a discipline that begins to demonstrate not only the uselessness, but the impossibility of a sovereign point of view, of a point of a *sovereign's* point of view, upon the totality of the State that is his to govern.[10]

Listeners attuned to Foucault's patterns of speech would have recognized in this last trope a familiar Foucauldean theme. The "point of view of the sovereign" not only carried echoes of the "place of the king," but directly referenced what Foucault had called as late as 1977 "the eye of power."[11]

To call economics an "atheist discipline" was to say that it denied the very possibility of a sovereign or godlike point of view, of a fixed point from which to gain purchase on a "totality" of social forces. Modern liberalism emerged, Foucault alleged, to formulate the incompatibility between, on one hand, the nontotalizable multiplicity characteristic of subjects of interest (or economic subjects), and, on the other hand, the totalizing unity of the juridical sovereign. The liberal critique revealed the inadequacy of a governmental discourse which had believed a sovereign center capable of monitoring—and thereby controlling—a society of independently-functioning individuals.

To present such an argument was to speak, as Foucault so often did, in two registers. In the first, he was describing the process through which these discursive positions—that is, those positing the possibility of panopticism—were called into question historically. In the second, he was transcribing the process within which, in his own thought, these same discursive positions were being called to account. Foucault's enthusiasm for the discourse that had critically undermined "the eye of power" sounded, in this sense, very much like an effort at self-criticism.

The Birth of Biopolitics was Foucault's first public settling of accounts with the disciplinary hypothesis. It was his first effort to liquidate a position that had earned him a great deal of notoriety, and to speak in a new way about individuals. On the surface, the course grew directly out of the "reason of state" narrative of the 1978 lectures. Beneath that surface continuity, this was a bold departure into the uncharted territory of subjectivity. Stark verification of this new tack came in autumn of the same year. In an October 1979 interview, Foucault declared, "[w]e should liberate ourselves from the kind of subjectivity of which the psychoanalysts treat: namely, psychological subjectivity." The implication—that there exist other and better types of subjectivity that might be worth embracing—was noteworthy. But even more so was Foucault's assertion that "[w]e are prisoners of certain conceptions of ourselves and of our conduct," and that, as such, "[w]e should liberate our subjectivity, our relation to ourselves."[12]

IN THE AUTUMN of 1979, Foucault was in northern California. Touring and offering guest lectures at Berkeley and Stanford, he experienced a rock star's reception from admiring American audiences. The talks that Foucault gave provided the opportunity for thousands to acquaint themselves with the philosopher's recent projects. Yet the most telling insights into his new trajectory came in the course of small and informal discussions—question-and-answer sessions to which Foucault was often invited by the philosophy departments of the universities that he visited.

It was with the intent of allowing Foucault and the analytical philosopher John Searle to hash out ideas that Berkeley hosted such a session in late October of 1979. During a trip to Japan the preceding year, Foucault had earnestly described his own project as "the analytical philosophy of politics."[13] Searle, who was the author of *Speech Acts: An Essay in the Philosophy of Language* and *Expression and Meaning: Studies in the Theory of Speech Acts*, rightly felt that his work was in dialogue with what Foucault had done throughout the 1960s and into the 1970s.

Searle himself did not ask pointed questions, leaving that role to Paul Rabinow and Hubert Dreyfus, the event's organizers.[14] Dreyfus pressed Foucault on the notion of the "last stages of man" and the disappearance of the subject, as described in *The Order of Things*. Foucault, speaking in English, responded with an unflinching critique of his own philosophical positions of the late 1960s. The claims of *The Order of Things*, he said, needed to be understood within the context of the conjunctures of that moment in France: that is to say, the existence of an "apocalyptic schema" in which it appeared that something was ending and something new about to begin. This impression, he added, was only reinforced by the advent of May 1968.[15]

Dreyfus then steered the discussion toward what he believed to be Foucault's current avenue of research. Why, he asked, had Foucault not written a methodological book like *The Archaeology of Knowledge* that would deal with genealogy? Foucault replied that this was, in fact, his aim, and that his reference in *The History of Sexuality, Volume I*, to a future work with the title *The Power of Truth* (*Le pouvoir de la vérité*) signaled the intention to write just such a genealogical treatise. "*Le pouvoir de la vérité*, that would be the genealogy, the problem of why, in our society . . . why everything has to integrate into certain kinds of true discourses which are supposed to be sciences. It would have been also the institutionalization of truth in our society."[16]

Two things are worth noting about this passage. The first is the description of this proposed genealogical treatise, which bears slight resemblance to what Foucault had actually practiced under the name of genealogy. *Discipline and Punish*, for instance, can hardly be called the effort to understand the institutionalization of truth. The second, just as important, is the use of the past conditional. *The Power of Truth* was a book that, in another time, Foucault would have written—but that no longer appeared to hold much interest for him. Genealogy was already yesterday's concern.

What Foucault *was* interested in researching, and the place at which he found himself intellectually in the wake of his course on modern liberalism, had been suggested two weeks earlier during a similar session at Stanford. "I am just now," Foucault told his small group of interlocutors, "studying the literature about confession." This included, "thousands and thousands of books" on the proper conduct of this procedure, "all the very complicated, very sophisticated apparatus of techniques to extract the truth from the soul and heart of people."[17]

It is likely that many of Foucault's listeners imagined the philosopher to be speaking lightly when he pointed to "the soul and heart" of those undergoing confession. This was, after all, the man who had written in *Discipline and Punish*, with the acerbity of which he alone among French intellectuals of his generation was capable, of "the soul, prison of the body."[18] Was there any reason to believe that he lent greater credence to the soul-idea now?

In fact, within twelve months Foucault would offer a remarkable reinterpretation of his comments in *Discipline and Punish*: "[O]f course, when I said that the soul was the prison of the body, it was a joke, of course. But the idea was that the body in this kind of discipline is defined and delimited by a kind of relation of the individual to himself."[19]

One would not need to look far to glean that Foucault had manifestly intended nothing like this meaning in *Discipline and Punish*, and that, here again, he was providing a creative reinterpretation of his past work in light of his present projects. But Foucault's statement is doubly significant as a marker of his changing perspective; it not only shows him backpedaling on the issue of the soul, it also shows him linking this question to the "relation of the individual to himself."

What is at stake in the study of confessional practices is neither the link between the individual and power, nor that between the individual and discourse. It is the link between the individual and himself. But what is *the relation of the individual to himself*? This was nothing other than the expression used by Foucault to define the term "subjectivity."[20] Confessional practices, then, were meant to shed light on the formation of subjectivity.

Was there, however, any reason to think that Foucault's mounting *interest* in the question of subjectivity was an indication of a changed *attitude* toward the subject? Again, Foucault's own public comments in the fall of 1979 suggested that there was. Asked at Stanford about certain political and social stances that he had taken during the 1970s, Foucault responded with a polite but strongly worded defense of personal ethics as a point of departure for philosophy and political action. He told his questioner:

> I don't hide the fact that certain of my choices about either psychiatry or repression of sexuality and so on had their root in my own life and in my own experience. And why not? And that, I think, is the . . . importance of, the characteristic of the emergence of subjectivity as a right and a theoretical field, and a political field. And that, I think, is characteristic of our society nowadays, that subjectivity has the right to assert itself, and to say, even in a very serious theoretic or political field, "that I cannot accept," "that I don't want," or "that I desire."[21]

An unusually revealing burst of emotion, Foucault's response made three things clear. It offered an apology—highly Nietzschean in its tone—for taste as an arbiter in matters of significance. It made the overt claim, turning on its head the argument of *Discipline and Punish*, that self-assertive subjectivity was characteristic of modern society. Finally, and most crucially, it made the implicit claim that the question of subjectivity was personally important to Foucault. For if his research agenda was driven by his own life and experience, what else was one to make of his decision to focus his future research on subjectivity? And that was precisely what his 1980 lecture course would do.

FOUCAULT'S 1980 CONTRIBUTION to the curriculum of the Collège de France upheld his tradition of proffering his ideas under misleading titles. *The Government of the Living*, much like its predecessor, sounded like an inquiry into modern biopolitics. In reality, it was a course on the evolution of religious doctrine, and Foucault's first unabashed foray into the ancient world.[22]

The Government of the Living set forth what was arguably the most complex and difficult topic upon which Foucault had ever lectured. He chose, as such, to open the course with a visual metaphor. Foucault placed his listeners in Rome, at the end of the second century, under the reign of the emperor Septimius Severus. He described for them the chamber in which Severus presented his edicts—the ceiling of which depicted the heavens at the hour of his birth. The intent of this arrangement, Foucault argued, was to demonstrate that Severus's reign was no matter of caprice, no mere act of men, but was founded in the stars and in the very necessity of the world. It was, at the same time, to show that the *logos* that resided in his edicts was the same one that ordered the universe. Finally, it was to reveal in advance the inevitability of his rule and the hopelessness of any effort that might be made to steal his throne.[23]

Thus, Foucault said, a past made up of chance actions, a present composed of uncertain and particular acts, and a future that could not be known, were transformed into necessities and presented—on the ceiling of the site of government—as a *truth*. Septimius Severus in his starry chamber captured perfectly, for Foucault, the set of interwoven ideas that formed the basis of the course. For the theme that *The Government of the Living* was meant to address was "how, in our civilization, we establish the relations between the government of men, the manifestation of truth in the form of subjectivity, and salvation for all and for each."[24]

This very dense prospectus needs to be taken piece by piece. For the moment, let us treat the first two parts—what Foucault called "the government of men" and "the manifestation of truth in the form of subjectivity."

Foucault's question was about the way in which links were forged between the government of men and the display of a purported truth—and in particular, a truth that comes in the form of subjectivity. Throughout Western history, Foucault was suggesting, rulers have legitimated their power of governance through reference to discourses: discourses that they often wielded exclusively, and which purported to speak a kind of truth. These "true discourses," unlike, say, the modern political discourse that gave rise to *reason of state*, cannot be explained in utilitarian terms, by their capacity to rationalize and render more efficient the workings of government. Often, in fact, they bore no relation to politics broadly considered. Astrology is a prime example: it enhanced the power and effectiveness of the rulers in no way. What it did was permit a kind of truth to be displayed—a completely gratuitous truth—the possession of which was meant to signal the fitness for rule of those who governed. This was the government of men by the manifestation of truth.

Where did subjectivity enter the picture? The answer is far from simple, and herein lay the importance of the vignette that Foucault had chosen to start the course. The truth that Septimius Severus chose to project over the heads of those he ruled was not an impersonal one—it was, on the contrary, the graphic rendering of his own existence. It was *his own* truth. So seriously did the emperor take this self-presentation, Foucault claimed, that he had one particular portion of his astral sky removed from the ceiling and hidden in a room to which only he had access. This was the section properly known as the "horoscope," or that which allows one to know the hour of death. As this patch of sky fixed the final destiny of the emperor, it was necessarily secret.[25]

Foucault wanted to examine the way in which the government of men was cemented by the revelation of "one's own truth." What he hoped to demonstrate—although he did not tell his audience as much until later in the course—was that the *modality* according to which men were governed by the revelation of truth underwent a very important change during the century after Severus. The Roman emperor found the truth of himself in the world: outside himself, above himself. His destiny was literally written in the stars. The practitioners of early Christianity, on the other hand, found their truth *within* themselves. They coaxed it forth with an elaborate series of confessional practices. This change, Foucault would argue, was of immense consequence for the emergence of the modern individual.

The effective government of men was, for the Roman of late antiquity as for the Christian of the patristic era, dependent upon the public revelation of the truth about oneself. But between these two styles of government, the nature of that public revelation underwent a complete reversal. Septimius Severus publicized a kind of truth that existed outside of himself in order to demonstrate his legitimacy as a governor of men. The Christian pastor, in contrast, summoned forth a unique truth from within each of those whose spiritual existence he governed.

The centerpiece of *The Government of the Living* was this transition. It was a course about the emergence of a particular (and historically resilient) kind of subjectivity: one that viewed the individual as the secret bearer of his own deep truth.

WAS FOUCAULT GENUINELY breaking with the past in his explorations of "government of men by the truth"? Would he have agreed that his analyses were moving beyond genealogy? The answer is an unequivocal yes. As Foucault proclaimed in the first lecture of the course, the government–truth dyad was meant as an explicit corrective to the idea of power–knowledge. Elaborating the notion of government of men by the truth was a way "of shifting things slightly in relation to the now worn and hackneyed theme of power–knowledge."[26]

It was a matter of recognizing, Foucault announced, that the idea of power–knowledge was itself an expedient. Power–knowledge, as Foucault had used it in his courses and book-length studies of the 1970s, was a corrective that had been devised in response to a particular problem in the discipline of the history of thought: namely, analysis in terms of ideology.[27] As Foucault had maintained from the time of *The Punitive Society* onward, the notion of ideology was an extremely limiting one, because it forced the historian to believe that power had but two options: either the mute force of violence, or the chattiness of ideology. This stark choice, Foucault had warned his audience in the spring of 1973, simply did not exist:

> Now, power is not caught in this dilemma: either to be exercised by imposing itself by violence, or to hide itself, and to get itself accepted by holding the chatty discourse of ideology. In fact, every point of exercise of power is at the same time a site of formation: not of ideology, but of knowledge. And on the other hand, every established knowledge permits and assures the exercise of a power.[28]

Foucault's advance, which was simple and revolutionary, had been to deny the utility of ideology as a concept, to deny the entire schema that opposed scientific "truth" on one hand to silence and falsehood on the other. The inextricability of power and knowledge from one another belied this dichotomous logic.[29]

But the problem of ideology-critique, Foucault felt in the spring of 1980, had been duly confronted. In that sense, power–knowledge had served its purpose. Its continued deployment promised only to cloud the issues. "I would say that it is essentially a matter," he told his listeners, "of passing from the notion of *power–knowledge* to the notion of *government by the truth* . . . of giving a positive and differentiated content to the term . . . to these two terms, power and knowledge."[30]

Here, Foucault was being earnest and disingenuous at the same time. Examining problems in the history of thought through the lens of "government" would restore "a positive and differentiated content" to the notions of power and knowledge by—to speak plainly—liquidating those terms. Foucault would continue to address questions of knowledge and power, but they had ceased to be the axis around which his work revolved.[31] If power still played a leading role in *The Government of the Living*, it was with Foucault's explicit disclaimer that "this notion of government . . . seems to me much more functional than the notion of power."[32] While critics have devoted scant attention to it, the words "power" and "knowledge" are almost entirely absent from the latter two volumes of *The History of Sexuality*.

The notion of government was valuable for the simple reason that it would reinsert the free individual back into historical analyses of thought.[33] "Government" was not *necessarily* anonymous and third-person: unlike "power" and "knowledge," the word "government" pointed toward an activity that could be exercised by an individual upon himself.[34] One governed others, but one also governed oneself. As a concept, government was far better suited to discern the role that the individual plays in the formation of his own subjectivity.

THE CONTENT OF *The Government of the Living* was, as noted above, exceedingly specific. Foucault sought to explain the shift from the kind of government-through-truth characteristic of the late pagan world to another, more sophisticated kind characteristic of early Christianity. The former style of government rooted itself in an external and visible order. The latter style was predicated upon the idea that each individual contains a truth within him, and that, moreover, his life can only be properly regulated when that truth is spoken aloud. This Christian government-through-truth was of tremendous historical importance because it was, a millennium and a half after its inception, still operative in the West.

It was, then, with his gaze focused directly on the present time that Foucault posed a series of questions to his listeners:

> Why, in what form, in a society like our own, does such a strong link exist between the exercise of power and the obligation for individuals to make of themselves, in procedures for the manifestation of truth . . . essential actors? What relation [exists] between the fact that one is a subject in a relation of power, and a subject by whom, for whom, and through whom the truth is manifest?[35]

Why, Foucault was asking, must we—in the twentieth century—engage in activities in which we speak the truth of ourselves aloud? Why do we experience a link between the functioning of power and the requirement to "tell the truth" about who we are? What is the nature of this link?

If these questions sounded familiar, it was because, to a certain degree, they were. Foucault had already framed them within the problematic of modern sexuality. In the closing section of *The History of Sexuality, Volume 1*, he had observed that it was the nature of the "dispositive of sexuality" to sustain a system in which sexuality was incessantly articulated in discourse and formulated in truth. At the same time, he had described "sex" as the "imaginary point fixed by the dispositive of sexuality, that each must pass in order to have access to his own intelligibility"—or, for that matter, " to his identity."[36]

Now, however, Foucault was turning for answers about the modern condition neither to the Classical era, nor to the period surrounding the French Revolution, historical moments that he had traditionally presented as the crucible of contemporary forms of power and discourse. Instead, he was looking all the way back to the ancient world and the first centuries of Christianity.

Perhaps more fundamentally, the "imaginary point" upon which Foucault centered his investigation was increasingly not "sexuality" but rather subjectivity *tout court*. Where he had formerly observed (in the dispositive of sexuality) an anomalous and uniquely modern configuration of power, the effect of which was to induce a torrent of confessional discourse, he now claimed to see a far more stable continuity. In this revised view, the discursive paradigm that forced out into the open the most intimate details of individuals' lives could not be directly attributed to "sexuality." This last was, instead, merely the most recent instance of a far older Western tradition: that of compelling the subject to speak its truth. Foucault's interest, as such, gradually shifted away from texts focused on sexuality and toward texts that spoke directly and without intermediary to the crafting of the individual spirit. As there will be occasion to show in the next chapter, this tendency would reach critical mass in 1982, when Foucault would entirely shelve materials dealing with sexuality in order to focus on properly philosophical texts—and specifically, on those confronting the link between subjectivity and truth.

For the time being, Foucault's concern was to investigate the patristic writings of Christianity. This was done with the intention of unearthing, within Christian thought and worship, the origins of a modern obligation: that requiring individuals to establish a permanent relation of knowledge with themselves.[37]

FOUCAULT WAS NEVER above revealing his frustration with critics who highlighted his lack of consistency. His tart injunction in the preface of *The Archaeology of Knowledge*—"Don't ask me who I am and don't tell me to stay the same"—remains well-known.[38] This ostensible commitment to intellectual homelessness was reiterated in *The Government of the Living*:

> For me, theoretical labor doesn't so much consist of establishing and fixing the set of positions to which I will hold myself, and, in the space between these supposedly coherent positions, forming a system. My problem—or the only possibility of theoretical labor that I see for myself —would be to leave the trace, according to the most intelligible design possible, of the movements thanks to which I am no longer where I once was.[39]

Foucault was casting a sly glance over his shoulder when he styled his methodology an "anarchaeology of knowledge."[40] And while the philosopher was unquestionably making a virtue of necessity by portraying his wanderings as essential to a greater personal project, we should keep his apologia in mind when we watch him at work in the spring of 1980.

The method that he brought to bear upon the texts and practices of early Christianity was quite unlike anything he had done before. Gone was any visible attempt to analyze undifferentiated discourse in terms of its objects, concepts, and strategies; gone, too, was the desire to reconstruct historical "dispositives" by decoding the interplay of power and knowledge within particular societies. Neither archaeological (in the tradition of *The Order of Things*), nor genealogical (in the spirit of *Discipline and Punish*), Foucault's efforts to study "the government of men by the truth" resembled nothing so much as standard intellectual history. He grappled with late antiquity— a period essentially alien to him—by interpreting and contextualizing doctrinal texts of established significance. Paul Rabinow and Hubert Dreyfus note in the introduction to their study of Foucault that their original title was "Michel Foucault: From Structuralism to Hermeneutics."[41] This suggests a high level of awareness of what Foucault was doing in the early 1980s.

Foucault began his historical narrative at the turning of the second and third centuries, or at the precise period in which Septimius Severus had ruled. In this period, Foucault argued, well apart from the world in which Severus moved, Christianity was undergoing a transformation. That transformation had to do with the sacrament of baptism. Baptism had appeared in the New Testament as a pure ritual, unadorned by spiritual avowals. It was a matter of descending into water, a way of symbolizing the acceptance of a new faith and a new life. In the course of the first two Christian centuries, it had gradually taken on additional roles: that of marking the faithful, of demonstrating second birth, and of celebrating illumination. But at the turning of the second and third centuries, sects within Christianity began to challenge the efficacy (and thus the necessity) of baptism. How, the gnostics of this period asked, could an impure and material substance like water possibly cleanse the soul, which was immaterial and pure?

Here, the theologian Tertullian entered the picture.[42] An apologist for orthodox Christianity, Tertullian wrote against these gnostic challenges.

In the process, he offered a radically new perspective on baptism—and through baptism, on the entire experience of Christian life. Tertullian admitted that descending into water in and of itself was merely an act, but maintained that it was a crucial one on the path to spiritual purity. With the Fall, he argued, the devil had established his kingdom in the hearts of men; the aim of baptism was to chase him out. The devil could not tolerate such an affront, and raged mightily as the day of baptism approached. The time of preparation for baptism was thus a time of danger, a period of intense spiritual combat. A Christian was never in greater danger than in the immediate approach to truth and liberation.

Tertullian's innovations, Foucault asserted, created the idea of "original sin," an element that had been absent from Christianity prior to that point. They also created, far more significantly, the notion that fear (*crainte*) should be maintained throughout the lifetime of the believer. That is to say, danger must remain constant; the Christian must never feel that he is safe. Conversion was a process and not an event. But such an idea, Foucault argued, not only ran counter to earlier gnostic belief; it also opposed Neoplatonistic and Stoic beliefs. All of these philosophical descendants of Greece held that there was a state of wisdom beyond which the individual was no longer vulnerable to temptation. A baptism that prepared the individual for a state of perpetual fear was thus a serious rupture. Within such a schema, the figure of the sage—who is wise and perfect—became unthinkable. A dramatics of struggle replaced a pedagogical dramatics of progressive illumination.[43]

The effects of this shift, Foucault argued, were far-reaching. Anchored in Christianity from the beginning of the third century onward, this perpetual fear "will clearly have an absolutely decisive importance throughout the history of what can be called subjectivity: that is to say, the relation of self to self, the exercise of self upon self, and the truth that the individual can discover within the depths of himself."[44]

It would have this importance not least because of the practical consequences that believers would derive from it. Preparation of the soul was necessary before baptism, and remains necessary after baptism. The sacrament does not efface faults and provide illumination; it gives individuals the capacity to fight against evil. One must continue to labor upon oneself, to sound one's own depths for outcroppings of evil upon which the spirit might founder. Perpetual fear engendered the notion that all of life should be a penitence. This preparation for baptism, now extended well beyond the singular instance of the sacrament, was *asceticism* in its pure sense: gymnastics for the unceasing struggle against evil. "The time of ascetics," Foucault claimed, "is in the process of disengagement from the time of illumination."[45]

Tertullian's texts represented a watershed moment in the history of Western subjectivity because they produced a diffraction in Western spirituality. The doctrines that he introduced, in other words, modified the conditions under which a subject was seen to become capable of gaining access to truth. From the time of Plato, the soul's accession to truth was a matter of conversion or *metanoya*: it was a unitary movement in which the soul pivoted upon itself and turned from the darkness to the light. This discovery of truth and light was simultaneously the discovery of the soul's own truth, because the soul was necessarily of the same nature as the being that illuminated it. It was with Tertullian, Foucault argued clearly and unambiguously, that this pedagogically oriented path to truth—a truth which was *out there*—reached its end. The "grand unitary series"—linking conversion, illumination, access to the truth, and the discovery of one's own truth—began to come apart. Thereafter, Christian thought started along a new path: one in which the soul must turn *within*, must constitute itself as the protagonist of a procedure in which it will constantly be an object of knowledge. "The sinner," as Tertullian wrote, "should cry his errors," and that his whole life long. Septimius Severus's world gave way to that of Augustine. For the entire West, a complex history of relations between subjectivity and truth was initiated.[46]

THE ANALYSIS THAT Foucault provided in *The Government of the Living* was noteworthy for three characteristics. The first of these concerned interpretation. What Foucault winkingly called his "anarchéologie du savoir" was an ambitious effort to look at a particular moment in the history of ancient thought. Description was to be carried out not in the familiar terms of power–knowledge, but rather in terms of the "government of men by the truth." As noted above, however, this method bore in practice a suspicious resemblance to traditional *histoire de la pensée*, the very discipline against which Foucault had written so many of his most powerful works. In *The Archaeology of Knowledge*, to take the clearest example, he had lambasted practitioners of the history of thought precisely because they *interpreted texts* rather than *analyzing discourse*. For these surface-skimming historians, the question was always "what, then, was being said in what was said?"[47] Interpretation explained nothing; it merely fueled the exponential proliferation of discourse, piling layer upon layer of meaning. Yet this meaning-question was invariably the one that Foucault posed in *The Government of the Living*. What was the meaning of the emperor's ceiling? To whom was Tertullian responding? What was Cassian trying to say in his *Institutions Cénobitiques*? Textual and contextual interpretation was at the heart of Foucault's method throughout the course.

This turn points directly toward the second noteworthy feature, which had to do with authorial agency. When Foucault argued that, in essence, Western subjectivity was transformed because Tertullian's ideas carried the day, he was a very long way from *The Order of Things*, with its stern demand not to treat works at the level of their content but at the level of the systematicity that links and determines them.[48] When he told his listeners that Tertullian's writings expressed that author's disagreement with contemporaneous views on baptism, he showed just how frayed his affinity with *The Archaeology of Knowledge* had become. The latter work excoriated historians who treated discourse "in such a way that they try to rediscover, beyond the statements themselves, the intention of the speaking subject, his conscious activity, [and] what he meant to say."[49] Authorial privileges that Foucault had scathingly revoked in works like "What Is an Author?" were, in this historical narrative, more than restored. Not only did individual speakers (as, for instance, Tertullian) have agency to "create" ideas outside of the boundaries of any normative episteme, they were also able to wield transformative power over subsequent thought. Authors *influenced*. Foucault had once laughed off the notion of influence as "too magical to bear proper analysis."[50]

Finally, Foucault demonstrated a newfound forthrightness in his treatment of subjectivity. The simple frequency of use of words like "soul," "subject," and "subjectivity" sufficed to differentiate *The Government of the Living* from earlier courses. But Foucault no longer even pretended that he was dealing with "political subjectivity" (or the political self-understanding of subjects in relation to their governments), as had been the case in *The Birth of Biopolitics*. His interest as a historical observer seemed instead to lie in subjectivity in the traditional philosophical sense: the subject as independent locus of experience. Those harboring this suspicion would only have found corroboration in his focus on practices like penitence and confession, in which individuals demonstrated volition and exercised choice.

But if we accept, as the evidence bids us, that the Foucault of 1980 had found room for interpretation, agency, and subjectivity, must we necessarily believe that he had found room for the independent subject as well? Publicly, Foucault was insistent that his views were unchanged, that he continued to have no truck with the subject as traditionally understood. He could claim with some justification that the study of the history of subjectivity—of the construction of particular kinds of subjects through discourse—proceeded in a straight line from his earlier projects, and was, in fact, what he had always done.

The crucial linking element, as he explained to his listeners in January of 1980, was a rigorous antirealism. His current work did not start from a universal conception of the subject and work backward to its historical antecedents; rather, it asked how we might understand *our particular* form of subjectivity based on the study of isolable historical practices. In the same way, he argued, *Madness and Civilization* did not start from the acknowledged fact of "madness." Instead, it began with the historical (and therefore contingent) singularity which was the practice of confinement. From there, it asked what the effects of this practice had been in the field of knowledge. It did not neglect, Foucault added, to ask what the effects of the practice were on the experience of the subject itself.[51]

Such was Foucault's explanation. But the parallel between *Madness and Civilization* and *The Government of the Living* arguably failed on two levels. Firstly, *Madness and Civilization*, Foucault's first book, was unlike any of its successors in that it employed the concept of "experience"—as in the lived experience of the subject. In this sense, it was misleading on Foucault's part to suggest that his work as a whole dealt with transformations in lived subjectivity. In reality, he had abandoned the concept of experience almost immediately after the publication of *Madness and Civilization*—and shunned it through the ensuing twenty years. On this crucial topic, more will be said in the following chapter.

Secondly, Foucault spoke as though he might remain agnostic on the actual existence of subjects (in the way that he remained uncommitted on the existence of madness). By this logic, his questions in *The Government of the Living* were addressed merely to the processes that he alternately called *subjectivation* and *assujetissement*; his concern for the process by which different forms of "subjectivity" were constituted likewise implied no belief in a "subject" per se. The subject was *not* to be understood as a natural substratum for surface qualities collected through practices: that would be a realist view. It continued to be understood as an entity wholly constructed in practices.[52]

Yet that purported attitude meshed poorly with the actual positions that Foucault staked out during this time. The dissonance was on display in "Truth and Subjectivity," a two-part lecture that Foucault delivered at Berkeley in October of 1980. In the past, he told his audience, he had "insisted maybe too much" on the centrality of practices of domination in the shaping of subjectivity. His work, he continued, had since forced a different view upon him:

> Analyzing the experience of sexuality and the history of the experience of sexuality, I became more and more aware that there are, in all societies, other types of techniques, techniques which permit individuals to effect a certain number of operations on their own bodies, on their souls, on their thoughts, on their own conduct, and in this manner . . . to transform themselves.[53]

This was a fascinating and original view, but also a troubling one. All societies possessed techniques that allowed individuals to effect operations upon their souls, thereby transforming themselves. But the question naturally followed: what individuals? What souls?

Foucault's way of posing the problem to his Berkeley audience tacitly assumed some kind of already-present subject that could act upon itself. The alternative—the notion of a non-subject that performs techniques upon itself—is contradictory. But on the other hand, if we truly are to believe that subjects are formed—all the way down—by techniques of subjectivation, how are we to make sense of the idea of *individuals who elect to engage in such techniques*? Or worse, not to engage in them? Foucault was caught in the same kind of conceptual problem when, two days later, he told a gathering of Berkeley professors that "[the relation] of the subject to himself . . . is the target of techniques."[54] But if subjectivity is the target of techniques rather than the product of techniques, then we are entitled to wonder where that subjectivity comes from in the first place.

Without acknowledging it, Foucault had posited a free subject prior to any "technical elaboration": a subject free to choose itself, to build its own *subjectival modality*. While he continued to claim, and perhaps to believe, that he was describing the construction of subjects through discourse, his arguments told otherwise. Peter Dews strikes at the heart of this conceptual confusion when he writes, "The obvious paradox of a reflexive account of self-construction is that the self must already exist in order to construct itself."[55] It was insufficient for Foucault to suggest that practices that had arisen anonymously "produced" the subject. Once *some kind* of subject was acknowledged to precede those practices—to reflect upon them and choose among them—then the notion that the subject was "produced" at all lost a great deal of its force. It essentially meant only that the subject was modified, or shaped. The definition of the subject that Foucault offered at the beginning of the 1980s, if it is to be judged coherent, necessarily carried within it the ideas of autonomy, reflexivity, and lived experience.

Let us, at the expense of tiresomeness, remark on the rapidity of the intellectual transformation. *Discipline and Punish* had described a process in which individuality and subjectivity were *literally* manufactured by an institutionalized and pervasive process of domination. No individual received the choice of whether or not to undergo discipline; and only through discipline did one become an individual. In contrast, the Foucauldean subject of 1980 was a free individual. It had the ability to pursue (or not pursue) techniques that would transform its subjectival modality—but which would not, one way or the other, disrupt its status as an independent locus of experience. Foucault's Christian disciple was a strong subject: the kind that, in years past, he had done his best to vanquish from the philosophical scene. The consequences of his appearance will form the subject of the final chapter.

—◆◆◆—

CHAPTER FIVE

Arts of Living

Antiquity, Modernity, and the Experience of Self

Once there exists, in a culture, a true discourse on the subject, what experience does the subject have of himself?[1]

THE PARAMOUNT CONCEPTUAL INNOVATION OF FOUCAULT'S LAST years was the idea of the *tekhnê peri ton bion*, or art of living. "Arts of living," he declared to his audience in 1981, represented a "minor genre" that, while absent today as an autonomous category of writing, was of considerable extent in the ancient world. These arts were a valued type of literature; essentially manuals, they offered cultured readers not a model of behavior to follow, but rather a set of "counsels on existence," or guidance on how to *be*.[2] Examples of such works included the *Oneirocritica* of Artemidorus of Daldis, a second-century text that used dreams as a path to fuller living;[3] and Xenophon's *Economics*, a treatise of the fourth century BC detailing the proper life-conduct of a head of household.[4] Foucault worked with these texts and others primarily by citing, interpreting, and commenting upon key passages within them. This hermeneutical approach, which is on display in *The Use of Pleasure* and *The Care of the Self*, allowed the philosopher to highlight what he viewed as crucial matters of dispute—or "problematizations"—as experienced by past societies.[5]

The conclusions that Foucault reached through the study of the arts of living tended to reinforce the methodological *volte-face* of 1980's *The Government of the Living*. Succinctly, Foucault increasingly believed—and said—that the relationship between the subject and truth was defined by widespread "practices of self": the kind of practices, that is, that arts of living would have permitted.[6] In this sense, his earlier works, in emphasizing the centrality of coercive practices, had been overhasty and potentially misleading.[7] By the mid-1980s, Foucault was prepared to travel even farther down this path of apostasy. He noted in 1984 that "We traditionally do the history of human existence starting from its conditions. . . . But it seems to me possible to do the history of existence as art and as style. Existence is the most fragile raw material of the human art; but it is also its most immediate given."[8]

To write the history of human existence not in terms of its conditions but as art and style: this was, for Foucault, practically to sever ties with his past. If anything had been a constant in Foucault's work, it was the determination to treat historical phenomena—be they discourses, objects, or even particular kinds of subjects—in terms of the conditions of their possibility. That effort was now to take a back seat to an analysis that treated the same phenomena as the result of free and creative activity. Lest Foucault leave any doubt as to where he stood on this question, he repeated on innumerable occasions during this period his desire that arts of living experience a renaissance in the present, and that we moderns learn to make an art of our existence.

Nothing would be simpler than to chalk up this change of direction to the influence of Nietzsche. For Nietzsche was, on the subject of life as art, characteristically unambiguous. Under the heading, *"One thing needful,"* he proclaimed to the readers of *The Gay Science*, "To 'give style' to one's character—a great and rare art!"[9] There is, moreover, at least limited textual evidence to suggest that Foucault placed his interest in arts of living under Nietzsche's banner.[10] Yet to argue—correctly—that Foucault followed Nietzsche in seeking to aestheticize life is nevertheless to offer an historical account of limited value. Nietzsche, as was suggested in Chapter 2, had such an immense impact upon Foucault, and that over the course of the latter's entire career, that "Nietzschean influence" will always be a rather poor and imprecise explanation for change in Foucault's ideas. The question needs to be: Why, *at this particular moment*, did the (manifestly Nietzschean) concept of an art of life move to the forefront of Foucault's concerns? And even more importantly: What was the significance of the turn to the arts of living in Foucault's last years?

Historians have struggled to integrate the theme of the arts of living with Foucault's other great themes of the early 1980s, which was "Enlightenment." On a number of occasions during this period, Foucault spoke and wrote on the centrality of the Enlightenment—and specifically on the Kantian tradition of critique—in the formation of the modern mode of philosophical questioning. From Hegel to Habermas, Foucault declared, modern philosophy had been a continuous effort to comprehend the significance of the Enlightenment as an event; it had been that which attempted "to answer the question raised so imprudently two centuries ago: *Was ist Aufklärung?*"[11] A considerable literature has proliferated around these Enlightenment texts by Foucault.[12] While the best of this scholarship has helped to dispel the myth that Foucault's interest in the Enlightenment was a kind of "deathbed conversion,"[13] it has been less successful at delineating connections between, on one hand, the historico-critical investigations of modern society that Foucault proposed, and on the other the studies of ancient asceticism in which he was actually engaged.

As this chapter will show with reference to Foucault's major works, occasional writings, published interviews, and unpublished lecture courses from the Collège de France, Foucault's enthusiastic embrace of "arts of living" was the flip side of the project that Foucault called "the problem of today": namely, carrying forward the post-Kantian philosophical task of questioning the present in order to render it more livable. Arts of living, Foucault wanted to suggest, were entirely possible in the modern world; it was the right of every individual to define the modality of his existence, to choose his way of being and relating to others. To pursue life as an art was, in fact, to tear oneself free from those discourses that would colonize one's experience of self with the language of truth.[14] Such a position was an index of the centrality of strong subjectivity to the philosopher's late work. For the dying Foucault, the possibility of societal transformation in the present was linked not simply to the genealogical disassembly of modern configurations of power; it was intimately tied to the creative activity of strong and free individuals intent upon living their lives as works of art.

WHAT, PRECISELY, WERE arts of living? As Foucault noted in *The Use of Pleasure*, they were to be understood as a set of *practices*: practices that, at one time, had enjoyed a considerable importance within Western societies. They could be defined as:

> intentional and voluntary practices by which men not only fix rules of conduct for themselves, but seek to transform themselves, to modify themselves in their singular being, and to make of their life a work that bears certain aesthetic values and responds to certain criteria of style.[15]

This definition, while brief, contains four discrete parts. Firstly, arts of living are described as intentional (*réfléchies*) and voluntary. They are—and here, Foucault leaves no room for doubt—a matter of choice on the part of their participants. Secondly, they enable men to fix *for themselves* rules of conduct. Thirdly, they enable men to seek to transform themselves, to change their very being. Finally, they enable men to turn their life into a work: an object that might be judged according to aesthetic and stylistic categories.

Arts of living were discursive. They were embodied in a literature that had enjoyed immense popularity. They were also, Foucault argued, not a retrospective invention of the historian, but rather an actors' category. For the student who wished to understand ancient morality, he told interviewer François Ewald in 1984, the compilation of a list of prohibitions would miss the essential:

> It seems to me more in accord with the domains with which I dealt and the documents of which I disposed to think this morality in the very form in which contemporaries had reflected upon it: that is to say, in the form of an *art of existence*, or let us rather say of a *technique of life*.[16]

The moral question as it faced free men of antiquity was not how one might conform one's actions to a more or less rigid code. Rather, it was how to govern one's own life so as to give it the most beautiful form possible—be it in the eyes of others, of posterity, or of oneself. In attempting to reconstruct the historical circumstances in which these arts flourished, Foucault's object was thus "the formation and development of a practice of self, the objective of which is the constitution of oneself as the laborer of the beauty of one's own life."[17]

Arts of living as they existed in the ancient world, Foucault told his audience in January of 1981, were less concerned with teaching one what to *do* than with teaching one how to *be*. Rather than providing a model of behavior or choreographing a set of gestures, ancient arts of living aided individuals to modify and model their being itself. Such arts ideally allowed one to acquire a set of qualities. These qualities were neither aptitudes, nor precisely "virtues," but rather attributes of being. Foucault called the aggregate of acquired qualities, "modalities of experience." Tranquility, beatitude, and happiness represented three of the most sought-after modalities of experience.[18] An art of living should, in addition, permit the individual to acquire a certain "ontological status." By this, Foucault meant that it should open to the individual a modality of experience qualifiable in terms of, say, tranquility, happiness, or beatitude.

The kinds of procedures through which these arts brought about change in individuals, Foucault said, were three: *mathesis*, *melete*, and *askesis*. Each procedure was situated on a different axis. *Mathesis*, or learning, concerned the relation of the self to others. As it was judged impossible to accede to the arts of living in isolation, the relation of the master to disciple was constitutive. *Melete*, or meditation, concerned the relation of the self to truth. It was necessary not merely to learn, but to interiorize. Hence, teachings must be made into one's own truth through a rigorous process of reading, memorization, and self-interrogation. Finally, *askesis*, or exercise, dealt with the relation of self to self. It was the labor of testing and self-trial, the proof that one was progressing in one's art. Foucault christened these three kinds of procedures "technologies of the self," emphasizing by this choice of words that these were well-developed and systematized practices. As the three elements on the path to wisdom, he asserted, they were present in every art of living.[19]

If, as we have seen, Foucault felt that he had neglected the study of self-initiated practices in the past, he was determined to make up for lost time.

He now discovered arts of living to be integral not only to his own project, but to those of his contemporaries. Thus, of K. J. Dover's landmark 1978 work *Greek Homosexuality*, he announced, "[Dover] recounts the singular history of a sexual choice which, within a given society, was a mode of life, culture, and art of oneself."[20] And while arts of living had lost a great part of their importance and even their autonomy during the course of the Middle Ages, Foucault claimed, they had by no means disappeared. Burckhardt's *Civilization of the Renaissance in Italy*, he suggested, had underlined just how vibrant such practices remained on the threshold of modernity.[21] Stephen Greenblatt's 1980 *Renaissance self-fashioning* had accomplished much the same thing.[22]

ARTS OF LIVING were, then, at the center of the investigations that Foucault aimed to conduct in the early 1980s. They would serve as the base material and guiding thread in his 1981 course at the Collège de France, entitled *Subjectivity and Truth*. This, in turn, doubled their importance, as *Subjectivity and Truth* provided essential raw material for both *The Use of Pleasure* and *The Care of the Self*. For it was the case, Foucault told his audience, that the link between subjectivity and "truth," while not visible only in arts of living, was nevertheless on display there in a particularly vivid way. They constituted, as such, an especially rich and interesting body of documentation for the general problem posed by the course.[23]

If students of Foucault sensed a certain lack of detachment in the philosopher's pursuit of the "arts of living" idea, they would not have been deceived. His comments beyond the auditorium walls—like those he made during a December 1981 interview with German film director Werner Schroeter—were striking: "The art of living is the art of killing psychology, of creating with oneself and with others unnamed individualities, beings, relations, qualities. If one can't manage to do that in one's life, that life is not worth living."[24] The Greeks, Foucault added, had understood that an existence could be a perfect and sublime work (*oeuvre*), "while we have completely forgotten it, especially since the Renaissance."[25] Uncharacteristic flashes of emotion like this one revealed that this was a matter in which the philosopher was personally invested. For the attention that

Foucault paid to antique arts of living cannot be wholly understood within the context of his early-1980s research itinerary. Rather, it merged almost seamlessly into his contemporary social and personal concerns.

Chief among these concerns—however surprising it seemed—was the search for a modern morality. Foucault, it will be recalled, had argued in *The Order of Things* that modern thought was incapable of generating a coherent morality.[26] He compounded this statement in a spring 1968 interview, stating pithily that, "morality has ceased to exist in the course of the twentieth century."[27] Yet by the end of the 1970s, Foucault began to show signs of wavering on this point (as on so many others). As early as 1977, the language of ethics began to infiltrate his working vocabulary. In his preface to the English edition of Deleuze and Guattari's *Anti-Oedipus*, he called the book, "the first book of ethics to be written in France in quite a long time." It was, he wrote, a kind of ethical treatise showing us how to unburden ourselves of the "fascism" that, against our will perhaps, inhabits our words and acts.[28]

More tantalizing, perhaps, was the precise wording that Foucault used. *Anti-Oedipus*, he wrote, was an "*art of living* counter to all forms of fascism."[29] Being anti-oedipal had become, for many, "a life style, a way of thinking and living." These were atypical expressions for the philosopher. Was there a link between Foucault's reconsideration of the idea of a *modern* ethics and the notion of arts of living?

For Foucault, apparently, the link was very clear. "Paying a modest tribute to Saint Francis de Sales," he wrote, "one might say that Anti-Oedipus is an introduction to the non-fascist life." The reference here was to Francis de Sales' 1604 *Introduction à la vie dévote*, a work that had never once figured in any of Foucault's studies.[30] Yet de Sales's *Introduction* would, in 1981, provide the material for the opening vignette of *Subjectivity and Truth*.[31] It was Foucault's shining exemplar of a *modern* art of living. Foucault's reconsideration of the very possibility of an ethics was thus contemporaneous with his discovery of the genre of the art of living.[32]

For Foucault came to believe, with a fervor that only increased during his last years, that arts of living had a valuable contribution to make to the modern world. In particular, he saw the potential for great breakthroughs in the treatment of questions of morality—and particularly sexual morality —via the adoption of the *perspective* contained within arts of living.

The moral experience of our culture, which derived from Christianity, featured a universal moral subject and a singular moral code to which all were expected to submit. This configuration, said Foucault, was not only unsatisfying but patently catastrophic. And for that very reason, he added,

> a certain number of questions are posed to us today in the very terms in which they were posed in Antiquity. Research into styles of existence as different from one another as possible seems to me to be one of the points where contemporary research got its start in the efforts of certain erstwhile groups.[33]

To the extent that ethical questions were ones in which what was at stake was the way in which free individuals related to one another, Foucault suggested, the ancient arts of living—while not directly imitable—had the potential to speak to our situation.[34] In rethinking how we might live and how we might *live with each other*, the ancient way of posing the question was quite fertile.

And yet, he lamented to Hubert Dreyfus and Paul Rabinow in 1983, modern individuals live in a way that scarcely recognizes the possibility of free creation. "We have hardly any remnant of the idea in our society," he told them, "that the principle work of art which one has to take care of, the main area to which one must apply aesthetic values is oneself, one's life, one's existence."[35] If the idea had briefly resurfaced during the Renaissance, and again in the form of nineteenth-century dandyism, these were but episodes. The concept of fashioning oneself—or by extension, of fashioning original ways to relate to others—remained alien to the modern world.

What did Foucault imagine a modern art of living would look like? He provided valuable hints during an October 1981 interview with a representative of the gay review *Christopher Street*. Deflecting a question about the value of legal changes in the status of homosexual couples, Foucault stated, "rather than arguing that individuals have fundamental and natural rights, we should perhaps try to imagine and create a new right of relations." A *creative* effort rather than a defensive one, he argued, might render unnecessary the "relationally impoverishing institutions" that currently prevented multiple kinds of interpersonal relations from existing.

Integrating the practice of homosexual love into preexisting cultural fields was not enough; "it is a matter of creating new cultural forms."[36]

Foucault expressed himself in similar fashion in the course of a June 1982 interview with *The Advocate*. Asked whether the homosexual movement was making progress, Foucault replied that there had unquestionably been a genuine process of liberation at the beginning of the 1970s; he noted, however, that the situation had not yet stabilized, and that rather than accepting a status quo based on rights and tolerance, it would be preferable to take an additional step forward. One path to this, he affirmed, would be "the creation of new forms of life, of relations, of friendships, in society, art, and culture: new forms that will be put into practice through our sexual, ethical and political choices."[37] It should not be a matter of self-defense, but rather of self-assertion. And that assertion should itself be understood less as the affirmation of an identity than as the propagation of a creative force. We don't need, Foucault explained, to discover that we are homosexuals; "We should instead create a gay way of life."[38]

Crafting new cultural forms, beautifying life, and creating new kinds of relations: these were, in Foucault's mind, inseparable from the idea of elaborating a modern ethics. Hence, when challenged by Dreyfus and Rabinow as to how an ethics might be built in an age that recognized the historical contingency of all such structures, Foucault replied quite naturally, "But couldn't everyone's life become a work of art?"[39] The distance between an existential ethics and an aesthetics of existence had, for Foucault, shrunk to nothing. To constitute *ourselves* as moral agents through the living of life as an art-object: these were two sides of the same coin.

If Dreyfus and Rabinow were skeptical, it was not because they doubted Foucault's sincerity in posing the question of ethics in this way. Rather, it was because, in the San Francisco Bay Area of the early 1980s, the paradigm that Foucault described seemed anything but foreign. They chided: "Of course, that kind of project is very common in places like Berkeley where people think that everything from the way they eat breakfast, to the way they have sex, to the way they spend their day, should itself be perfected."[40]

Foucault, unfazed and unpersuaded, clarified his position. There was a critical difference, he explained, between *creating oneself* and *seeking one's truth*. The former was an open-ended artistic effort that promised both freedom and beauty; the latter, which defined the "California cult of the self," was indexed to a process of discovery, and to the idea that one's "true self" was determinate and knowable. People who view the elaboration of self in this way, Foucault explained, "think that if they do what they do, if they live as they live, the reason is that they know the truth about desire, life, nature, body, and so on."[41] Arts of living were about dispensing with such alleged truths.

DREYFUS AND RABINOW may have been off the mark in their understanding of arts of living. They were nevertheless onto something when they drew connections between Foucault's new conceptual apparatus and Berkeley. Foucault's intellectual evolution in the late 1970s and early 1980s arguably owed more to developments at Berkeley than any other place on the globe, Paris included.

Foucault first visited California in the spring of 1975. He was immediately taken with it. Warm weather, widespread drug use, small communities experimenting with alternative ways of life, and the highly developed gay bathhouse culture of San Francisco: all of these things made California an exceedingly congenial environment for the philosopher, and of this he made no secret.[42] The American West Coast was also a welcome retreat from Paris, where, from the beginning of the 1980s onward, Foucault rarely passed more than the four months required by his teaching commitment.

Previous observers have stressed the importance of this permissive California environment in shaping Foucault's trajectory during the last half-decade of his life. The social atmosphere, as Dreyfus and Rabinow had intuited, was unquestionably important. What has been less appreciated is the impact of Foucault's institutional connection with the University of California at Berkeley. As the foregoing chapter noted, Foucault gave numerous lectures at Berkeley during the late 1970s and early 1980s. He also took part in colloquia focused on his own work;[43] hosted informal discussions with the representatives of various departments;[44] collaborated with Berkeley professors Dreyfus and Rabinow in the authorship of a major study on his thought;[45] and even led an extended public lecture series on truth-telling in the ancient world.[46] To describe Foucault's routine in the half-decade from 1979 to 1983 as a fall term in Berkeley and a spring term in Paris would not be a gross exaggeration.

There is powerful evidence that Foucault's Berkeley colleagues—spanning a range of disciplines—were integral to the thought process that went into his final works. Greenblatt, a professor of English, was clearly thinking in the same direction that Foucault was. Dreyfus and Rabinow, a philosopher and an anthropologist respectively, were, for their part, forcing Foucault to clarify his ideas, challenging the coherence of his archaeological vision, and subtly pushing him toward a Heideggerian language that was not his own. But the most significant of these Berkeley associates was Peter Brown, a man whose name was often on Foucault's lips in the early 1980s.[47] Brown, a respected historian of the late antique and early medieval world, was, during the period of Foucault's visits, a critical part of the Berkeley Department of History. In his landmark 1978 work *The Making of Late Antiquity*, Brown had set down a simple and compelling account of early-Christian religious transformation.[48] The book provided a visible link between Brown's longstanding interests and Foucault's nascent ones.

Yet the sheer amount of overlap between Brown's work and, for instance, Foucault's course on *The Government of the Living* should give us pause.[49] Both offered narratives set in the third century of the Christian era; both concerned the shift from pagan to Christian religiosity; both dealt with ancient sexuality; both investigated the emergence of a kind of consciousness that weighed its thoughts and searched itself for evil content. A perusal of the second half of Brown's work—a book only one hundred pages long in total—reveals practically the entire cast of characters of Foucault's course: Cyprian, Tertullian, Christian baptism, asceticism, *anachoresis*, even the obscure dream-treatise of Artemidorus.[50] Given that Foucault did all of his lecturing and writing on the ancient world *after* 1978, it is difficult to escape the conclusion that the philosopher owed Brown an even greater amount than he ultimately acknowledged.

Moving beyond mere content, Foucault seems to have latched onto Brown's core concept: *style*. At least one interlocutor felt this connection at the time, remarking to Foucault in 1984 that not he but Peter Brown was the first to have introduced the notion of style into the study of antiquity. Foucault concurred, saying, "[t]he use that I make of 'style,' I have borrowed in large part from Peter Brown."[51] In *The Making of Late Antiquity*, Brown had defined the shift from pagan religiosity in Late Antique Egypt to a recognizably Christian religiosity in terms of a change of style. "The 'style' of religious life of the late second and third centuries," he wrote, "was that the frontier between the divine and the human had lain tantalizingly open." Inasmuch as that state of affairs had rapidly changed in the course of a generation, Brown claimed, it was because ascetic monks, "fought against their own past, and they did so by creating *a new style of religious life*, that was the antithesis of that against which they had rebelled."[52] Keeping in mind Foucault's earlier comment about his debt to Brown, it is clear that this notion of a *style*—an assertive and freely chosen life-aesthetic, yet one that had the power to transform the world in its image—was of great utility to the philosopher.

FOUCAULT CERTAINLY RECOGNIZED that, in confronting the question of arts of living, he was operating outside of his traditional hunting grounds. *The Use of Pleasure* contained the philosopher's acknowledgment that he was "neither Hellenist nor Latinist," but that he had nevertheless felt it vital to confront ancient texts.[53] If he had succeeded, over a half-decade, in acquiring what he felt to be "a sufficient familiarity" therewith, it was, he declared in 1983, through the assistance of a handful of associates. Three of the scholars so named, unsurprisingly, were Berkeley professors: Brown, whose works, advice, and conversation had been "of enormous assistance"; and Dreyfus and Rabinow, whose questions and reflections had forced Foucault to sharpen his vision and reformulate his methodology.[54] The other two figures who came in for mention were both colleagues of Foucault at the Collège de France, where Paul Veyne held the Collège's chair in Roman history, and Pierre Hadot studied the history of ancient thought.

Veyne, who was the author of an influential study of Roman civic culture and a highly regarded treatise on historiography, had joined the faculty of the Collège de France in 1976.[55] Foucault considered the historian a valuable resource in his study of ancient societies and cultures,[56] and had frequented his office since early 1978.[57] In that same year, Veyne published an essay entitled, "Foucault Revolutionizes History." Its argument—that Foucault's antirealism represented a major theoretical insight for practicing historians—veiled the fact that Veyne was elucidating and magnifying ideas that Foucault had only half-articulated. When Veyne wrote that the philosopher's method consisted "of understanding that things are nothing more than the objectifications of determinate practices—of which the determinations must be brought to light," he expounded the latter's ideas at once more concisely and more forcefully than Foucault himself had ever done.[58] Foucault's subsequent public formulations of his antirealist theses bore the stamp of Veyne's silent elaboration.[59] "His influence upon these pages," Foucault wrote candidly in the prefatory essay to the 1984 *Sexuality* volumes, "would be difficult to circumscribe."[60]

Yet if Veyne contributed to the methodology and factual background of Foucault's late studies, Pierre Hadot may be said to have given directly to the fund of themes. Hadot spent much of his career at the École Pratique des Hautes Études in Paris, writing and lecturing on neoplatonic philosophy during the Hellenistic period. In 1976, Hadot published a piece on the notion of "spiritual exercises" in the ancient world. As Hadot had occasion to note after Foucault's death, the latter was "particularly interested" in three of the article's ideas:

> the description of ancient philosophy as an art, style, or way of life; the attempt I made to explain how modern philosophy had forgotten this tradition, and had become almost entirely a theoretical discourse; and the idea I sketched out in the article . . . that Christianity had taken over as its own certain techniques of spiritual exercises, as they had already been practiced in antiquity.[61]

Each of these ideas is present in a robust and unmistakable form in Foucault's 1981 course, *Subjectivity and Truth*. As none of them is discernible in *The Government of the Living*, we may assume that Foucault acquainted himself with Hadot's work sometime between April and October of 1980.[62] Arnold I. Davidson relates the passionate enthusiasm that Foucault felt for Hadot's work in 1982.[63]

However dissatisfied Hadot may have ultimately been with the use to which Foucault put his ideas—he felt the latter to have placed too great an emphasis on the "self" and not enough on the transcendence of self—there is little question that they were a great catalyst for Foucault's thinking.[64] Transmuted into "practices of the self," Hadot's concept of spiritual exercises gave substance and structure to the phenomena that Foucault had treated in *The Government of the Living* under the rubric of "avowal" (*l'aveu*), and the "putting-into-discourse of oneself" (*mise-en-discours de soi-même*), or *exagoresis*. Even more crucially, Hadot's concept of a philosophical way of life allowed Foucault to inject into his history of Western subjectivity a moment of genuine freedom.

The Government of the Living, it will be remembered from Chapter 4, had moved directly from the "worldly subjectivity" characteristic of the age of Severus to the "deep subjectivity" characteristic of the age of Augustine. In both cases, the subject was called upon to recognize and proclaim a "truth" about itself: the only difference was that, in the former case, that truth was perceived to come from without; in the latter case, from within. Fortified by Hadot's concepts, Foucault was emboldened in the 1981 *Subjectivity and Truth* to present a different narrative. In this version, there was a period several centuries in length in which, for at least a privileged portion of the citizenry, it was possible to craft one's existence according to principles of beauty. Spiritual exercises in the service of arts of living—arts, as noted above, practiced freely and voluntarily[65]—yielded a conjuncture in which individuals *made* rather than *discovered* themselves. "Prediscursive" subjects chose practices that would enable them to acquire particular, and desirable, subjectival modalities. If this conjuncture had come apart with the emergence of a more austere, late-pagan spirituality, it remained the case that it had not been wholly eradicated.

To RECAP, THEN: arts of living as they were practiced during Classical antiquity were concerned with crafting one's being so as to attain a particular and desired ontological status. Such "modalities of being" included beauty, tranquility, gracefulness, and any of a number of other attributes. These were to be obtained by the more or less frequent application of techniques of the self, or what Hadot had called "spiritual exercises." An art of living was thus a *tekhnê* in the proper Greek sense of that term: a skill, a *savoir-faire*. The practitioner was not concerned, as Kant would be two millennia later, to universalize the rule of his actions. On the contrary, he made an ethical subject of himself "by an attitude and by a research that *individualizes* his action, modulates it, and can even, by lending it a rational and reflective structure, give it a unique splendor."[66]

If *Subjectivity and Truth* had concerned itself with documenting and describing the existence of an historical conjuncture defined by these arts, then Foucault's 1982 course, *The Hermeneutics of the Subject*, would offer an account of that conjuncture's slow dissolution. *The Hermeneutics of the Subject*, which formed a considerable part of the groundwork for *The Care of the Self*, focused its attention on the world of the second century C. E. Like Brown's *The Making of Late Antiquity*, it emphasized not the breaks but the continuities between the late-pagan and early-Christian periods. It was also, as Foucault announced during his first lecture, an effort to address the question of subjectivity in general terms, rather than through the lens of sexuality as had been the case in *Subjectivity and Truth*.[67]

What Foucault sought to demonstrate in the 1982 course was the gradual transformation, within the late-pagan world and prior to the ascendancy of the Christian faith, of certain themes that had enjoyed a long existence. In particular, it was a question of the erosion of the concept of the art of living. Foucault claimed that the arts of living had experienced a metamorphosis in the course of the second century. The techniques of the self (which, again, were the subcomponents of all such arts, and intended as a *means*) increasingly developed a life and a momentum of their own. Spiritual exercises became a significant goal in their own right.

This transformation carried with it a progressively smaller emphasis on the aesthetics of life, a progressively greater emphasis on self-assessment and self-discovery. "At a certain moment," Foucault declared, "the problem of an aesthetics of existence is covered over by the problem of purity."[68] The phenomenon of performing a labor upon oneself—of monitoring oneself and maintaining one's purity—increasingly detached itself from the personal stylization that it had been intended to serve.[69] Hence, within the arts of living, "the notion of exercising a perfect mastery over oneself soon became the main issue." That these arts were ultimately overshadowed and liquidated by the very techniques of the self that comprised them was, for Foucault, one of the most important evolutions of antiquity.[70]

The transition from arts of living to the narrower "care of the self" may be viewed as the theme of the latter two *Sexuality* volumes taken as a whole.

The Use of Pleasure covered the era defined by an aesthetic of existence, while *The Care of the Self* looked to the ensuing period. But it should be remembered that the full scope of Foucault's intended project never appeared in print. His aim, had he lived, was more ambitious than the positing of a binary historical model. For the thesis that Foucault developed in *The Hermeneutics of the Subject* held that the evolutionary trend continued. Techniques of the self did not die with the emergence of Christianity; rather, they continued to hypertrophy. The claim was a subtle one. Christianity, Foucault argued, revealed not the termination but the intensification of the late-pagan focus on practices of the self.

The Christian "culture of the self," like the thought of its great pagan predecessors Seneca and Epictetus, was not a function of individualism but of critical attention to interior life.[71] Like Stoic and Epicurean practitioners of techniques of the self, Christian directors of conscience worked by guiding initiates to survey themselves, to sift their thoughts, and to acknowledge what they discovered there.[72] Christianity's interrogation of the self was, however, far more harrowing. From the perspective of the extension of techniques of the self, Christianity carried quantitative change to the point of qualitative difference: "This new Christian self had to be *constantly* examined because in this self were lodged concupiscence and desires of the flesh. From that moment on, the self was no longer something to be made but something to be renounced and deciphered."[73] Decipherment of one's own inner truth with an eye to self-renunciation: this was precisely what Foucault termed "the hermeneutics of the subject."

And while this hermeneutics was the lineal descendant of the art of living, it was, as Foucault believed he had amply demonstrated, wholly distinct in its approach and in its aims. Far from providing the tools for the construction of one's own mode of being, the hermeneutics of the subject demanded that one solemnly acknowledge the "true" self that one already was—and then only to revile and renounce it.

THE HISTORICAL TRANSFORMATION that substituted the hermeneutics of the subject for the Classical arts of living was, Foucault argued, of profound consequence. For the subjectivity proper to modern Western thought was constituted "the day that *bios* ceased to be what it had been for so long in Greek thought, namely the corollary of a *tekhnê*; when bios (life) ceased being the corollary of a *tekhnê*, to become the form of a test of self."[74]

The truly determinant shift, according to Foucault, was thus the one that had taken place in the second century, within pagan philosophy. The colonization of arts of living by "the care of the self" (*epimeleia heautou*)—which is to say, the transformation of life (*bios*) from the corollary of an art (*tekhnê*) into the object of a test (*épreuve*)—ensured the emergence of the modern "deep" subject, even if the full elaboration of that type of subjectivity would require several additional centuries.[75] The sinful Christian self was a mere subset of this profound, truth-bearing subject.

The crux, for Foucault, was the very notion that the subject possessed a truth, and that this truth could be attained through a process of introspection and discovery. If *tekhnê* had represented art, creativity, and expression, then *épreuve* was the overthrowing of all of these things: it was science, discovery, and reflection. It was the triumph of the metaphysical conception of truth in the realm of human existence.

The search begun, it was not difficult to see that the "art versus science" distinction ran through much of Foucault's recent work—even, arguably, as a kind of tacit and unacknowledged normativity. Already in the first volume of *The History of Sexuality*, Foucault had emphasized the sharp divide between the *ars erotica* as practiced in numerous Asian civilizations, and the *scientia sexualis* that dominated the West.[76] While the book rendered illegitimate any possible statement of preference for one such structure over another, it also visibly aligned the *ars erotica* (in which "truth is extracted from pleasure itself") with the beneficent "economy of bodies and pleasures" in which we were permitted to hope. The *scientia sexualis*, on the other hand, was the clear villain of the piece, submitting us to the "austere monarchy of sex" and "the infinite task of forcing forth its secret and extorting from this shadow the truest of confessions."[77]

By the early 1980s, this "art versus science" distinction had, if anything, become sharper. Foucault increasingly spoke of the creative and the analytical as distinct, even unrelated categories. Here, morality-as-art was the test case. "My idea," he declared in 1983, "is that it's not at all necessary to relate ethical problems to scientific knowledge."[78] Morality could be "a very strong structure of existence, without any relation with the juridical per se, with an authoritarian system, with a disciplinary structure."[79] The notion of creation was as positively charged as the notion of discovery was negatively charged. As Peter Dews observes, "Foucault's task, in his late work, will be to articulate the concepts of subjectivity and freedom in such a way as to avoid any suggestion that such freedom must take the form of the recovery of an authentic 'natural' self."[80]

If Foucault opposed what he termed the contemporary Californian cult of the self, it was precisely because of its propensity in this direction. "[O]ne is supposed," he lamented, "to discover one's true self, to separate it from that which might obscure or alienate it, to decipher its truth thanks to psychological or psychoanalytic science." Such was the bitter fruit of the second-century transformation that he had studied.[81]

It is noteworthy that, during this time, when Foucault reiterated his rejection of the Sartrean conception of subjectivity, he did it not on the grounds that Sartre had posited a unified subject (for this had ceased to be a point of contention), but rather on the grounds that the core of Sartre's subject was *authenticity*. Authenticity, as adequacy to one's true self, could never capture the richness and diversity of the possible relations between an individual and himself.[82] Foucault's comments on this point are telling:

> I think that the only acceptable practical consequence of what Sartre has said is to link his theoretical insight to the practice of creativity—and not of authenticity. From the idea that the self is not given to us, I think that there is only one practical consequence: we have to create ourselves as a work of art.[83]

Inasmuch as Sartre's thought remained valuable, it was because it deemed creativity a worthy problem for philosophy. To carry forward that line of questioning, Foucault asserted, would be to investigate the ways in which it was possible not to create works of art, but to create *ourselves* as works of art.

A listener hearing these comments in 1983 would rightly have sensed that Foucault's vision of the autonomous individual had undergone a substantial rehabilitation. The project of self-creation—"without," as Foucault had said, "any relation with the juridical per se, with an authoritarian system, with a disciplinary structure"—sounded not a little like existentialism. That impression would only be reinforced by the philosopher's contemporary comments on a pivotal concept: experience.

WHAT EXPERIENCE, FOUCAULT asked in the opening lecture of *Subjectivity and Truth*, does the subject have of himself once a "true discourse" on the subject exists in his culture?[84] From the listener's perspective, this was an eye-opening question, not least in its casual implication that one might speak of *a* subject *prior* to the appearance of a discourse that purported to reveal the truth about subjects. But even more immediately striking in Foucault's question was the deployment of the concept of "experience."

Experience was not a new concept in Foucault's thought, but rather a very old one. As the preceding chapter noted, Foucault made ample reference to "experience" in his earliest works, and most notably in *Madness and Civilization*. There, his stated aim was to recover whatever might be available to us of the *experience* of madness across the centuries. This project was, as historical inquiry demanded, to be conducted through an empirical examination of the texts of the nascent psychiatric discipline and the records of places of detention. It was not to be imagined, however, that these documents in any way exhausted the lived experience of the mad. On the contrary, Foucault wrote, "madness, as a domain of experience, is never exhausted in the medical or para-medical knowledge of it that one may gain."[85] He was compelled to consult the documentary record, but the experience of madness had been transcribed there in a language not its own.

The category of experience was thus an important one to the early Foucault. And if the philosopher spoke of experience, it was because he, like the existentialist thinkers who had not yet ceded the field in 1961, was concerned with the subject's encounter with the world—with "the lived" (*le vécu*). An excerpt from a 1964 interview is revealing on this point:

M. Demonbynes: . . . May I ask you to what extent, in your opinion, Nietzsche had the experience of madness? . . . Have I understood you properly? Because you have unquestionably spoken of this experience of madness. Is this really what you meant?

M. Foucault: Yes.

M. Demonbynes: . . . Do you believe that one can really have. . . . That great spirits like Nietzsche can have "the experience of madness"?

M. Foucault: I would say to you: yes, yes.[86]

Experience was, seemingly, the lived encounter with the world in its many facets—as it accrued to individuals. Any suggestion that such a notion was problematic to Foucault is undercut by the literally hundreds of references to "experience" in *Madness and Civilization*.

Yet problematic it rapidly became. In Foucault's writings after 1964, the word "experience" virtually disappeared as a term of art.[87] By the time that *The Order of Things*—with its thesis of the disappearance of man—went to press in 1966, any language tasting even remotely of the transcendental had been meticulously purged from his conceptual arsenal. Foucault was conceding past error when he wrote in the preface to *The Archaeology of Knowledge*:

In a general way, *Madness and Civilization* gave much too great a role— and an enigmatic role at that—to what found itself designated as an "experience," showing thereby how close I remained to admitting an anonymous and general subject of history.[88]

This kind of self-critique suggests an intimate awareness on Foucault's part of the inextricability of the notion of experience from traditional under-standings of subjectivity. Throughout his later career, as such, he would routinely pillory the concept of experience, and ask pardon for having had the poor judgment to employ the term himself.[89]

This is what makes the reemergence of "experience" within Foucault's thought at the beginning of the 1980s so interesting, and such a tangible marker of his evolving attitude toward the subject. Having explicitly associ-ated the concept of experience with Sartrean thought ("an anonymous and general subject of history") and with such "empty" (and patently existen-tialist) concepts as time and being, Foucault now reclaimed experience for his own—and this precisely within the context of his first overt study of subjectivity. Listeners who sensed Foucault's thought careening toward the path of his old nemesis might have been forgiven their bewilderment.

Foucault was assuredly *not* postulating a universal consciousness or a subject of history. Yet the idea of experience had newfound appeal to him as a way of describing—just as he might have at the beginning of his career—the individual's lived encounter with the world. "Experience" was, we may say, directly opposed to "system" in Foucault's thought. The two could not coexist, and never had coexisted. When one used the language of system, one was looking at the subject from *without*, as a position or node. Conversely, when one used the language of experience, one was looking at the subject from *within*, as an actor. Whereas system had been a way of treating the subject as a kind of epiphenomenon, experience represented the acknowledgement that the interior dimension was as valid and necessary as the exterior dimension in the study of ourselves; that "art and style" were as vital as "conditions." The last four years of Foucault's life witnessed a dramatic move in the direction of experience; he was, in his final courses at the Collège de France, Professor of the History of *Systems* of Thought more in name than in fact.

WHAT, THEN, WAS the significance of Foucault's question? Why did he inquire after the experience of the subject in a culture that has generated a "true discourse" about subjects? It was to demonstrate, as Foucault had done in every one of his studies, that such a state of affairs was not "necessary"; that it was instead simply specific. The idea of a "knowable subject" was historically contingent, fragile, and amenable to change. The import of Foucault's question lay in the twentieth century, not in the second century.

If the experience of the subject, from antiquity to the present day, was one in which the subject was perceived to possess a singular and profound truth, then that was a misfortune—but not a destiny. The experience need not remain as it was. There were other, perhaps better, experiences of one's own subjectivity. As the study of ancient arts of living showed, there had been other ways of conceptualizing selfhood that were not dependent upon bondage to a "true" self. That alone would be sufficient to demonstrate that other ways could be found in the present.

Here, then, was the intimate bond with Foucault's writings on the Enlightenment. Since 1978, Foucault had returned again and again—though never in a systematic way—to what he called the philosophical problem of the "present moment."[90] The essential idea in each of these interventions was that Kant, with his "Was ist Aufklärung?" of 1784, had inaugurated an era in which the central preoccupation of philosophy was the interrogation of the historical present. Hence, Hegel, Marx, Nietzsche, Weber, Horkheimer, and Habermas could all be seen as perpetuators of a Kantian project: one that moved the attention of philosophy from the eternal to "what we do today."[91]

Kant had ushered in what Foucault believed to be the quintessentially "modern" attitude. That attitude was encapsulated in the famous *aude sapere*. It was a recognition of the surpassing of intellectual minority; it entailed perpetual self-questioning. In this latter sense, it transcended philosophy and flavored all aspects of modern culture. "For the attitude of modernity," Foucault wrote, "the high value of the present is indissociable from a desperate eagerness to imagine it . . . otherwise than it is, and to transform it not by destroying it but by grasping what it is."[92] Modernity put self-knowledge in the service of a transformative effort.

No better exemplar of the post-Kantian attitude could be found, argued Foucault, than Baudelaire. For Baudelaire, the essence of the modern artist was his willingness to transfigure the world, and to do so in a way that was not mere negation of the real, but rather "a difficult interplay between the truth of what is real and the exercise of freedom." This was equally true of the individual at large:

> Modern man, for Baudelaire, is not the man who goes off to discover himself, his secrets and his hidden truth; he is the man who tries to invent himself. This modernity does not "liberate man in his own being"; it compels him to face the task of producing himself.[93]

The attitude of modernity, Foucault noted in carefully chosen language, was tied to "an indispensable asceticism": one in which, rather than accepting oneself, one "[took] oneself as object of a complex and difficult elaboration."

Here, then, were central motifs of the 1981 and 1982 courses—only transferred to "modernity." The primacy accorded to art (and not science); the indispensability of asceticism; the partisanship for self-production over self-discovery: all of this was directly imported from the study of the arts of living and their successors. It was a remarkable, even brazen, act of intellectual legerdemain on Foucault's part. Modernity, which the philosopher had presented throughout his career as an era defined by rationalization (in forms of discourse, in the functioning of power, and elsewhere), was here recast as an attitude: an attitude, moreover, defined by the "ascetic elaboration of self" through *art*.[94]

While Habermas and a number of his followers saw "What Is Enlightenment?" as a kind of end-of-the-day concession speech,[95] it was in reality something of an argumentative coup for Foucault. Three moves are worth noting. Firstly, by defining the Enlightenment tradition as "the permanent reactivation of an attitude"—one that manifested itself in critique of the historical present—Foucault situated himself squarely within the philosophical tradition that his opponents alleged him to menace. Secondly, by positing a laudable post-Kantian ethos that operated through innovation and not discovery, he provided normative grounding for his (obvious) preference for arts of living over the hermeneutics of the self:[96] the latter, in its infinite task of scrutiny, merely took things as they were, while the arts of living—with their imperative to craft one's self in a state of autonomy—manifested a Königsbergian intellectual maturity. Finally, by issuing an ironic echo of Habermas's call to uphold the Enlightenment tradition (which, translated into Foucault's terms, became a call to transfigure ourselves and our historical moment), he made the idea of an art of living something relevant to the present. All three of these moves converged when Foucault wrote of Enlightenment-inspired critique: "I shall thus characterize the philosophical ethos appropriate to the critical ontology of ourselves as a historico-practical test of the limits that we may go beyond, and thus as *work carried out by ourselves upon ourselves as free beings*."[97]

TO BE MODERN was, thus, to scrutinize and destabilize our present, so that we might, as "free beings," craft ourselves in such a way as to transcend it. Enlightenment *meant autonomous subjects living their lives as art*.

While Foucault's last works have generally not been read in this way—the temptation being to read them as if the philosopher still clung to his "strong" genealogical views on power and subjectivity—he showed great determination, in his final years of life, to make just this point. Did Foucault actually think of the arts of living and the critical ontology of ourselves as a single issue? Perhaps the most striking piece of evidence in this regard is the philosopher's lecture of January 5, 1983: the two-hour introductory piece to his course of that year, *The Government of the Self and of Others*. A single oral presentation, this lecture nevertheless contained near-complete versions of both "What is Enlightenment?" *and* the introduction to *The Use of Pleasure*. Foucault presented, that is to say, his preface to the study of the aesthetics of existence and his account of the Enlightenment ethos as a single thread.[98]

On the question of individual liberty, Foucault sounded at times during his last years like the risen Sartre. He told one interviewer, "I believe solidly in human liberty."[99] In a discussion with Paul Rabinow conducted shortly before his death, he made the profoundly unarchaeological statement: "Thought is liberty in relation to what one does, the movement by which one detaches oneself from it, constitutes it as an object and reflects upon it as a problem."[100] In the final interview that he gave, Foucault said that he had undertaken the study of antiquity "in order to see how sexuality was *manipulated, lived, and modified by a certain number of actors*."[101] Choice, freedom, reflection, experience, agency: these were the undisguised hallmarks of Foucault's last philosophical interventions.

In parallel, it is clear that Foucault continued to use not simply positive but hortatory language when speaking about the crafting of life, noting during one interview that rule-based morality was disappearing in the modern world, and that "to this absence of morality responds, or should respond, a research effort which is that of an aesthetic of existence."[102] He was emphatic that he lived his own life according to these principles. Asked to what extent he was involved in the homosexual movement in France, he replied that he held himself aloof from movements of sexual liberation; "For me," he added, "sexuality is a matter of one's way of living, it points back to the technique of the self."[103]

For Foucault, the philosophical advances that had been made in the course of his lifetime—he remained too modest to say *made by himself*—were major steps on the path to individual freedom. If the Nietzschean dream of life as art was closer today, it was because philosophy had rendered individuals more aware of the fragility of that which constrained them. From this, the possibility of determining one's own existence followed naturally.[104]

Had the philosopher been able to keep to path that he himself had blazed? Had he lived life as art? He seemed, at the end, to think so. "My books," he said, "are, in a sense, fragments of autobiography."[105] Was there coherence, he was asked, to the struggles in which he had engaged? There was none, he responded, save that of his own life.[106]

Conclusion
Foucault's Pendulum

FOR THE INTELLECTUAL HISTORIAN, IT IS AN INESCAPABLE FACT THAT the great bulk of scholarship conducted on Michel Foucault is in the English language. That Foucault himself was exceedingly comfortable speaking and working in the English-speaking world has certainly played a part in this. The centrality to Foucault's work of California—as a site of social experimentation, as an academic hub, and as a place where the philosopher formed close and lasting intellectual partnerships—is clear, and bears, through his interpreters, strongly on his subsequent reception. In his last years, Foucault also gave courses at the University of Vermont, and lectured extensively at universities throughout the American northeast. Foucault's spiritual home was, by the end, unquestionably in North America. An exchange from a 1982 interview is revealing:

Stephen Riggins: You don't match up with the image of the refined Frenchman who practices the art of living well. You're also the only Frenchman I know who's told me that he preferred American cuisine.

Foucault: Yes, that's true! A good club sandwich with a Coca-Cola, there's nothing like it! It's true. With ice cream, of course.[1]

In another interview conducted the same year, Foucault declared that he had always felt himself poorly integrated into French social and intellectual life, and that, had the possibility occurred to him at a younger age, he would have emigrated to the United States.[2]

But if it is the case that, since his death in 1984, Foucault has experienced divergent destinies in France and in the English-speaking world, part of that is to be attributed to the intellectual politics of the 1980s, so markedly different on the two sides of the Atlantic. In America, as François Cusset has ably demonstrated, Foucault's prominence surged as the large-scale appropriation of his ideas, both inside and outside of academia, provided the theoretical grounding for a decade of identity politics.[3] In France, on the other hand, Foucault's reputation as a thinker and public intellectual went into eclipse almost immediately after his death. Here, the temper of the moment was in opposition to the perceived intellectual excesses of the late 1960s and early 1970s, and sympathetic to a liberal critique that, in Paris if not elsewhere, had the air of novelty. As Mark Lilla argues, the 1981 election of François Mitterand, far from heralding *la gauche au pouvoir*, marked the rapprochement of the French revolutionary tradition with the liberal institutions of the Fifth Republic. What the ensuing two decades witnessed was "the almost universal abandonment of the Hegelian, Marxist, and structuralist dogmas that nourished intellectual contempt for liberalism after the war."[4] In this twilight of idols, the author of *The Order of Things* and *Discipline and Punish* was not spared.

The breakthrough work for the emergence of a confident and articulate French liberalism was Luc Ferry and Alain Renaut's 1985 *La pensée 68: Essai sur l'anti-humanisme contemporain*.[5] In this groundbreaking and contentious work, Ferry and Renaut, like Marcel Gauchet, Pierre Manent, and a considerable number of recent French thinkers, self-consciously rehabilitated a set of concepts that had seemed irretrievably lost at the end of the 1960s. History, the subject, rights, *man* himself: in the course of the 1980s and 1990s, all of these returned to the center of philosophical questioning in France.[6]

The achievement of *La pensée 68* was to draw a hard line between the vital liberal–republican tradition in France on one side, and the illiberal and pernicious aberration that the thought of the generation of 1968 represented on the other. In this intellectual revolt against the fathers, it was essential for Ferry and Renaut to depict the leading figures of the preceding generation—Foucault, Derrida, Bourdieu, and Lacan—as practitioners of a rigorous and consistent antihumanism: as deniers, that is, of man, the subject, and liberty. Likewise, it was necessary to treat "la pensée 68" as a fundamentally static body of thought, incapable of meaningful self-critique. Hence, Ferry and Renaut could, in concluding their analysis of Foucault's late writings on subjectivity, shrug off the philosopher's late-career changes of orientation as so much window-dressing. New words, they argued, masked the same old Foucault:

> The previous positions are preserved . . . in their entirety, while at the same time benefiting from an effect of language that, in dangling the theme of the search for new subjectivities, allows [Foucault] to jump on the bandwagon of the return to the subject and to mask everything that is so deeply outmoded about his discourse.[7]

The adoption of this new vocabulary and voice, Ferry and Renaut suggested, carried with it the ancillary benefit of camouflaging the contradiction that necessarily existed in criticizing modernity (with its concomitant concepts of humanism and subjectivity) while at the same time embracing the discourse of human rights. Foucault's seeming "advance" to an ethics of self was thus, as Ferry and Renaut suggested, in reality "a desperate attempt to mask the immense gap that had opened up between him and the evolution of ideas and morals."[8]

For Ferry and Renaut, as for others within the neoliberal current, Foucault's "French Nietzscheanism," like that of his contemporary Jean-François Lyotard, represented a positive threat to human rights and to republican values. As Ferry and Renaut observed:

> The antihumanism of the thought of '68 opens onto "barbarism," not in the sense that it would unleash untold torrents of violence, but in that its intended trial of subjectivity destroys any possibility of genuine dialogue between consciousnesses that might be able to think their differences on the basis of identity: once all that remains to each of us is the exacerbation of individual differences, the other becomes the "entirely other," the "*bar-bar*-ian."

The practical consequence of Foucault's antisubjectivity was—as Ferry and Renaut believed Foucault's criticisms of Habermas amply demonstrated— a profound mistrust of *intersubjectivity*, and a belief that any claim thereunto was "utopian." That such a path of thought was politically corrosive seemed manifest to these authors. If they congratulated Foucault upon any aspect of his philosophical practice, it was that he had "so assiduously cultivated the inconsequence" of his own ideas that he had defended human rights and the Republic in spite of himself.[9]

Foucault, had he been alive to respond, would doubtless have countered that a "positive" theory never ensures positive political results, and that no theory's historical appropriation can be foreseen.[10] That he was not alive helps to explain how Ferry and Renaut's work was able to exercise the influence that it did over Foucault's posthumous reputation in France. While the neoliberal critique of Foucault is incisive on a number of points, what the present volume should have demonstrated is that it nevertheless proceeds from a serious misrepresentation of his work, and particularly the later portion thereof. What Ferry and Renaut offered their readers was a caricature of Foucault's thought: one that emphasized the profoundly antihumanist sentiments of the 1960s, while ignoring or challenging the sincerity of his subject-centered work of the 1980s.

Part of what this work has attempted to show is that nothing could be more unreasonable than the attempt to flatten down Foucault's thought into a single, coherent project. What we see over the course of Foucault's career is not the consistent advocacy of a pointed philosophical message (as, for instance, the dissolution of the subject), but rather a succession of near-independent probings into questions that, for the moment, had captured the philosopher's imagination. In this sense, Gary Gutting is on much firmer ground than Ferry and Renaut when he argues that:

> Foucault's work is at root ad hoc, fragmentary and incomplete. Each of his books is determined by concerns and approaches specific to it and should not be understood as developing a theory or a method that is a general instrument of intellectual progress.[11]

In Isaiah Berlin's terminology, Gutting tells us, Foucault is a fox and not a hedgehog. And while Gutting may put the case a touch strongly, the core assertion that he makes is critical to comprehending Foucault's work. Foucault never wrote the same book twice. *Madness and Civilization*, which sought, in a particularly stirring way, to restore the voices of the voiceless, was asking fundamentally different questions from *The Archaeology of Knowledge*, which proclaimed the essential anonymity of all speech. Neither work is directly comparable to *The Use of Pleasure*, which found in the voices of the past an exhortation to a richer social world in the present. And what is true of these particular works is true of Foucault's oeuvre generally.

How are we to understand the changeability, the centerlessness of Foucauldean thought? Manifestly, there is no one simple answer. Yet we move closer to making sense of the philosopher's trajectory when we recognize that, as a thinker, Foucault was exceedingly *permeable*. He liked to paint himself as an outsider and as one who worked against the grain of his times, and this self-characterization is not without a bit of truth: he shunned institutional commitments, traveled as much as his work allowed, and steered clear of much that was fashionable. As the foregoing chapters have demonstrated, however, Foucault was at every moment of his career highly attuned both to the prevailing intellectual mood and to the needs and expectations of his audience. It was the nature of his philosophical practice to enter a community, imbibe its concepts, deploy them in a powerful and original way—and then move on when the tides changed.

The first community of thought in which he found a home and welcome was a literary one, defined by Blanchot, Bataille, and the *Tel Quel* authors. His work of this period, accordingly, bore a distinctly literary stamp, and shared the preoccupations—experience, language, limits—of his fiction-writing colleagues. If the structuralist wave, with which he rapidly affiliated himself, enabled Foucault to speak in a new voice to a new set of listeners, it also virtually required him to abandon certain philosophical positions, like the centrality of experience or the importance of the gaze, that had become inconvenient. This pattern would repeat itself in the wake of May 1968. Where the Foucault of *The Order of Things* excoriated the modern-day followers of Marx and tentatively praised those of Freud, the radicalized and Deleuze-inspired Foucault of the early 1970s made precisely the opposite choices, adopting Marxian rhetoric and dismissing the "repressive hypothesis." The wheel turned yet again with the emergence of *la nouvelle philosophie* in the late 1970s, and several times more before

Foucault's death in 1984. At every point, Foucault's essential openness to the new ideas and currents flowing around him, coupled with his remarkable ability to rapidly master new conceptual languages, drove his thought in new and unforeseen directions.

Naturally, amidst this perpetual self-reinvention, Foucault's position on subjectivity did not remain static. In his earliest writings, including *Madness and Civilization* and many of the shorter pieces that followed in its wake, Foucault showed his commitment to something like a traditional subject: an independent and autonomous locus of experience. That kind of subjectivity not only disappeared from his work during the second half of the 1960s, but actually served as the target of a series of devastating attacks. The concept of experience was, in a succession of works that increasingly bore the stamp of the triumphant structuralist movement, officially banished from Foucault's conceptual vocabulary and consigned (along with "creativity," and all other terms redolent of agency) to the trash-heap. Experience was recognized as subjective and interior—the province of the *for-itself*. Archaeology, like the genealogy that would follow and build upon it, was committed not to experience but to an anonymous systematicity that generated meaning *while avoiding* the notion of an experience-laden subject. As Foucault could write in 1972, "What counts in the things said by men is not so much what they might have thought behind or beneath them, but *that which systematizes them from the outset.*"[12]

Foucault's works from the decade spanning 1966 to 1976—*The Order of Things, The Archaeology of Knowledge, Discipline and Punish*, and the first volume of *The History of Sexuality*—each, in slightly modulated ways, dissected the notion of the individual subject as agent or patient. The philosopher certainly did not misspeak when he described his thought from this period as the interrogation of system. The logic of these critiques was, while differing in its object, always essentially the same: the phenomena under examination represented some portion of a great system, or what we might call an immanent material totality. This system was self-governing in the sense that it transformed itself over time. It also produced a number of effects—works of philosophy, for instance, or institutions like the prison— that appeared to be the products of conscious and purposeful action, but were in the fact the result of the play of anonymous forces. These systemic "surface effects," whether viewed as discourse-objects or power-objects, succeeded in bearing meaning without meaning's first being imparted to them by any subject. Subjects were not the makers of these objects, but were rather co-produced *alongside* the objects by the selfsame processes.

Foucault's notoriety as a thinker continues to derive from the positions that he theorized in the works of this fruitful decade.[13] With Foucault's political and philosophical projects of the late 1970s, however, came an increasing interest in questions that refused to be bound by the logic of the immanent material totality. On the political level, his part in the contentious debate over the significance of the *nouveaux philosophes* divided Foucault from the French left—and even from his own recent theses on the disciplinary society—and drove him toward a rights-oriented position in which the treatment of the individual was the ultimate marker of a regime's acceptability. On the philosophical level, his attention began a slow migration away from the social, and toward the experience of religion and of spirituality. Already by 1978, it was clear to Foucault that the study of the history of sexuality upon which he had embarked would be incomplete and misleading if he failed to pause, backtrack, and examine the role of Christian confession in the construction of the modern sexual subject.[14] But the doctrines, institutions and rituals of Christianity quickly proved too narrow to accommodate the breadth of his passion for "spirituality," a term by which he understood the transformation of one's own being with the goal of *opening oneself* to the discovery of truth.

Taking these shifts into account, Foucault's fascination with the Iranian Revolution of 1978–79 seems a natural development. He saw there, or believed he saw, not only an unarmed population courageously opposing its dictatorial rulers, but also a religious movement that was a kind of "political spirituality." As he would say in an 1979 interview:

> In rising up, the Iranians said to themselves (and perhaps this is the soul of uprisings): "we must change, certainly, the regime. . . . But above all, *we must change ourselves.* Our way of being, our relation to others, to things, to eternity, to God, etc., all must be completely changed, and *there won't be any real revolution save on the condition of this radical change in our experience.*" I think it's there that Islam played a role. . . . religion was for them like the promise and the guarantee of finding something that would radically *change their subjectivity.*[15]

The Iranians' hunger for personal freedom was indivisible, in Foucault's eyes, from their desire to live in such a way that their subjectivity was transformed, that their experience was opened up to new dimensions, and that the pathways of their lives gave forth onto truths that modernity itself had blocked and obscured.

In Foucault's analysis of the Iranian events, as in nearly all of the work that he would undertake after 1978, the critical perspective was the reverse of what one had come to expect from him. Rather than starting from an immanent totality and demonstrating the ways in which that totality produced individual subjects as the result of its functioning, *Foucault started from the standpoint of the individual.* He treated subjects not as the secondary manifestations of a more primary network, but rather as primary entities in themselves. It was not the functioning of power that made Iranians into the vital (and inflamed) subjects that they were; it was the accumulated behavior of Iranian subjects—desirous of effecting their own self-transformation—that stilled and then reconfigured the mechanisms of power. Within a year, Foucault would undertake to study this relationship for its own sake, examining in *The Birth of Biopolitics* the "liberal governmentality" in which outcomes were generated by the combined actions of individual actors, rather than by the desires of the center or the systematicity of the whole.

It is no exaggeration to say that, in Foucault's last works, his commitment to system gave way before his equally significant (but long-dormant) commitment to experience. To treat phenomena in terms of experience was to treat them as lived events. It was to understand them from the position of interiority, rather than from the famous standpoint of "exteriority" that, for its many vicissitudes of meaning, had remained the fixed star of Foucault's thought. As Martin Jay has recently argued:

> in his final work, Foucault came to focus his attention on the constitution of the subject of knowledge in such a way that experience once again began to resist reduction to [its] conditions, whether understood in terms of epistemic discourses or apparatuses of power. In so doing, he returned to his earlier fascination for Bataille's notion of inner experience, while at the same time reproducing some of the unresolved tensions that critics like Habermas had discerned in Bataille's approach to the issue.[16]

Experience was the province of an active, autonomous, reflective subject. It was that which allowed the Iranian subject to examine his own condition and then act. It was that which permitted the free citizen to craft his selfhood according to the principles of art. Experience was certainly historically dependent, but it is incorrect to imagine that, for the Foucault of the early 1980s, it was constructed by practices; it was, rather, that which made practice possible.

That Foucault did not himself acknowledge a change of direction in his work should not give surprise. As there has been repeated occasion to show, Foucault's intellectual modus operandi was, on the one hand, frequently to assert his right to change his mind; and on the other always to reinterpret his past achievements in light of his current projects, so as to give the impression of a consistent and coherent oeuvre. This amusing personal contradiction was tremendously empowering for Foucault, because it allowed him to undertake philosophical leaps at which a more fastidious thinker would have balked—without once having to "renounce" the works that, objectively speaking, he had surpassed.[17] In this as in most things, Foucault was a great student of Nietzsche, who wrote, "Convictions are prisons. . . . Freedom from convictions of any kind, the *capacity* for an unconstrained view, *pertains* to strength."[18]

Many historians who have not shared the political agenda of Ferry and Renaut have nevertheless echoed the pair's conclusions. That is, they have minimized the significance of Foucault's late espousal of a more robust conception of subjectivity, either because they have lacked the evidence—specifically, the lecture courses from 1979 and after—that would have revealed the enormity of the shift; or else, like Ferry and Renaut, they have simply doubted the sincerity of the philosopher's transformation. The result has been that Foucault's philosophical career has read like a kind of arrow's flight: a straight trajectory, an unwavering determination to deconstruct the subject. Habermas found the archery metaphor valuable enough to title his posthumous analysis of Foucault's project, "Taking Aim at the Heart of the Present."[19]

As we have seen, the history of Foucault's intellectual project—the term itself is misleading—is far from a straight line. A more accurate depiction might be the swing of a pendulum. Foucault started from a position that admitted the possibility of subjectivity: arguably, it was his awareness that certain kinds of subjects had been suppressed merely because of the label that one affixed to them—"mad," "demented," "enraged"—that motivated him to write in the first place. He ended, nearly a quarter-century later, at a position that looked not a little like his starting-point: acknowledging the existence of prediscursive subjects, enraptured by literature, politically unaffiliated, and pledged to a kind of experience that pushed the limits of the known. In the period in-between, Foucault created the twentieth century's most devastating critique of the free subject—and then, in a voice that by the end trembled from pain and debility, liquidated it. For the notion of the end of subjectivity had offered a kind of cold clarity, as well as an immensely thought-provoking lens through which to view the world. But ultimately, only the notion of strong subjectivity proved *warm* enough to accommodate an overwhelming passion for life and an inextinguishable belief in the primacy of human liberty.

Notes

NOTES FOR THE INTRODUCTION

1. Arnold I. Davidson, "Structures and Strategies of Discourse: Remarks Towards a History of Foucault's Philosophy of Language," in Davidson, ed., *Foucault and His Interlocutors* (Chicago: University of Chicago Press, 1997), 1. Davidson's course, "Historical Epistemology," taught at Harvard University in the fall of 1999, was the author's introduction to Foucault, and to the French epistemological tradition that nourished his thought.

2. "L'homme disparaît en philosophie, non pas comme objet de savoir mais comme sujet de liberté et d'existence." "Foucault répond à Sartre," *La Quinzaine littéraire* 46, March 1–15, 1968, 20–22; reprinted in *Dits et écrits, t. I*, 692.

3. See François Dosse, *The History of Structuralism* (Minneapolis: University of Minnesota Press, 1997). Dosse's work excels at depicting the breadth of what might be called the "anti-subjective" impulse; it is especially strong on the heroic years of high structuralism during the mid-1960s. See also Edith Kurzweil, *The Age of Structuralism: Lévi-Strauss to Foucault* (New York: Columbia University Press, 1980); and John Sturrock, ed., *Structuralism and Since* (Oxford, UK: Oxford University Press, 1979). Terence Hawkes, *Structuralism and Semiotics* (London: Routledge, 1997) is a short and helpful introduction to the intellectual foundations of structuralist thought; Patrick Sériot, *Structure et totalité: les origines intellectuelles du structuralisme en Europe centrale et orientale* (Paris: Presses Universitaires de France, 1999) provides a more thorough version of the same.

4. The transition from rigorously "structural" thought to what is called post-structuralism is, however, adroitly handled in Manfred Frank, *What Is Neo-Structuralism?* (Minneapolis: University of Minnesota Press, 1989). Frank's account is, in addition, the most penetrating analysis to date of the specifically philosophical dimension of anti-subjectivity.

5. "Non, non je ne suis pas là où vous me guettez, mais ici d'où je vous regarde en riant." Foucault, *L'archéologie du savoir* (Paris: Gallimard, 1969), 28. All translations of Michel Foucault are my own, unless otherwise noted.

6. On the emergence of *Tel Quel*, see especially Danielle Marx-Scouras, "Requiem for the Postwar Years: The Rise of *Tel Quel*," *The French Review*, February 1991, 407–416; and Marx-Scouras, *The Cultural Politics of Tel Quel* (College Park, PA: Pennsylvania State University Press, 1996). See also Philippe Forrest, *Histoire de Tel quel: 1960–1982* (Paris: Éditions du Seuil, 1995); Patrick ffrench, *The Time of Theory: A History of Tel Quel (1960–1983)* (Oxford, UK: Clarendon Press, 1995). Valuable insider perspectives are provided by Marcelin Pleynet, *Le plus court chemin: De Tel quel à L'Infini* (Paris: Gallimard, 1997); and Jean Thibaudeau, *Mes années Tel quel: mémoire* (Paris: Ecriture, 1994).

7. "une sorte d'extraordinaire convergence, isomorphisme, résonance." "Débat sur le poésie," *Tel Quel* 17, Spring 1964, 69–82; reprinted in *Dits et écrits, t. I*, 423. The theme of the conference, which included among its participants Philippe Sollers, Marcelin Pleynet, Jean-Pierre Faye, and Edoardo Sanguinetti, was, "Une littérature nouvelle?" Foucault pointed to the problems of experience, of contestation, and of limit as elements that linked his own project with that of the writers around him. At another point in the conference, he would suggest the common themes of madness, transgression, and language. See "Débat sur le roman," op. cit.; reprinted in *Dits et écrits, t. I*, 366–6–367.

8. "n'est pas un langage de la subjectivité; il s'ouvre et, au sens strict, 'donne lieu' à quelque chose qu'on pourrait désigner du mot neutre d'*expérience*. . . . C'est que l'écart de la distance et les rapports de l'aspect ne relèvent ni de la perception, ni des choses, ni du sujet, ni non plus de ce qu'on désigne volontiers et bizarrement comme le "monde"; ils appartiennent à la dispersion du langage." Foucault, "Distance, aspect, origine," *Critique* 198, November 1963, 931–945; reprinted in *Dits et écrits, t. I*, 311; italics mine.

9. Alan Megill—interested, like most early commentators on Foucault, primarily in the philosopher's left-critical works of the mid-1970s—presents the dominant view of *Raymond Roussel* when he asserts that the work stands in no obvious relation to books like *Discipline and Punish*. Megill's decision to omit *Raymond Roussel* entirely from his study is emulated by most critics. See Alan Megill, *Prophets of Extremity: Nietzsche, Heidegger, Foucault, Derrida* (Berkeley, CA: University of California Press, 1985). Yet it is clear that *Raymond Roussel* already contains, as no prior work by Foucault can be said to, the central intuition that will animate every one of

Foucault's books through *The History of Sexuality*: namely, that what appears to bear the marks of a founding subjectivity (be it a text, a discourse, or a social "dispositive,") is, in fact, the anonymous product of the material interaction of meaningless elements. As Foucault would write in 1976, power is exercised with visible objectives, but, "cela ne veux pas dire qu'il résulte du choix ou de la décision d'un sujet individuel." In the rationality of power, "la logique est encore parfaitement claire, les visées déchiffrables, et pourtant, il arrive qu'il n'y ait plus personne pour les avoir conçues et bien peu pour les formuler." Foucault, *Histoire de la sexualité I: La volonté de savoir* (Paris: Gallimard, 1976), 125. Social strategies, like Roussel's texts, emerge without the intermediary of a strategist.

10. "prendre une phrase au hasard—dans une chanson, sur une affiche, sur une carte de visite; la réduire en ses éléments phonétiques, et avec ceux-ci reconstruire d'autres mots qui doivent servir de trame obligée. Tous les miracles microscopiques . . . ne sont que les produits de décomposition et de recomposition d'un matériel verbal pulverisé, jeté en l'air, et retombant selon des figures qu'on peut dire, au sens strict, 'disparates.'" Foucault, "Pourquoi réédite-t-on l'oeuvre de Raymond Roussel? Un précurseur de notre littérature moderne," *Le Monde* 6097, August 22, 1964, 9; reprinted in *Dits et écrits, t. I*, 451.

11. "l'improbable rencontre," Ibid.

12. Philippe Sollers, "Logicus Solus," *Tel Quel* 14, Summer 1963, 46–50.

13. "L'effondrement de la subjectivité philosophique, sa dispersion à l'intérieur d'un langage qui la dépossède, mais la multiplie dans l'espace de sa lacune, est probablement une des structures fondamentales de la pensée contemporaine." Foucault, "Préface à la transgression," *Critique* 195–196, August–September 1963, 751–769; reprinted in *Dits et écrits, t. I*, 270.

14. It would be more precise still to say that Foucault and the *Tel Quel* writers each partook, albeit in different ways, of a form of secondhand Heideggerianism that derived from Blanchot and Emmanuel Levinas.

Heidegger's vision of the *es gibt* (or "there is") was transformed in Levinas's writings of the mid-1940s into an "il y a," a kind of anonymous and impersonal being, a "universal absence [that] is in turn a presence." That presence was modeled on the experience of absolute darkness. Emmanuel Levinas, "There Is: Existence without Existents," in Seán Hand, ed., *The Levinas Reader* (Oxford: Blackwell, 1989), 30.

Levinas's concept of the "il y a" was itself shaped in part by Blanchot's visceral description of darkness in his 1941 *Thomas L'Obscur*. Blanchot had written: "La nuit était plus sombre et plus pénible qu'il ne pouvait s'y attendre. L'obscurité submergeait tout, il n'y avait aucun espoir d'en traverser les ombres, mais on en atteignait la réalité dans une relation dont l'intimité était bouleversante. . . . ce n'était pas qu'il vît quelque chose, mais ce qu'il regardait, à la longue le mettait en rapport avec une masse nocturne qu'il percevait vaguement comme étant lui-même et dans laquelle il baignait." Maurice Blanchot, *Thomas L'Obscur* (Paris: Gallimard, 1950), 19. Blanchot considered Levinas's notion of the "il y a"—that is, enveloping absence experienced as presence—to be of great significance. In Blanchot's thought, the idea of the all-encompassing absence/presence would come to take the form of a language in which the writer dissolves. He wrote in 1955: "The writer belongs to a language which no one speaks, which is addressed to no one, which has no center, and which reveals nothing. He may believe that he affirms himself in this language, but what he affirms is altogether deprived of self.... Where he is, only being speaks—which means that language doesn't speak any more, but *is*.... To write is to make oneself the echo of what cannot cease speaking." Blanchot, *The Space of Literature* (Lincoln, NE: University of Nebraska Press, 1982), 27. This last idea was to prove particularly fertile for French thought in the 1960s.

15. Foucault, "L'homme est-il mort?" *Arts et Loisirs* 38, June 15–21, 1966, 8–9; reprinted in *Dits et écrits, t. I*, 569.

16. "Voilà bien des années que la philosophie française n'avait produit d'ouvrage aussi magistral, aussi impressionant d'érudition et de style, et aussi apparement original que *Les mots et les choses* de Michel Foucault. On sait que de pareils compliments peuvent laisser présager des critiques: sur ce point nous ne manquerons pas à l'habitude, mais notre controverse, pour radicale qu'elle se veuille, devra être prise d'abord comme un homage a l'ampleur d'un monument dont nous tenterons de prendre toute la mesure." Michel Amiot, "Le relativisme culturaliste de Michel Foucault," *Les Temps Modernes* 248, January 1967, 1285.

17. Jean Lacroix, "La fin de l'humanisme," *Le Monde*, June 9, 1966; cited in Eribon, *Michel Foucault*, 159–160.

18. "[l]a mode est aux structuralismes." Jean-Marie Domenach, "Le système et la personne," *Esprit* 360, May 1967, 771–772.

19. "Une entreprise convergente vise à renverser l'ordre des termes sur lequel vivait jusqu'à présent la philosophie, et à nier l'activité autonome de conscience: je ne pense pas, *je suis pensé*; je ne parle pas, *je suis parlé*; je n'agis pas; *je suis agi*. C'est du langage que tout part, et c'est au langage que tout retourne. Le Système, qui se saisit à travers lui, est proclamé maître de l'homme." Ibid., 771–772.

20. "métaphysique du Système"; "pensée froide, impersonnelle,"; "édifiée à l'écart de tout sujet, individuel ou collectif, et niant à la fin la possibilité même d'un sujet capable d'expression et d'action autonomes." Ibid., 772.

21. Sartre, "Jean-Paul Sartre répond," *L'Arc* 30, October 1966, 88.

22. This is a central argument of Dreyfus and Rabinow, *Michel Foucault: Beyond Structuralism and Hermeneutics* (Chicago: University of Chicago Press, 1983); see also

Béatrice Han, *Foucault's Critical Project: Between the Transcendental and the Historical* (Stanford, CA: Stanford University Press, 2002).

23. See "Foucault répond à Sartre," *La Quinzaine littéraire* 46, March 1–15, 1968, 20–22; reprinted in *Dits et écrits, t. I*, 696. Asked about the seemingly greater propensity to progressive political action of existentialist thought when compared to his own thought, Foucault responded: "La différence n'est pas en ceci que nous aurions maintenant séparé le politique du théorique, c'est au contraire dans la mesure où nous rapprochons au plus près le théorique et le politique que nous refusons ces politiques de la docte ignorance qui étaient celles, je crois, de ce qu'on appelait l'engagement."

24. Davidson notes of this "hybrid period" in Foucault's work that, "Foucault had not yet worked out his strategic analysis of power and still employs a Marxist terminology that he will later forcefully criticize." Davidson, *Foucault and His Interlocutors*, 15.

25. The literature on Foucauldean genealogy is voluminous and still growing. See, for a sample, Rudi Visker, *Michel Foucault: Genealogy as Critique* (New York: Verso, 1995); C. G. Prado, *Starting with Foucault: An Introduction to Genealogy* (Boulder, CO: Westview Press, 1995); Michael Mahon, *Foucault's Nietzschean Genealogy: Truth, Power, and the Subject* (Albany: State University of New York Press, 1992); Nancy Fraser, "Foucault on Modern Power: Empirical Insights and Normative Confusions," *Praxis International* 1, no. 3, October 1981, 272–287; Todd May, *Between Genealogy and Epistemology* (University Park: Pennsylvania State University Press, 1993); François Ewald, "A power without an exterior," in Timothy J. Armstrong, ed., *Michel Foucault, Philosopher* (New York: Routledge, 1992), 169–175; Bryan S. Turner, "The Disciplines," in Barry Smart, ed., *Michel Foucault: Critical Assessments*, vol. IV (London: Routledge, 1995), 372–387.

26. Mark Lilla offers a brief account of Foucault's engagement during this period in *The Reckless Mind: Intellectuals in Politics* (New York: New York Review Books, 2001), 152–156. Slightly fuller is Maria Bonnafous-Boucher, *Un liberalisme sans liberté: Pour une introduction du terme de 'libéralisme' dans la pensée de Michel Foucault* (Paris: L'Harmattan, 2001).

27. The *nouveaux philosophes* included Guy Lardreau, Christian Jambet, Bernard-Henri Lévy, and André Glucksmann.

28. See, however, Georg Stauth, "Revolution in Spiritless Times: An Essay on Michel Foucault's Enquiries into the Iranian Revolution," in Barry Smart, ed., *Michel Foucault: Critical Assessments*, vol. III, 379–401. Stauth's contention that, "Foucault's deep concerns with the cultural meaning of Islam . . . ultimately contradict his own critique of Western rationalisation, of profundity, of 'depth,'" (396) is insightful. See also Janet Afary and Kevin B. Anderson, *Foucault and the Iranian Revolution* (Chi-

cago: University of Chicago Press, 2005). While it had not yet appeared at the time of this book's completion, Afary and Anderson's book promises to greatly expand our understanding of Foucault's engagement with the Tehran uprising, as well as the attractions that it held for him.

29. Foucault pressed the new theocratic government of Iran to respect the rights of alleged political criminals. See Foucault, "Lettre ouverte à Mehdi Bazargan," *Le Nouvel Observateur* 753, April 14–20, 1979, 46; reprinted in *Dits et écrits, t. II*, 780–782. He also joined in the defense of the Vietnamese boat people, aligning himself in June of 1981 with the International Committee Against Piracy. He declared at the Geneva press conference announcing the committee's creation: "Il existe une citoyenneté internationale qui a ses droits, qui a ses devoirs et qui engage à s'élever contre tout abus de pouvoir, quel qu'en soit l'auteur, quelles qu'en soient les victimes." Foucault, "Face aux gouvernements, les droits de l'homme," *Libération* 967, June 30–July 1, 1984, 22; reprinted in *Dits et écrits, t. II*, 1526.

30. A notable exception is Marcio Alves da Fonseca's thorough *Michel Foucault e o Direito* (São Paulo: Editora Max Limonad, 2002).

31. "un détour [. . .] pour retrouver l'individu, au-delà des mécanismes du pouvoir." "Une esthétique de l'existence," *Le Monde* July 15–16, 1984; reprinted in *Dits et écrits, t. II*, 1551.

32. En admettant—et je l'admets!—que j'aie pratiqué avec *Les Mots et les Choses*, l'*Histoire de la Folie*, même avec *Surveiller et Punir* une étude philosophique essentiellement fondée sur un certain usage du vocabulaire, du jeu, de l'expérience philosophique et que je m'y sois livré pieds et poings, il est certain que, maintenant, j'essaie de me déprendre de cette forme-là de philosophie." Foucault, "La retour de la morale," *Les nouvelles littéraires* 2937, June 28–July 5, 1984, 36, in *Dits et écrits, t. II*, 1516.

33. Gary Gutting, "Introduction: Michel Foucault: A User's Manual," in *The Cambridge Companion to Foucault* (Cambridge, UK: Cambridge University Press, 1994), 24.

34. Foucault, "Polemics, Politics and Problematics," in Paul Rabinow, ed., *The Foucault Reader* (New York: Pantheon, 1984), 388; italics mine.

35. Foucault, "Une érudition étourdissante," *Le Matin* 278, January 20, 1978, 25; reprinted in *Dits et écrits, t. II*, 503–505. While the subject of Foucault's article was historian Philippe Ariès, he was speaking as much for himself as for Ariès when he wrote that "[l]a mort est bien plus qu'un rite de passage vers un autre monde; c'est toute une manière de vivre—de vivre sa mort et celle des autres."

36. Foucault, "Un plaisir si simple," *Le Gai Pied* 1, April 1, 1979, 1, 10; reprinted in *Dits et écrits, t. II*, 777.

37. Foucault, "Le langage à l'infini," 278–279; Foucault, *L'archéologie du savoir* (Paris: Gallimard, 1969), 274.

Part One: Discourse

CHAPTER 1. SURFACE EFFECTS

1. "Le point de rupture s'est situé le jour où Lévi-Strauss pour les sociétés et Lacan pour l'inconscient nous ont montré que le *sens* n'était probablement qu'une sorte d'effet de surface, un miroitement, une écume . . ." Michel Foucault, "Entretien avec Madeleine Chapsal," *La Quinzaine littéraire* 5, May 16, 1966, 14–15; reprinted in Foucault, *Dits et écrits, t. II* (Paris: Gallimard, 2001), 542.

2. David Macey, *The Lives of Michel Foucault* (New York: Vintage, 1995), 160.

3. On 1966 as the *annis mirabilis* of French structuralism, see François Dosse, *History of Structuralism* (Minneapolis: University of Minnesota Press, 1997).

4. See, for example, Jean-Marie Domenach, "Le système et la personne," *Esprit* 360, May 1967, 771–780; and Sylvie Le Bon, "Un positiviste désesperé: Michel Foucault," *Les Temps Modernes* 248, January 1967, 1299–1319. Didier Eribon's chapter, "Ramparts of the Bourgeoisie," offers a detailed account of both the immense success experienced by *The Order of Things*, and of the widespread criticism that ensued. See Didier Eribon, *Foucault* (Cambridge, MA: Harvard University Press, 1991), 155–186.

5. "le dernier barrage que la bourgeoisie puisse encore dresser contre Marx." "Jean-Paul Sartre répond," in *L'Arc* 30, October 1966, 87–88.

6. While no in-depth analysis of the Sartre–Foucault encounter currently exists, several authors have described the major events. Thomas R. Flynn offers an interpretation of the philosophers' mutual barbs in Flynn, *Sartre, Foucault, and Historical Reason* (Chicago: University of Chicago Press, 1997), 244–253. Neil Levy, in a chapter entitled "The Nineteenth-Century Man Versus the Magic Lantern," provides a somewhat fuller account of their confrontation—with the aim, however, of highlighting the civility that prevailed between the two thinkers in the longer term. See Neil Levy, *Being Up-to-Date* (New York: Peter Lang, 2001), 17–26.

7. Foucault, *Les mots et les choses* (Paris: Gallimard, 1966), 7.

8. Jorge Luis Borges, "John Wilkins' Analytical Language," in *Selected Non-Fictions*, ed., trans. Eliot Weinberger (New York: Viking, 1999), 231.

9. Foucault, *Les mots et les choses*, 366.

10. "qui prend pour objet l'homme en ce qu'il a d'empirique." Ibid., 355.

11. Foucault, *Naissance de la clinique* (Paris: Gallimard, 1963), vi.

12. Ibid., xv.

13. The strongest book on Foucault's archaeology remains Gary Gutting, *Michel Foucault's Archaeology of Scientific Reason* (Cambridge, UK: Cambridge University

Press, 1989). Gutting sees archaeology as a concrete method of historical analysis, developed ad hoc to deal with particular problems in the history of thought. He is, as such, skeptical of the account offered by Hubert Dreyfus and Paul Rabinow, in which Foucault's archaeological project is fundamentally a response to questions launched by twentieth-century philosophers and social scientists. (Hubert Dreyfus and Paul Rabinow, *Michel Foucault: Beyond Structuralism and Hermeneutics*, Chicago: University of Chicago Press, 1983). While Gutting's perspective provides an extremely valuable corrective, it arguably leads him to undervalue the points of contiguity between Foucault's project and contemporary philosophical discourse—like that of Sartre. See also Joseph Cronin, *Foucault's Antihumanist Historiography* (Lewiston, NY: The Edwin Mellen Press, 2001).

14. "Une réforme de la monnaie, un usage bancaire, une pratique commerciale peuvent bien se rationaliser, se développer, se maintenir ou disparaître selon des formes propres; ils sont toujours fondés sur un certain savoir: *savoir obscur qui ne se manifeste pas pour lui-même* en un discours, mais dont les nécessités sont identiquement les mêmes pour les théories abstraites ou les spéculations sans rapport apparent à la réalité." Foucault, *Les mots et les choses*, 179; italics mine.

15. "Dans une culture et à un moment donné, il n'y a jamais qu'une épistémè, qui définit les conditions de possibilité de tout savoir." Ibid.

16. "tout l'*épistémè* de la culture occidentale se trouv[ait] modifiée dans ses dispositions fondamentales"; "modifications qui ont altéré le savoir lui-même, à ce niveau archaïque qui rend possibles les connaissances et le mode d'être de ce qui est à savoir." Ibid., 68.

17. Ibid., 318–323. "celui pour qui la représentation existe, et qui se représente lui-même en elle." It was to introduce this challenging idea that Foucault had begun the work with an excursus on Velasquez's *Las Meninas*. The latter painting provided, as Foucault saw it, the ideal metaphor for representation in the classical period, because within it all the moments of representation (painter, canvas, spectators, observers of spectators, mirror) are made visible, but that which would tie them all together, the figure around which the work invisibly revolves—namely, the king—cannot be shown *within* the picture. "La place du roi" is outside of Velasquez's painting: it is, in fact, in the spot where the living observer of the painting is standing.

18. "Avant la fin du XVIIIe siècle, l'*homme* n'existait pas. . . . L'*épistémè* classique s'articule selon des lignes qui n'isolent en aucune manière un domaine propre et spécifique de l'homme. . . . l'homme, comme réalité épaisse et première, comme objet difficile et sujet souverain de toute connaissance possible, n'y a aucune place." Ibid., 319–321.

19. Ibid., 324. Foucault would reiterate his argument with extreme clarity in a 1967 interview: "[L]'homme est apparu comme un objet de science possible—les sciences

de l'homme—et en même temps comme l'être grâce auquel toute connaissance est possible. L'homme appartenait donc au champ des connaissances comme objet possible et, d'autre part, il était placé de façon radicale au point d'origine de toute espèce de connaissance." "Che cos'è Lei Professor Foucault?" *La Fiera letteraria* 39, September 28, 1967, 11–15; reprinted as "Qui êtes-vous, professeur Foucault?" in *Dits et écrits, t. I*, 636.

20. "un être tel qu'on prendra en lui connaissance de ce qui rend possible toute connaissance." Foucault, *Les mots et les choses*, 329.

21. "L'homme, s'étant constitué quand le langage était voué à la dispersion, ne va-t-il pas être dispersé quand la langage se rassemble?"; "une figure entre deux modes d'être du langage." Ibid., 397–398.

22. This view is on display in Foucault, "Le langage de l'espace," *Critique* 203, April 1964, 378–382; reprinted in *Dits et écrits, t. I*, 436.

23. In a 1967 interview, Foucault would say, "mon objet n'est pas le langage mais l'archive, c'est-à-dire l'existence accumulée des discours." "Sur les façons d'écrire l'histoire," *Les Lettres françaises* 1187, June 15–21, 1967, 6–9; reprinted in *Dits et écrits, t. I*, 623.

24. "Pendant une longue période, il y a eu en moi une espèce de conflit mal résolu entre la passion pour Blanchot, Bataille et d'autre part, l'intérêt que je nourrissais pour certaines études positives, comme celles de Dumézil et de Lévi-Strauss, par example. Mais, au fond, ces deux orientations . . . ont contribué dans une égale mésure à me conduire au thème de la disparition du sujet." "Qui-êtes vous, professeur Foucault?" in *Dits et écrits, t. I*, 642.

25. As David Macey observes of this period, "the emphasis on the literary fades and . . . Foucault begins to move away from the Blanchot-like contention that 'language is all' to a broader notion of Discourse." Macey, *The Lives of Michel Foucault*, 200.

26. "le magnifique et pathétique effort d'un homme du XIXe siècle pour penser le XXe siècle." "L'homme est-il mort?" *Arts et Loisirs* 38, June 15–21, 1966, 8–9, reprinted in *Dits et écrits, t. I*, 569–570.

27. "l'obstacle têtu qui s'oppose obstinément à une pensée prochaine"; "A tous ceux qui veulent encore parler de l'homme, de son règne ou de son libération, à tous ceux qui posent encore des questions sur ce qu'est l'homme en son essence, à tous ceux qui veulent partir de lui pour avoir accès à la vérité, . . . qui ne veulent pas penser sans penser aussitôt que c'est l'homme qui pense." Foucault, *Les mots et les choses*, 353–354.

28. Foucault liked to claim in later years that he had never been a structuralist, and had never applied the methods and concepts of structuralism. This was not the way he viewed the matter when structuralism was young. In a 1967 interview, he asserted: "Ce que j'ai essayé de faire, c'est d'introduire des analyses de style

structuraliste dans des domaines où elles n'avaient pas pénétré jusqu'à présent, c'est-à-dire dans le domaine de l'histoire des idées, l'histoire des connaissances, l'histoire de la théorie. Dans cette mesure, j'ai été amené à analyser en termes de structure la naissance du structuralisme lui-même." Foucault, "La philosophie structuraliste permet de diagnostiquer ce qu'est 'aujourd'hui,'" *La Presse de Tunisie* April 12, 1967, 3; reprinted in *Dits et écrits, t. I*, 611.

29. "on était très, très loin de la génération précédente, de la génération de Sartre, de Merleau-Ponty." "Entretien avec Madeleine Chapsal," 541.

30. "[N]ous, nous nous sommes découvert autre chose, une autre passion: la passion du concept et de ce que je nommerai le 'système.'" Ibid., 542.

31. See Roland Barthes, "Eléments de sémiologie," *Communications* 4, 1964, 91–135; and Barthes, *Système de la mode* (Paris: Éditions du Seuil, 1967).

32. See Jean Baudrillard, *Le système des objets* (Paris: Gallimard, 1968).

33. See André-Pierre Arnal et al., *Supports/Surfaces: 1966–1974* (Saint-Etienne: Musée d'art moderne Saint-Etienne, 1991). Claude Viallat (1936–) adopted a procedure that involved the Warholesque repetition of stamped patterns upon cloth; unlike Warhol's, Viallat's stamps were nonfigurative. The "frameworks" of Daniel Dezeuze (1942–) embraced gridlike forms while calling into question the traditional supports of visual art: the canvas and paint. Marc Devade (1943–1983), an affiliate of *Tel Quel*, built upon the earlier efforts of American expressionist painters, producing canvases that were rigorously rectilinear. Devade wrote in 1970, "The production-process of painting is indissolubly linked to the production of 'forms' across the plane. The plane-base structure is nothing outside of the formal effects it produces. . . . The author-actor-spectator of this mise-en-scène is none other than its own structure elaborating itself, playing itself in a mechanical programme of which we are the contingent readers. A programme that is the sum of the painting's formal elements." Marc Devade, "Chromatic Painting: Theorem written through painting," in Patrick ffrench and Roland-François Lack, eds., *The Tel Quel Reader* (London: Routledge, 1998), 185–187. See also Yve-Alain Bois, "Les années supports/surfaces," *ArtForum International* 37, issue 4, December 1998, 119–120.

34. "une matrice carrée engendrant la narration et sa refléxion." Philippe Sollers, *Nombres* (Paris: Editions du Seuil, 1968), back cover; and Sollers, "Lois," *Tel Quel* Summer 1971, 3–9.

35. Le point de rupture s'est situé le jour où Lévi-Strauss pour les sociétés et Lacan pour l'inconscient nous ont montré que le *sens* n'était probablement qu'une sorte d'effet de surface, un miroitement, une écume, et que ce qui nous traversait profondément, ce qui était avant nous, ce qui nous soutenait dans le temps et l'espace, c'était le *système*. "Entretien avec Madeleine Chapsal," 542.

36. "Avant toute existence humaine, toute pensée humaine, il y aurait déjà un savoir, un système, que nous redécouvrons." Ibid., 543. In 1967, Foucault would declare, "Le système, c'est actuellement notre forme majeure d'honnêteté." Foucault, "La philosophie structuraliste permet de diagnostiquer ce qu'est 'aujourd'hui,'" 610.

37. "le type d'intelligibilité qui s'exprime dans les structuralismes." Paul Ricoeur, "La structure, le mot, l'événement," *Esprit* 360, May 1967, 801.

38. "C'est un peu cette méthode," he noted, "que j'ai essaie d'introduire dans l'histoire des idées, des sciences et de la pensée en général." Foucault, "Linguistique et sciences sociales," *Revue tunisienne de sciences sociales* 19, December 1969, 248–255; reprinted in *Dits et écrits, t. I*, 866. Similarly, in a 1967 interview, Foucault declared: "[L]a critique contemporaine . . . est-elle en train de formuler sur les textes divers qu'elle étudie, ses textes-objets, une sorte de combinatoire nouvelle, Au lieu d'en reconstituer le secret immanent, elle se saisit du texte comme d'un ensemble d'éléments (mots, métaphores, formes littéraires, ensemble de récits) entre lesquels on peut faire apparaître des rapports absolument nouveaux dans la mesure où ils n'ont pas été maîtrisés par le projet de l'écrivain et ne sont rendus possibles que par l'oeuvre elle-même en tant que telle. Les relations formelles qu'on découvre ainsi n'ont été présentes dans l'esprit de personne, elles ne constituent pas le contenu latent des énoncés, leur secret indiscret; elles sont une construction, mais une construction exacte sitôt que les relations ainsi décrites peuvent être assignées réellement aux matériaux traités." "Sur les façons d'écrire l'histoire," 620.

39. See Foucault, "L'arrière-fable," *L'Arc* 29, May 1966, 5–12; reprinted in *Dits et écrits, t. I*, 534–541.

40. "Foucault ne nous dit pas ce qui serait le plus intéressant: à savoir comment chaque pensée est construite à partir de ces conditions, ni comment les hommes passent d'une pensée à une autre. Il lui faudrait pour cela faire intervenir la praxis, donc l'histoire, et c'est précisément ce qu'il refuse"; "Mais il remplace le cinéma par la lanterne magique, le mouvement par une succession d'immobilités." "Jean-Paul Sartre répond," *L'Arc* 30, October 1966, 87.

41. "Or une pensée vraiment originale n'est jamais attendue"; "une synthèse éclectique où Robbe-Grillet, le structuralisme, la linguistique, Lacan, *Tel Quel* sont utilisés tour à tour pour démontrer l'impossibilité d'une réflexion historique." Ibid., 87–88.

42. "Il s'agit de constituer une idéologie nouvelle, le dernier barrage que la bourgeoisie puisse encore dresser contre Marx." Ibid., 88.

43. "un moment du pratico-inerte"; "Le progrès, c'est le développement de l'ordre"; "Il s'applique parfaitement à l'idée que les structuralistes se font de la diachronie: l'homme est en quelque sorte développé par le développement même de la structure. Moi, je ne crois pas que l'histoire puisse se réduire à ce processus interne. L'histoire, ce n'est pas l'ordre. C'est le désordre. Disons: un désordre rationnel. Au

moment même où elle maintient l'ordre, c'est-à-dire la structure, l'histoire est déjà en train de la défaire." Ibid., 90.

44. See Foucault, "Monstrosities in Criticism," *Diacritics* 1, Autumn 1971, 57–60; reprinted as "Les monstruosités de la critique," in *Dits et écrits, t. I*, 1082–1091; "Foucault Responds," *Diacritics* 2, Winter 1971, 60; reprinted as "Foucault répond," in *Dits et écrits, t. I*, 1107–1108.

45. See Foucault, "Michel Foucault Derrida e no kaino," *Paideia* 11, February 1, 1972, 131–147; reprinted as "Réponse à Derrida," in *Dits et écrits, t. I*, 1149–1163.

46. "Depuis dix-huit mois, je me garde de toute réplique, car je travaille à donner une réponse à des questions qui m'ont été posées, à des difficultés que j'ai rencontrées, à des objections qui ont été formulées—et entre autres celles de Sartre." Foucault, "Une mise au point de Michel Foucault," *La quinzaine littéraire* 47, March 15–31, 1968, 21; reprinted in *Dits et écrits, t. I*, 697.

47. "la loi de ce qui peut être dit, le système qui régit l'apparition des énoncés comme événements singuliers." Foucault, *L'archéologie du savoir* (Paris: Gallimard, 1969), 169–170.

48. Ibid., 32–34.

49. On Foucault's central category of the discursive formation, see B. Brown and M. Cousins, "The Linguistic Fault: The Case of Foucault's Archaeology," in Barry Smart, ed., *Michel Foucault: Critical Assessments, Vol. II* (London: Routledge, 1994), 186–208.

50. "tant de choses dites, par tant d'hommes depuis tant de millénaires, n'ont pas surgi selon les seules lois de la pensée, ou d'après le seul jeu des circonstances, qu'elles ne sont pas simplement la signalisation, au niveau des performances verbales, de ce qui a pu dérouler dans l'ordre de l'esprit ou dans l'ordre des choses; mais qu'elles sont apparues grâce à tout un jeu de relations qui caractérisent en propre le niveau discursif; qu'au lieu d'être des figures adventices et comme greffées un peu au hasard sur des processus muets, elles naissent selon des régularités spécifiques; bref, que s'il y a des choses dites—et celles-là seulement—il ne faut pas en demander la raison immédiate aux choses qui s'y trouvent dites ou aux hommes qui les ont dites, mais au système de discursivité, aux possibilités et aux impossibilités énonciatives qu'il ménage." Foucault, *L'archéologie du savoir*, 170.

51. "Il ne s'agit pas de transférer au domaine de l'histoire, et singulièrement de l'histoire des connaissances, une méthode structuraliste qui a fait ses preuves dans d'autres champs d'analyse"; "Ce que j'ai essayé de faire, c'est d'introduire des analyses de style structuraliste dans des domaines où elles n'avaient pas pénétré jusqu'à présent, c'est-à-dire dans le domaine de l'histoire des idées, l'histoire des connaissances, l'histoire de la théorie." See endnote 27 above. The willingness to sacrifice consistency for argumentative gain would be a recurrent theme throughout Foucault's career.

52. "Jean-Paul Sartre répond," 87.

53. "Aux derniers flâneurs, faut-il signaler qu'un 'tableau' . . . c'est formellement une 'série de séries'? En tout cas, ce n'est point une petite image fixe qu'on place devant une lanterne pour la plus grande déception des enfants, qui, a leur âge, préfèrent bien sûr la vivacité du cinema." Foucault, *L'archéologie du savoir*, 19.

54. Jean-Paul Sartre, *Critique of Dialectical Reason, Volume I* (New York: Verso, 2004), 53.

55. "L'histoire continu, c'est le corrélat indispensable à la fonction fondatrice du sujet." Foucault, *L'archéologie du savoir*, 21–22.

56. "Derrière le systèm achevé, ce que découvre l'analyse des formations, ce n'est pas, bouillonante, la vie elle-même, la vie non encore capturée; c'est une épaisseur immense de systématicités, un ensemble sereé de relations multiples." Ibid., 101.

57. "On demeure dans la dimension du discours." Ibid.

58. "cet ouvrage, comme ceux qui l'ont précédé, ne s'inscrit pas—du moins directement ni en première instance—dans le débat de la structure (confrontée à la genèse, à l'histoire, au devenir); mais dans ce champ où se manifestent . . . les questions de l'être humain, de la conscience, de l'origine, et du sujet." Ibid., 26.

59. Foucault had given voice to this idea in 1967. Pressed by an interviewer on Sartre's claims about the need to reconcile the synchronic and the diachronic, he responded: "selon moi, le vrai problème aujourd'hui est constitué seulement en apparence par le rapport entre synchronie et diachronie. La discussion semble en effet se développer sur ce thème. . . . La polémique, à l'inverse, est apparue est a atteint assez récemment un degré d'intensité élevé, lorsque nous avons mis en cause quelque chose d'autre: non point la diachronie au profit de la synchronie, mais la souveraineté du sujet, ou de la conscience." "Qui êtes-vous, professeur Foucault?" 636–637.

60. I am indebted to Arnold I. Davidson for the use of the expression "hostile inter-locutor" to describe Foucault's imaginary adversary in this encounter.

61. "A l'instar d'une certaine forme de linguistique, vous avez cherché à vous passer du sujet parlant; vous avez cru que qu'on pouvait décaper le discours de toutes ses références anthropologiques, et le traiter comme s'il n'avait jamais été formulé par quiconque, comme s'il n'était pas né dans des circonstances particulières, comme s'il ne s'adressait à personne." Foucault, *L'archéologie du savoir*, 260.

62. "Vous avez raison: j'ai méconnu la transcendance du discours; j'ai refusé, en le décrivant, de le referer à une subjectivité." Ibid.

63. These "acceptable" structuralist practices pointed respectively to the works of Saussure, Lévi-Strauss, Lacan, Dumézil, and Barthes. That structuralism was ac-ceptable "quand le structuraliste reste conscient des limites de la méthode" was precisely the point that Sartre had made in the *L'Arc* interview.

64. "Permettez-moi . . . de vous dire comment j'ai entendu votre discours de tout à l'heure. 'Bien sûr, disiez-vous en sourdine, nous sommes désormais contraints, malgré tous les combats d'arrière-garde que nous avons livrés, d'accepter qu'on formalise des discours déductifs; . . . Bien sûr, il nous a fallu abandonner tous ces discours que nous ramenions autrefois à la souveraineté de la conscience.'" Foucault, *L'archéologie du savoir*, 263.

65. "affranchir l'histoire de la pensée de la sujetion transcendentale"; "un anonymat auquel nulle constitution transcendentale n'imposerait la forme du sujet," Ibid., 264–265.

66. "Vous faites vous-même un étrange usage de cette liberté que vous contestez aux autres"; "oubliez-vous le soin que vous avez pris d'enfermer le discours des autres dans des systèmes de règles? Oubliez-vous toutes ces contraintes que vous décrivez avec méticulosité? N'avez-vous pas retiré aux individus le droit d'intervenir personnellement dans les positivités où se situent leurs discours?" Ibid., 271.

67. With minor modifications, the text of the closing statement had, in fact, appeared within a separate published essay. See "Réponse à une question," *Esprit* 371, May 1968, 850–874; reprinted in *Dits et écrits, t. I*, 722–723.

68. "Eh quoi! tant de mots entassés, tant de marques déposées sur tant de papier et offertes à d'innombrables regards, . . . une piété si profonde attachée à les conserver et les inscrire dans la mémoire des hommes,—tout cela pour qu'il ne reste rien de cette pauvre main qui les a tracées, de cette inquiétude qui cherchait à s'apaiser en elles, et de cette vie achevée qui n'a plus qu'elles désormais pour survivre? . . . . Il faudrait admettre que le temps du discours n'est pas le temps de la conscience porté aux dimensions de l'histoire, ou le temps de l'histoire présent dans la forme de la conscience? Il faudrait que je suppose que dans mon discours il n'y va pas de ma survie?" Foucault, *L'archéologie du savoir*, 274.

69. Sartre, *Search for a Method* (New York: Vintage, 1963), 161.

70. Sartre, *Nausea* (New York: New Directions, 1964), 175–177.

71. "je découvris que le Donateur, dans les Belles-Lettres, peut se transformer en son propre Don, c'est-à-dire en objet pur. Le hasard m'avait fait homme, la générosité me ferait livre; je pourrais couler ma babillarde, ma conscience, dans des caractères de bronze, remplacer les bruits de ma vie par des inscriptions ineffaçables, ma chair par un style, les molles spirales du temps par l'éternité." Sartre, *Les mots* (Paris: Gallimard, 1964), 160.

72. "Je renais, je deviens enfin tout un homme, pensant, parlant, chantant, tonitruant, qui s'affirme avec l'inertie péremptoire de la matière." Ibid., 161.

73. "Je fais, je ferai des livres"; "il s'y projette, s'y reconnaît; seul, ce miroir critique lui offre son image." Ibid., 211.

74. "Il faudrait que je suppose que dans mon discours il n'y va pas de ma survie?";
"les fables même qu'on leur racontait dans leur enfance." Early in the first section
of *The Words*, Sartre had described the experience of having fables read to him as
a child. Sartre, *Les mots*, 34–35.

75. "ce discours où ils veulent pouvoir dire immédiatement, sans distance, ce qu'ils
pensent, croient ou imaginent." Foucault, *L'archéologie du savoir*, 274.

76. "sans équipment, sans outillage, je me suis mis tout entier à l'œuvre pour me sauver
tout entier. Si je range l'impossible Salut au magasin des accessoires, que reste-t-
il? Tout un homme, fait de tous les hommes et qui les vaut tous et que vaut
n'importe qui." Sartre, *Les mots*, 212–213.

77. "Le discours n'est pas la vie: son temps n'est pas le vôtre; en lui, vous ne vous
réconcilierez pas avec le mort; il se peut bien que vous ayez tué Dieu sous le poids
de tout ce que vous avez dit; mais ne pensez pas que vous ferez, de tout ce que
vous dites, un homme qui vivra plus que lui." Foucault, *L'archéologie du savoir*, 275.

78. Gilles Deleuze, *Foucault* (Minneapolis: University of Minnesota Press, 1988), 1–22.

79. "on peut dire que le savoir, comme champ d'historicité où apparaissent les sciences, est libre de toute activité constituante, affranchi de toute référence à une
origine ou à une téléologie historico-transcendantale, détaché de tout appui sur
une subjectivité fondatrice." Foucault, "Sur l'archéologie des sciences. Réponse au
Cercle d'épistémologie," *Cahiers pour l'analyse* 9, Summer 1968, 9–40; reprinted in
Dits et écrits, t. I, 759.

80. Foucault, *L'archéologie du savoir*, 101.

81. In this sense, Ian Hacking partially misrepresents Foucault's position when, in
his 1979 essay "Michel Foucault's Immature Science," he describes the discursive regularities that determine systems of possibility as "a sort of 'depth knowledge.'" It is true that the governing principles are not *articulated* within the system
of thought—but neither do they exist outside of it as a conditioning framework.
See Ian Hacking, *Historical Ontology* (Cambridge, MA: Harvard University Press,
2002), 91–95.

82. George Steiner, "The Mandarin of the Hour: Michel Foucault," *The New York Times
Book Review*, February 28, 1971, 23–31.

CHAPTER 2. RESTRUCTURING

1. "Les notions fondamentales qui s'imposent maintenant ne sont plus celles de la
conscience et de la continuité . . . ce ne sont pas celles non plus du signe et de la
structure. Ce sont celles de l'événement et de la série, avec le jeu des notions qui
leur sont liées; régularité, aléa, discontinuité, dépendance, transformation." Michel
Foucault, *L'ordre du discours* (Paris: Gallimard, 1971), 58.

2. "la description de cette ensemble, cette masse extraordinairement vaste, massive, complexe, de choses qui ont été dites dans une culture, en l'occurrence dans notre culture à nous. . . . c'est ça que j'entends en gros par archéologie." Foucault, "Discussion à propos de l'Archéologie du savoir," audio cassette available in the IMEC archive, Paris, France, document C. 120.

3. "les limites de l'énonciabilité." Foucault, Letter to Daniel Defert. Cited in *Dits et écrits, t. I*, 36.

4. "dans toute société la production du discours est à la fois contrôlée, sélectionnée, organisée et redistribuée par un certain nombre de procédures qui ont pour rôle d'en conjurer les pouvoirs et les dangers." Foucault, *L'ordre du discours*, 10–11.

5. In *The Birth of Tragedy* (1871), Friedrich Nietzsche posited a Socratic rupture in the Greek worldview. Before Socrates, it was both possible and legitimate to interpret existence otherwise than through the categories of critical rationality; after Socrates (and up through Nietzsche's own time), critical rationality held the field unchallenged. This idea was carried further in *Beyond Good and Evil* (1886), in which Nietzsche suggested that philosophers are bearers of a malign "will to truth"—a will that is itself a perverted version of the will to power. Martin Heidegger, in a series of works beginning with *Being and Time* (1927), lamented the progressive "forgetting of Being" that had overtaken the West in the wake of the post-Socratic conceptualization of Being as "presence."

6. "partage historique"; "Tout se passe comme si, à partir du grand partage platonicien, la volonté de vérité avait sa propre histoire, qui n'est pas celle des vérités contraignantes: histoire des objets à connaître, histoire des fonctions et positions du sujet connaissant, histoire des investissements matériels, techniques, instrumentaux de la connaissance." *L'odre du discours*, 19.

7. "le déroulement continu d'une nécessité idéale"; "traiter, non pas des représentations qu'il peut y avoir derrière les discours, mais des discours comme des séries régulières et distinctes d'événements." Ibid., 61.

8. For comparison, see Foucault, *L'archéologie du savoir* (Paris: Gallimard, 1969), 42.

9. Ibid., 23.

10. "le *hasard*, le *discontinu* et la *matérialité*." Foucault, *L'ordre du discours*, 61.

11. "*La transformation d'une pratique discursive* est liée à tout un ensemble souvent fort complexe de modifications qui peuvent se produire soit hors d'elle . . . soit en elle . . . soit à côté d'elles [*sic*]. . . . Ces principes d'exclusion et de choix . . . ne revoient pas à un sujet de connaissance (historique ou transcendantal) qui les inventerait successivement ou les fonderait à un niveau originaire; ils désignent plutôt *une volonté de savoir, anonyme et polymorphe*, succeptible de transformations régulières." Foucault, "La volonté de savoir," *Annuaire du Collège de France, 71e année, Histoire des systèmes de pensée, année 1970–1971*, 246. Cited in Foucault, *Dits et écrits, t. I*, 1109; italics mine.

12. See also Jürgen Habermas, *The Philosophical Discourse of Modernity* (Cambridge, MA: MIT Press, 1992), 266–268. Habermas makes the very similar claim that Foucault's archaeological method, as deployed in *The Order of Things*, generated conflicts that could only be resolved through the turn to Nietzsche and the introduction of causality via the external dimension of power.

13. Hubert L. Dreyfus and Paul Rabinow, *Michel Foucault: Beyond Structuralism and Hermeneutics* (Chicago: University of Chicago Press, 1983), 81. The italics in the citation from Foucault are Dreyfus and Rabinow's.

14. Ibid., 83.

15. Ibid., 84–85.

16. Ibid., 100. During the silence in question, it should be noted, Foucault published two books, produced more than seventy shorter published pieces, and delivered four semester-length lecture courses at the Collège de France.

17. Ibid., 106.

18. Béatrice Han, *Foucault's Critical Project: Between the Transcendental and the Historical* (Stanford, CA: Stanford University Press, 2002), 66.

19. Ibid., 77.

20. Ibid., 77, 99.

21. "Autre trait caractéristique: l'analyse des énoncés les traite dans la forme systématique de l'*extériorité*. . . . Pour restituer les énoncés a leur pure dispersion. Pour les analyser dans une extériorité sans doute paradoxale puisqu'elle ne renvoie à aucune forme adverse d'intériorité." Foucault, *L'archéologie du savoir*, 158; italics mine.

22. "Quatrième règle: celle de l'*extériorité*: ne pas aller du discours vers son noyau intérieur et caché, vers le cœur d'une pensée ou d'une signification qui se manifesteraient en lui; mais, à partir du discours lui-même, de son apparition et de son régularité, aller vers ses conditions externes de possibilité, vers ce qui donne lieu à la série aléatoire de ces événements et qui en fixe les bornes." Foucault, *L'ordre du discours*, 55.

23. "Quant au principe d'*extériorité*: jamais je n'ai essayé de faire l'analyse du texte à partir du texte lui-même. . . . J'ai essayé de lever le principe de la textualité en me plaçant dans une dimension qui était celle de l'histoire . . . j'ai essayé de repérer les événements discursifs qui ont leur lieu non pas à l'intérieur même du texte ou de plusieurs textes, mais qui ont lieu dans le fait de la fonction ou du rôle qui sont donnés à différents discours à l'intérieur d'une société. Passer hors du texte pour retrouver la fonction du discours à l'intérieur d'une société, c'est là ce que j'appelle le principe de l'extériorité." Foucault, *La volonté de savoir. Cours au Collège de France: 1970–71*. Edited and prepared by Jacques Lagrange. Available in printed form, archives of Bibliothèque Générale du Collège de France; italics mine.

24. "j'ai essayé de montrer comment [la] connaissance de l'ordre des choses et de l'ordre des hommes . . . ne naissait que comme prétexte à partir d'une césure économique et politique." Ibid.

25. "[l]e marxisme est dans la pensée du XIXe siècle comme poisson dans l'eau: c'est-à-dire que partout ailleurs il cesse de respirer." Foucault, *Les mots et les choses: une archéologie des sciences humaines* (Paris, Gallimard, 1966), 274.

26. "La critique de la raison dialectique, c'est le magnifique et pathétique effort d'un homme du XIXe siècle pour penser le XXe siècle. En ce sens, Sartre est le dernier hégélien, et je dirai même le dernier marxiste." "L'homme est-il mort?" *Arts et Loisirs* 38, June 15–21, 1966, 8–9; reprinted in *Dits et écrits, t. I,* 569–570.

27. "Marx ne représente pas une coupure épistémologique." "Sur les façons d'écrire l'histoire," *Les Lettres françaises* 1187, June 15–21, 1967, 6–9; reprinted in *Dits et écrits, t. I,* 615.

28. "un marxisme mou, fade, [et] humaniste." "En intervju med Michel Foucault," *Bonniers Litteräre Magasin,* March 1968, 203–211; republished as "Interview avec Michel Foucault," in *Dits et écrits, t. I,* 682.

29. Daniel Defert, "Chronologie," in *Dits et écrits, t. I,* 44–45; this is now the Université de Paris VII – Vincennes.

30. David Macey, *The Lives of Michel Foucault* (New York: Vintage, 1993), 219.

31. Ibid., 221.

32. Ibid., 224–225.

33. Didier Eribon, *Foucault,* translated by Betsy Wing (Cambridge, MA: Harvard University Press, 1991), 202–206. Placed alongside these courses, Foucault's own offerings on Nietzsche, "the end of metaphysics," and "the epistemology of the sciences of life" were quaint.

34. Ibid., 206.

35. Macey, *The Lives of Michel Foucault,* 226.

36. Foucault, "Qu'est-ce qu'un auteur?" *Bulletin de la Société française de philosophie,* 63e année, no. 3, July–September 1969, 73–104; reprinted in *Dits et écrits, t. I,* 833.

37. "[l]a conscience civile de la bourgeoisie parlementaire." Foucault, "Médecins, juges et sorciers au XVIIe siècle," *Médecine de France* 200, 1er trimestre 1969, 121–128; reprinted in *Dits et écrits, t. I,* 787.

38. "Or voilà que, portés par les développements récents, de nouveaux problèmes sont apparus: non plus quelles sont les limites du savoir (ou ses fondements), mais quels sont ceux qui savent? Comment se fait l'appropriation et la distribution du savoir? *Comment un savoir peut-il prendre place dans une société,* s'y développer, mobiliser

des ressources *et s'y mettre au service d'une économie?*" "Le piège de Vincennes," *Le Nouvel Observateur* 274, February 9–15, 1970, 33–35; reprinted in *Dits et écrits, t. I*, 939; italics mine.

39. "[leur] enseignement, au fond, n'était rien d'autre que le renouvellement et la re-production des valeurs et des connaissances de la société bourgeoise"; "la bourgeoisie est un système qui a une énorme capacité d'adaptation"; "la société capitaliste [a] totalement dépossédé l'écriture"; "Maintenant le moment n'est-il pas venu de passer aux actions véritablement révolutionnaires?" Foucault, "Kyôki, bungaku, shakai," *Bungei* 12, December 1970, 266–285; republished as "Folie, littérature, société," in *Dits et écrits, t. I*, 983–995.

40. "Je n'ai pas systématisé les relations entre les formations discursives et les forma-tions sociales et économiques, dont l'importance a été établie par le marxisme d'une façon incontestable." "Entrevista com Michel Foucault," in J. G. Merquior and S. P. Rouanet, *O Homen e o Discurso (A Arquelogia de Michel Foucault)* (Rio de Janeiro: Tempo Brasileiro, 1971), 17–42; republished as "Entretien avec Michel Foucault," in *Dits et écrits, t. I*, 1025.

41. "[l]a société industrielle capitaliste ne pouvait tolérér l'existence des groupes de vagabonds"; "une armée de réserve de la force du travail"; "un avatar de nos sociétés capitalistes." Foucault, "Kyôki to shokai," *Misuzu* December 1970, 16–22; republished as "La folie et la société," in *Dits et écrits, t. I*, 1003.

42. "La justice pénale n'a été produite ni par le plèbe, ni par la paysannerie, ni par le prolétariat, mais bel et bien par la bourgeoisie." "Sur la justice populaire: Débat avec les maos," *Les Temps modernes* 310 *bis*, June 1972, 355–366; reprinted in *Dits et écrits, t. I*, 1225.

43. "Elle est un des instruments du pouvoir, et l'un des plus démesurés. De quel droit le pouvoir la met-il au secret?" Foucault, "La prison partout," *Combat* 8335, May 5, 1971, 1; reprinted in *Dits et écrits, t. I*, 1061.

44. "la lutte politique prise comme lutte de classe." "Par-delà le bien et le mal," *Actuel* 14, November 1971, 42–47; reprinted in *Dits et écrits, t. I*, 1094–1095.

45. Foucault addresses them accordingly in his preface to the brochure *Enquête dans vingt prisons*, Paris, "Intolérable" collection, no. 1, May 28, 1971, 3–5; reprinted in *Dits et écrits, t. I*, 1063: "à travers toutes ces institutions et sous des masques différents, une oppression s'exerce qui est à sa racine une oppression politique. Cette oppression, la classe exploitée a toujours su la reconnaître."

46. This would, of course, be the central argument of Foucault's 1976 *History of Sexu-ality, Volume 1*.

47. Gilles Deleuze and Félix Guattari, *Anti-Oedipus: Capitalism and Schizophrenia* (Min-neapolis: University of Minnesota Press, 1983), 1.

48. Gilles Deleuze, "Foucault and the Prison," *History of the Present*, vol. 2, 1986, 1, 2, 20–21; reprinted in Barry Smart, ed., *Michel Foucault: Critical Assessments*, Vol. III (London: Routledge, 1994), 268.

49. Deleuze was an official, if sporadic, participant in the seminar of Foucault's 1971 course at the Collège de France, *Penal Theories and Institutions*. (Foucault, "Théories et institutions pénales," *Annuaire du Collège de France*, 1971–1972, 283–386; reprinted in *Dits et écrits, t. I*, 1260.)

50. "Si la lecture de vos livres (depuis le *Nietzsche* jusqu'à ce que je pressens de *Capitalisme et Schizophrénie*) a été pour moi si essentielle, c'est qu'ils me paraissent aller très loin dans la position de ce problème: sous ce vieux thème du sens, signifié, signifiant, etc., enfin la question du pouvoir, de l'inégalité des pouvoirs, de leurs luttes. Chaque lutte se développe autour d'un foyer particulier de pouvoir." "Les intellectuels et le pouvoir," *L'Arc* 49: *Gilles Deleuze*, 2nd trimester 1972, 3–10; reprinted in *Dits et écrits, t. I*, 1181.

51. "On ne sait peut-être toujours pas, ce qu'est le pouvoir"; "Et Marx et Freud ne sont peut-être pas suffisants pour nous aider à connaître cette chose si énigmatique, à la fois visible et invisible, présente et cachée, investie partout, qu'on appelle le pouvoir. La théorie de l'État, l'analyse traditionnelle des appareils d'État n'épuisent sans doute pas le champ d'exercice et de fonctionnement du pouvoir." Ibid., 1180–1181.

52. "systèmes de pouvoir"; "dans tout le réseau de la société." Ibid., 1176–1181. Just how completely Foucault called into question suppositions he had until quite recently entertained—and how rapidly he achieved what is recognizably his mature formulation of the concept of power—can be judged from the ensuing excursus: "On sait bien que ce ne sont pas les gouvernants qui détiennent le pouvoir. Mais la notion de 'classe dirigeante' n'est ni très claire ni très élaborée. 'Dominer', 'diriger', 'gouverner', 'groupe au pouvoir', 'appareil d'État', etc., il y a là tout un jeu de notions qui demandent à être analysées. De même, il faudrait bien savoir jusqu'où s'exerce le pouvoir, par quels relais et jusqu'à quelles instances souvent infimes, de hiérarchie, de contrôle, de surveillance, d'interdictions, de contraintes. Partout où il y a du pouvoir, le pouvoir s'exerce. Personne à proprement parler n'en est le titulaire."

53. On this conception, see Deleuze, "Faille et feux locaux," in *L'île déserte et autres textes* (Paris: Éditions de Minuit, 2002), 217–225.

54. Deleuze, *Anti-Oedipus: Capitalism and Schizophrenia*, 2.

55. See, for example, Foucault, *La société punitive. Cours au Collège de France 1972–1973*. Unedited. Available in recorded form (13 cassettes), archives of Bibliothèque Générale du Collège de France, lecture of March 28, 1973.

56. Defert, "Chronologie," 49.

57. "grands parmi les grands"; "un jour, peut-être, le siècle sera deleuzien." Foucault, "Theatrum philosophicum," *Critique* 282, November 1970, 885–908; reprinted in *Dits et écrits, t. I*, 943–944.

58. Deleuze, *Logique du Sens* (Paris: Éditions de Minuit, 1969), 295.

59. Claire Colebrook, *Gilles Deleuze* (London: Routledge, 2002), 6.

60. The parallels between Deleuze and Nietzsche on this point are evident. As Dreyfus and Rabinow observe of the genealogical method, "[t]he world is not a play which simply masks a truer reality that exists behind the scenes. It is as it appears. This is the genealogist's insight." (Dreyfus and Rabinow, *Michel Foucault: Beyond Structuralism and Hermeneutics*, 109) Foucault, who credited Deleuze with "une patience de généalogiste nietzschéen," undoubtedly recognized the homology. (Foucault, "Theatrum philosophicum," 955) What is noteworthy is that Foucault's engagement with Nietzsche in "Nietzsche, Genealogy, History," postdates this long examination of *The Logic of Sense* and *Difference and Repetition* by several months. Foucault only looked at the question of immanence from a Nietzschean perspective after having thoroughly explored it from a Deleuzian one. This is why Foucault's discussion of Nietzsche in "Nietzsche, Genealogy, History" is riddled with Deleuzian expressions like "le discontinu," "[le] hasard," and "l'aléa singulaire de l'événement." (Foucault, "Nietzsche, Genealogy, History," *Hommage à Jean Hyppolite*, Paris P.U.F., coll. "Épiméthée, 1971, 145–172. Reprinted in *Dits et écrits, t. I*, 1015–1016.)

61. "Au lieu de dénoncer une fois encore la métaphysique comme oubli de l'être"; "discours de la matérialité des incorporels." Foucault, "Theatrum philosophicum," 947.

62. "dans la direction paradoxale au premier regard d'un *matérialisme de l'incorporel.*" Foucault, *L'ordre du discours*, 60; italics mine.

63. Deleuze, *Logique du Sens*, 13–21.

64. "penser l'événement pur"; "L'événement—la blessure, la victoire-défaite, la mort—est toujours effet, bel et bien produit par les corps qui s'entrechoquent, se mêlent ou se séparent; mais cet effet, lui, n'est jamais de l'ordre des corps." Foucault, "Theatrum philosophicum," 949. To this difficult notion is appended the further explanation: "Imaginons une causalité coudée; les corps, en se heurtant, en se mêlant, en souffrant, causent à leur surface des événements qui sont sans épaisseur, sans mélange, sans passion, et ne peuvent donc plus être cause; ils forment entre eux une autre trame ou les liaisons relèvent d'un quasi-physique des incorporels, de la métaphysique."

65. "Les notions fondamentales qui s'imposent maintenant ne sont plus celles de la conscience et de la continuité . . . ce ne sont pas celles non plus du signe et de la structure. Ce sont celles de l'événement et de la série." Foucault, *L'ordre du discours*, 58; italics mine.

66. Ibid., 59. Foucault hybridizes the vocabulary of archaeology with that of *The Logic of Sense*: "Si les discours doivent être traités d'abord comme des ensembles d'événements discursifs, quel statut faut-il donner à cette notion d'événement qui fut si rarement prise en considération par les philosophes? Bien sûr l'événement n'est ni substance ni accident, ni qualité ni processus; l'événement n'est pas de l'ordre des corps. Et pourtant il n'est point immatériel; c'est toujours au niveau de la matérialité qu'il prend effet, qu'il est effet; il a son lieu et il consiste dans la relation, la coexistence, la dispersion, le recoupement, l'accumulation, la sélection d'éléments matériels; il n'est point l'acte ni la propriété d'un corps; il se produit comme effet et dans une dispersion matérielle."

67. "pour n'avoir plus de visage." Foucault, *L'archéologie du savoir*, 28.

68. "c'est la solution anthropophagique, où l'absorption permet à la fois l'assimilation et la neutralisation de cette force. L'autre solution consiste à essayer de vaincre l'hostilité de cette force. . . . Cette pratique de l'exclusion, il l'apelle anthropoémie (du grec *émein*, vomir): maîtriser les forces dangereuses de notre société, c'est, non pas les assimiler, mais les exclure." Foucault, *La société punitive. Cours au Collège de France: 1972–73*. Edited and prepared by Jacques Lagrange. Available in printed form, archives of Bibliothèque Générale du Collège de France, lecture of January 3, 1973, 1–2.

69. "Cette notion d'exclusion me paraît d'abord une notion trop 'large' et, surtout, composite et artificielle"; "les buts, les rapports, les opérations spécifiques du pouvoir à partir de quoi précisément se fait l'exclusion"; "dans cette notion, on laisse porter à la société en général la responsabilité du mécanisme par lequel l'exclu se trouve exclu. Autrement dit, . . . l'exclusion a l'air de se référer à quelque chose comme un consensus social qui rejette, alors que derrière cela il y a peut-être un certain nombre d'instances parfaitement spécifiées et par conséquent, définissables, de pouvoir qui sont responsables du mécanisme de l'exclusion." Ibid., 3.

70. "Je le dis autant mieux, que moi-même, j'en ai fait usage et, peut-être, abus." Ibid., 2.

71. "comme des instruments qui ont eu historiquement leur importance"; "du pouvoir plutôt que de la loi, du savoir plutôt que de la représentation." Ibid., 6–7.

Part Two: Power

CHAPTER 3. PLANETARY FORCES

1. "Est revenu l'âge de Candide où l'on ne peut plus écouter l'universelle petite chanson qui rend raison de tout. . . . La morale du savoir, aujourd'hui, c'est peut-être de rendre le réel aigu, âpre, anguleux, inacceptable." Michel Foucault, "La grande

colère des faits," *Le Nouvel Observateur* 652, May 9–15, 1977, 84–86; reprinted in *Dits et écrits, t. II* (Paris: Gallimard, 2001), 277.

2. Foucault, "L'esercito, quando la terra trema," *Corriera della sera* 103, no. 228, September 28, 1978, 1–2; republished as "L'armée, quand la terre tremble," in *Dits et écrits, t. II*, 662–669.

3. Earlier in the year, Foucault accepted the offer of his onetime publisher, Rizzoli, to serve as a regular contributor for the Italian daily *Corriera della sera*. His desire, briefly realized, was to equip a team of reporter-intellectuals able to travel the world and describe the emergence of ideas out of real events and confrontations. "One must attend at the birth of ideas and the explosion of their force," he wrote, "and thus not in the books that enunciate them, but in the events in which they manifest their force." Foucault, "Les 'reportages' d'idées" in *Dits et écrits, t. II*, 706–707. Other contributors to the resulting series of articles included Alain Finkielkraut and André Glucksmann; projected articles by Susan Sontag, Ronald Laing, Jorge Semprun, and Arpad Ajtony never appeared.

4. "depuis dix mois, la population s'oppose à un régime qui est parmi les mieux armés du monde et à une police qui est parmi les plus redoutables. Cela les mains nues, sans recours à la lutte armée, avec une obstination et un courage qui immobilisent l'armée sur place." Foucault, "Una rivolta con le mani nude," *Corriere della sera* 103, no. 261, November 5, 1978, 1–2; republished as "Une révolte à mains nues," in *Dits et écrits, t. II*, 701.

5. "un mouvement traversé par le souffle d'une religion qui parle moins de l'au-delà que de la transfiguration de ce monde-ci." Foucault, "Il mitico capo della rivolta dell'Iran," *Corriera della sera* 103, no. 279, November 26, 1978, 1–2; republished as "Le chef mythique de la révolte de l'Iran," in *Dits et écrits, t. II*, 716. Michiel Leezenberg provides a concise analysis of what he views as Foucault's misunderstanding of shi'ism in James Bernauer and Jeremy Carrette, eds., *Michel Foucault and Theology: The Politics of Religious Experience* (Burlington, VT: Ashgate, 2004), 99–115.

6. "Un fait doit être clair: par 'gouvernement islamique', personne, en Iran, n'entend un régime politique dans lequel le clergé jouerait un rôle de direction ou d'encadrement." Foucault, "À quoi rêvent les Iraniens?" *Le Nouvel Observateur* 727, October 16–22, 1978, 48–49; reprinted in *Dits et écrits, t. II*, 691.

7. Quand je suis parti d'Iran, la question qu'on me posait sans cesse était bien sûr: 'Est-ce la révolution?'. . . . Je n'ai pas répondu. Mais j'avais envie de dire: ce n'est pas une révolution, au sens littéral du terme: une manière de se mettre debout et de se redresser. C'est l'insurrection d'hommes aux mains nues qui veulent soulever le poids formidable qui pèse sur chacun de nous, mais plus particulièrement, sur eux, ces laboureurs de pétrole, ces paysans aux frontières des empires: le poids de l'ordre du monde entier. *C'est peut-être la première grande insurrection contre les*

systèmes planetaires, la forme la plus moderne de la révolte la plus folle. Foucault, "Le chef mythique de la révolte de l'Iran," 716; emphasis mine.

8. "celui d'un affranchissement à l'égard de tout ce qui marque dans leur pays et dans leur vie quotidienne la présence des hégémonies planétaires." Ibid., 715.

9. "Il n'y a, certes, aucune honte à changer d'opinion; mais il n'y a aucune raison de dire qu'on en change lorsqu'on est aujourd'hui contre les main coupées, après avoir été hier contre les tortures de la Savak"; "[l]a spiritualité à laquelle se référaient ceux qui allaient mourir est sans commun mesure avec le gouvernement sanglant d'un clergé intégriste." Foucault, "Inutile de se soulever?" *Le Monde* May 11–12, 1979, 1–2; reprinted in *Dits et écrits, t. II*, 793. The Savak was the secret police apparatus of the Shah's government.

10. "Au pouvoir, il faut toujours opposer des lois infranchissibles et des droits sans restriction." Ibid., 794.

11. "Je crois qu'aujourd'hui l'individualité est complètement contrôlée par le pouvoir, et que nous sommes individualisés, au fond, par le pouvoir lui-même. Autrement dit, je ne pense nullement que l'individualisation s'oppose au pouvoir, mais, au contraire, je dirais que notre individualité, l'identité obligatoire de chacun est l'effet et un instrument de pouvoir." Foucault, "Loucura, uma questão de poder," *Jornal do Brasil* November 12, 1974, 8; republished as "Folie, une question de pouvoir," in *Dits et écrits, t. I* (Paris: Gallimard, 2001), 1530–1531.

12. "l'ensemble des techniques en vertu desquelles les systèmes de pouvoir ont pour objectif et résultat la singularisation des individus." Foucault, "Incorporación del hospital en la tecnología moderna," *Revista centro-americana de Ciencias de la Salud* 10, May–August 1978, 93–104; republished as "L'incorporation de l'hôpital dans la technologie moderne," in *Dits et écrits, t. II*, 516–517.

13. Foucault, "Pouvoir et corps," *Quel corps?* 2, September–October 1975, 2–5, reprinted in *Dits et écrits, t. I*, 1625.

14. "[l]'individu, c'est . . . une réalité fabriquée par cette technologie spécifique de pouvoir qu'on appelle la 'discipline'." Foucault, *Surveiller et punir* (Paris: Gallimard, 1975), 227.

15. "Chacun de nous," Foucault wrote, "a une biographie, un passé toujours documenté en un lieu quelconque. . . . Il y a toujours un organisme administratif capable de dire à n'importe quel moment qui est chacun de nous." Foucault, "Folie, une question de pouvoir," 1530–1531.

16. For many thinkers sympathetic to Foucault's overall line of research, this fact in itself renders his approach useless as a critical theory of society. If there is no way to separate the individual subject from the system that "produces" him, then there is no coherent way to speak about agency; if there is no way to sort out the dominators from the dominated, we have no normative grounds for action. For the clearest

version of this line of criticism, see Jürgen Habermas, *The Philosophical Discourse of Modernity* (Cambridge, MA: MIT Press, 1992), 266–295.

17. "un certain nombre de postulats qui ont marqué la position traditionelle de gauche." Gilles Deleuze, "Ecrivain non: un nouveau cartographe," *Critique* 343, December 1975, 1207–1227.

18. "les deux grands vaincus de ces quinze dernières années." Foucault, "Sur la sellette," *Les Nouvelles littéraires* 2477, March 17–23, 1975, 3; reprinted in *Dits et écrits, t. I*, 1592.

19. "Marx pensait—et il l'a écrit—que le travail constitue l'essence concrète de l'homme. Je pense que c'est là une idée typiquement hégélienne. Le travail n'est pas l'essence concrète de l'homme. Si l'homme travaille, si le corps humain est une force productive, c'est parce que l'homme est obligé de travailler. Et il y est obligé, parce qu'il est investi par des forces politiques, parce qu'il est pris dans des mécanismes de pouvoir." Foucault, "Dialogue on Power," in S. Wade, ed., *Chez Foucault* (Los Angeles: Circabook, 1978), 4–22; republished as "Dialogue sur le pouvoir" in *Dits et écrits, t. II*, 470.

20. "Qu'on ne me parle plus de Marx! . . . Moi, j'en ai totalement fini avec Marx." Claude Mauriac, *Le Temps immobile 3: Et comme l'espérance est violente* (Paris: Grasset, 1976), 581; cited in Daniel Defert, "Chronologie" in *Dits et écrits, t. I*, 64–65.

21. Foucault, "Hospicios. Sexualidade. Prisoẽs." *Revista Versus* 1, October 1975, 30–33; republished as "Asiles. Sexualité. Prisons," in *Dits et écrits, t. I*, 1647–1648.

22. "[c]'est comme si, enfin, quelque chose de nouveau sursigissait depuis Marx." Deleuze, "Ecrivain non: un nouveau cartographe," 1212.

23. On this subject, see Peter Starr, *Logics of Failed Revolt: French Theory after May '68* (Stanford, CA: Stanford University Press, 1995), 88–109; Starr argues persuasively that the Cultural Revolution served not only as a "screen for the projection of French cultural-political fantasies," but that "as both a hotbed of radical cultural democracy *and* the privileged site of strict fidelity to Marxist-Leninist doctrine, [the Cultural Revolution] allowed a significant number of Maoist militants to fantasize a squaring of one of twentieth-century European Marxism's most troublesome circles: its inability to reconcile the demands of revolutionary discipline with those of democratic, grass-roots participation in the revolutionary process" (90–91).

24. "Après la lecture de l'*Archipel du Goulag*, versons au compte du *crétinisme théorique* propre à notre siècle toutes les doctrines qui partent d'une Russie peu ou prou socialiste. Comment l'expérience sensible d'un fascisme devient-elle la méditation intellectuelle du socialisme? Comment la tête écoute-t-elle avec sérieux les philosophes du Kremlin quand sous les yeux les camps se découvrent? Comment peut-on parler à la fois du travail forcé et de la propriété collective des moyens de production? Comment l'esclavage mène-t-il à la société sans classes? Il suffit d'un

brin de théorie!" André Glucksmann, *La cuisinière et le mangeur d'hommes* (Paris: Seuil, 1975), 82–83.

25. "A échelles différentes, au gré des circonstances historiques et des coutumes locales, notre siècle produit et reproduit cette invention qui lui est propre: le camp de concentration." Ibid., 15–16.

26. "maisons de correction idéales"; "forteresses idéales." Ibid., 102–103.

27. "Pauvre Foucault, devenu le Bossuet de cette histoire universelle!" François Furet, "Faut-il brûler Marx?" in *Un itinéraire intellectuelle* (Paris: Calmann-Lévy, 1999), 531; see also André Glucksmann, "Réponses," *Tel Quel* 64, Winter 1975, 67–73, in which Philippe Sollers questioned Glucksmann on his decision "d'inscrire l'*Archipel du Goulag* dans le prolongement du travail inaugural de Foucault, *Histoire de la Folie*," as well as on his comparison of the seventeenth-century "great lockup" postulated by Foucault to the camps of the twentieth century. Glucksmann's responses, far from repudiating Foucault, attempted rather to co-opt arguments from the recently released *Discipline and Punish*.

28. "Nous avions fait l'épreuve d'une conversion, d'une révolution culturelle dont la morale n'a pas encore été tirée—dont on trouvera ici des rudiments. Nous en sortions brisés d'un échec qu'au vrai, tentant encore de le penser dans les pensées qui nous avaient perdus, nous ne comprenions pas. Nous croyions avoir touché le fond: savez-vous ces temps où tout vient à faire défaut, les nuits entières passées à pleurer à petit bruit, à petit flot, sur le passé sans remède." Christian Jambet and Guy Lardreau, *L'ange* (Paris: Grasset, 1976), 10.

29. "un autre monde, malgré tout, est possible." Ibid.

30. "le meilleur maître parmi les maîtres." Christian Jambet and Guy Lardreau, "L'ange entre Mao et Jésus," *Magazine littéraire* 112–113, May 1976, 54–57.

31. "Il faut que l'Ange vienne." Jambet and Lardreau, *L'ange*, 36.

32. "ne décide du meilleur maître qu'au moindre lot de torture, qui a la dignité de peser le maître selon la plus petite oppression qu'il nous promet." Jambet and Lardreau, "L'ange entre Mao et Jésus," 56.

33. "les plus antiques questions de la plus antique tradition." Bernard-Henri Lévy, "Les nouveaux philosophes," *Les nouvelles littéraires* 2536, June 10, 1976, 15–16.

34. Glucksmann, *Les maîtres penseurs* (Paris: Grasset, 1977), 47–49.

35. The polyvalence of this expression is muted somewhat in English. To get at the fullness of Glucksmann's intent, we might wish to combine the notions of "master thinkers," "thinking masters," and "thinkers of mastery."

36. "On voit que Marx vit dans un monde où l'histoire de chaque pays est 'incomplète'. L'histoire de l'Allemagne ne se singularise nullement par ce trait, vu que les seules

'œuvres complètes' de l'histoire, Marx les trouve dans sa tête et sur les rayons des bibliothèques où elles finissent toutes." Glucksmann, *Les maîtres penseurs*, 54.

37. "En fait," he wrote, "les maîtres penseurs ne parlent ni du bas, ni du haut, mais d'eux et de leur science"; "être écoutés." Ibid., 225.

38. "on fantasme une unité dont la perfection se nourrit de l'imperfection allemande." Ibid., 55.

39. Lévy clearly hoped that his readers would bridge the gap between the two phrases that his title evokes: Castoriadis's *Socialisme ou Barbarie* and Dubcek's "Socialism with a Human Face." The elided word is the same in both cases.

40. Lévy, *Barbarism with a Human Face* (New York: Harper & Row, 1979), ix–xi.

41. Ibid., ix.

42. Ibid., 113–121.

43. Ibid., 111, ix.

44. Ibid., 189–190, 193.

45. Ibid., x.

46. Ibid., 116.

47. "À mon avis, le rôle de l'intellectuel aujourd'hui doit être de rétablir pour l'image de la révolution le même taux de désirabilité que celui qui existait au XIXe siècle. Et il est urgent pour les intellectuels—à supposer, bien sûr, que les révolutionnaires et une couche populaire plus vaste leur prêtent l'oreille—de restituer à la révolution autant de charmes qu'elle en avait au XIXe siècle." Foucault, "Hanzai tosite no chishiki," *Jyôkyô* April 1976, 43–50; republished as "Le savoir comme crime," in *Dits et écrits, t. II*, 85–86.

48. "[l]a retour de la révolution, c'est bien notre problème. . . .Vous le savez bien: c'est la désirabilité même de la révolution qui fait aujourd'hui problème"; "Je n'ai pas de réponse." Foucault, "Non au sexe roi," *Le Nouvel Observateur* 644, March 12–21, 1977, 92–130; reprinted in *Dits et écrits, t. II*, 266–267.

49. "qu'il n'y a plus sur la terre un seul point d'où pourrait jaillir la lumière d'une espérance"; "Pour la première fois, la gauche, face à ce qui vient de se passer en Chine, toute cette pensée de la gauche européenne, cette pensée européenne révolutionnaire qui avait ses points de référence dans le monde entier et les élaborait d'une manière determinée, donc une pensée qui s'orientait sur des choses qui se situaient en dehors d'elles-mêmes, cette pensée a perdu les repères historiques qu'elle trouvait auparavant dans d'autres parties du monde. Elle a perdu ses points d'appui concrets." Foucault, "Die Folter, das ist die Vernunft," *Literaturmagazin* 8, December 1977, 60–68; republished as "La torture, c'est la raison," in *Dits et écrits, t. II*, 397–398.

50. "tout ce que cette tradition socialiste a produit dans l'histoire est à condamner." Ibid.

51. "des édifices théoriques importants et un peu solonnels"; "avec le stalinisme par exemple, la Chine également"; "Je crois que c'est l'échec des grands systèmes théoriques pour faire l'analyse politique actuelle, qui nous renvoie maintenant à une sorte d'empirisme, qui n'est pas très glorieux, l'empirisme des historiens." Foucault, "El poder, una bestia magnifica," *Quadernos para el dialogo* 238, November 19–25, 1977; republished as "Le pouvoir, une bête magnifique," in *Dits et écrits, t. II*, 377.

52. "un empiriste aveugle." Foucault, "Kenryoku to chi," *Umi* December 1977, 240–256; republished as "Pouvoir et savoir," in *Dits et écrits, t. II*, 404.

53. Foucault, "Vie des hommes infâmes," *Les Cahiers du chemin* 29, January 15, 1977, 12–29; reprinted in *Dits et écrits, t. II*, 237–253.

54. Foucault, "Introduction," *Herculine Barbin, dite Alexina B.* (Paris: Gallimard, 1978).

55. This idea, which stands behind Foucault's inaugural project of a history of madness, was equally present in his work with the G.I.P. (Groupe d'Information sur les Prisons). In both cases Foucault saw himself as working to give voice to the voiceless.

56. "traité du désespoir"; "les discours qui nous font tenir tranquilles sous le poids de leurs promesses." Foucault, "La grande colère des faits," 277.

57. *"Peu importe, un fait ne sera jamais rien par lui-même; écoute, lis, attends; ça s'expliquera plus loin, plus tard, plus haut."* Ibid.

58. "L'épreuve décisive pour les philosophes de l'Antiquité, c'était leur capacité à produire des sages. . . . à l'époque moderne, c'est leur aptitude à rendre raison à des massacres. Les premières aidaient l'homme à supporter sa propre mort, les secondes, à accepter celle des autres." Ibid., 278.

59. "Il s'agit pour [Glucksmann] de plaquer sur des idées les têtes de mort qui leur ressemblent." Ibid., 279.

60. *"pas du tout hégélien"*; "fait surgir au coeur du plus haut discours philosophique ces fuyards, ces victimes, ces irreductibles. . . .—bref, ces 'têtes ensanglantées' et autres formes blanches, que Hegel voulait effacer de la nuit du monde." Ibid., 278, 281.

61. Foucault, "Sur la justice populaire: Débat avec les maos," *Les Temps Modernes* 310 *bis*, June 1972, 355–366; reprinted in *Dits et écrits, t. I*, 1208–1237. It is an irony of history that one of Foucault's two interlocutors in this debate was radical Maoist André Glucksmann (alias "Gilles"), whose stance on popular justice was extremely severe.

62. "la dissidence de notre temps,"; "[l]e premier grand style romantique depuis 68." Philippe Sollers, "La révolution impossible," *Le Monde*, May 13, 1977.

63. "Ceci, qui est important, que les intellectuels qui veulent avant tout combattre le pouvoir d'Etat le feront désormais dans le langage qui convient, celui du libéralisme. La confusion de l'esprit libertaire et de l'esprit bolchévik, qui a défini la pensée sartrienne et la suite presque ininterrompue de ses erreurs politiques, est désormais impossible." Alain Touraine, "Intellectuels d'en haut et intellectuels d'en bas," *L'Arc* 70, December 1977, 87–91.

64. "le mérite subversif de précipiter notre rejet des dogmes de la religion de l'histoire." Jean Daniel, "Etre un intellectuel journaliste," *L'Arc* 70, December 1977, 84–86.

65. "une caricature grinçante et grimaçante." Jean-Marie Vincent, "Du Goulag à l'Abbaye de Vézelay," *Rouge* July 6, 1977, n.p.

66. "l'encombrement des marchés par les collages d'une pop'philosophie en plastique." Cornelius Castoriadis, "Les divertisseurs," *Le Nouvel Observateur* June 20, 1977.

67. Xavier Aubral and François Delcourt, *Contre la nouvelle philosophie* (Paris: Gallimard, 1977).

68. "leur pensée est nulle"; "LE maître, LE monde, LA rébellion, LA foi, etc.,"; "introduit en France le marketing littéraire ou philosophique"; "*le journalisme découvrait en lui-même une pensée autonome et suffisante*"; "la soumission de toute pensée aux médias"; "Ce qui me dégoûte est très simple: les nouveaux philosophes font une martyrologie, le Goulag et les victimes de l'histoire. Ils vivent de cadavres." Deleuze, "A propos des nouveaux philosophes et d'un problème plus général," *Minuit* 24, June 1977, n.p.

69. Ibid.

70. Didier Eribon, *Foucault* (Cambridge, MA: Harvard University Press, 1991), 258–262.

71. Foucault, *Securité, territoire, population. Cours au Collège de France: 1977–1978.* Unedited. Available in recorded form (10 cassettes), archives of Bibliothèque Générale du Collège de France, lecture of March 8, 1978.

72. Foucault, *Securité, territoire, population*, lecture of March 15, 1978.

73. Foucault, *Securité, territoire, population*, lecture of March 29, 1978.

74. "faire de la ville une sorte de quasi-couvent et du royaume une sorte de quasi-ville"; "rêve disciplinaire." Foucault, *Securité, territoire, population*, lecture of April 5, 1978.

75. Ibid.

76. "Telle est, je crois, dans cette question de l'autolimitation par le principe de la vérité, le point formidable que l'économie politique a introduit dans la présomption indéfini de l'état-police." Foucault, *Naissance de la biopolitique. Cours au Collège de France: 1978–1979.* Unedited. Available in recorded form (12 cassettes), archives of Bibliothèque Générale du Collège de France, lecture of January 10, 1979.

77. Foucault, "Conversazione con Michel Foucault," *Il Contributo*, January–March 1980, 23–84; republished as "Entretien avec Michel Foucault," in *Dits et écrits, t. II*, 909.

78. "se trouve effectivement pour nous posé actuellement dans notre actualité immédiate et concrète." Foucault, *Naissance de la biopolitique*, lecture of January 10, 1979.

79. Foucault, "Truth and Subjectivity," Howison Lecture delivered at Berkeley, California, October 20, 1980. Unedited. Available in transcription at Institut Mémoire de l'Édition Contemporaine (IMEC), Paris, France, Documents D. 1 and D. 2, 8.

80. Ibid.; emphasis mine.

81. "la conscience de soi du gouvernement." Foucault, *Naissance de la biopolitique*, lecture of January 10, 1979.

82. "[d]ans l'Iran du pétrole et de la misère, l'armée occupe une place très importante." Foucault, "L'armée, quand la terre tremble," in *Dits et écrits, t. II*, 665–666.

83. "la monarchie la plus policière du monde." Foucault, "Une révolte à mains nues," 703.

84. "J'ai eu alors le sentiment de comprendre que les événements récents ne signifiaient le recul des groupes les plus retardaires devant une modernisation trop brutale; mais le rejet, par toute une culture et tout un peuple, d'une *modernisation* qui est en elle-même un *archaïsme*." Foucault, "La scia ha cento anni di ritardo," *Corriera della sera* 103, no. 230, October 1, 1978, 1; republished as "Le chah a cent ans de retard," in *Dits et écrits, t. II*, 680.

85. "à cause de son principe même" Ibid., 680–682.

86. "Soljenitsyne à l'échelle planétaire"; "univers concentrationnaire." Foucault, *Naissance de la biopolitique*, lecture of February 14, 1979.

87. "pour acclimater le soulèvement à l'intérieur d'une histoire rationelle et maîtrisable." Foucault, "Inutile de se soulever?" 791.

88. "Ce qui se passe en Iran a de quoi troubler les observateurs d'aujourd'hui. Ils ne peuvent retrouver ni la Chine, ni Cuba, ni le Viêt-nam, mais un raz de marée sans appareil militaire, sans avant-garde, sans parti." Foucault, "Une révolte à mains nues," 701.

89. Foucault, "Lettre ouverte à Mehdi Bazargan," *Le Nouvel Observateur* 753, April 14–20, 1979, 46; reprinted in *Dits et écrits, t. II*, 780–782.

90. "Il faut—et c'est impèrieux—donner à celui que l'on poursuit, le plus de moyens de défense et le plus de droits possible"; "Pour un gouvernement, il ne saurait y avoir de 'dernier des hommes'." Ibid., 782.

91. Lévy, *Barbarism with a Human Face*, 197.

Part Three: Subjects

CHAPTER 4. DEEP SUBJECTS

1. "La subjectivation de l'homme occidental, elle est chrétienne, elle n'est pas gréco-romaine." Michel Foucault, *Du Gouvernement des vivants. Cours au Collège de France: 1979–1980.* Unedited. Available in recorded form (12 cassettes), archives of Bibliothèque Générale du Collège de France, lecture of March 12, 1980.

2. "à ce qui reste tranquille, il ne faut pas toucher." Foucault, *Naissance de la biopolitique. Cours au Collège de France: 1978–1979.* Unedited. Available in recorded form (12 cassettes), archives of Bibliothèque Générale du Collège de France, lecture of January 10, 1979.

3. "ont pour maillon central ce quelque chose qu'on appelle *la population*"; "C'est une fois qu'on aura su ce que c'était que ce régime gouvernementale appelé [libéral], qu'on pourra, me semble-t-il, saisir ce qu'est la biopolitique." Ibid.

4. "La 'discipline' ne peut s'identifier ni avec une institution ni avec un appareil; elle est un type de pouvoir, une modalité pour l'exercer, comportant tout un ensemble d'instruments, de techniques, de procédés, de niveaux d'application, de cibles; elle est une 'physique' du pouvoir, une technologie." *Surveiller et punir,* 251.

5. "On s'est dit alors: à travers une réflexion sur le libéralisme, Foucault va nous donner un livre sur la politique. Le libéralisme semblait aussi un détour pour retrouver l'individu, au-delà des mécanismes du pouvoir." "Une esthétique de l'existence," *Le Monde* 15–16 July 1984, xi; reprinted in *Dits et écrits, t. II,* 1551–1552.

6. Foucault, *Naissance de la biopolitique,* lecture of March 28, 1979.

7. Foucault, *Naissance de la biopolitique,* lecture of April 4, 1979.

8. "Ils sont, deux structures hétérogènes." Foucault, *Naissance de la biopolitique,* lecture of March 28, 1979.

9. "On connaît votre contentieux avec le sujet phénoménologique. À cette époque-là, on commençait à parler d'un sujet de pratiques, et la relecture du libéralisme s'était faite un peu autour de cela." "Une esthétique de l'existence," 1551.

10. "L'économie est une discipline athée, l'économie est une discipline sans Dieu, l'économie est une discipline sans totalité, l'économie est une discipline qui commence à manifester non seulement l'inutilité, mais l'impossibilité d'un point de vue souverain, d'un point de vue *du* souverain, sur la totalité de l'état qu'il a à gouverner." Foucault, *Naissance de la biopolitique,* lecture of March 28, 1979.

11. See Foucault, "L'oeil du pouvoir," Interview with J.-P. Barou and M. Perot. In Jeremy Bentham, *Le Panoptique* (Paris: Belfond, 1977), 9–31; reprinted in *Dits et écrits, t. I,* 190–207.

12. "[n]ous devons nous libérer du type de subjectivité dont traitent les psychanalystes, à savoir la subjectivité psychologique"; "[n]ous sommes prisonniers de certaines conceptions de nous-mêmes et de notre conduite"; "[n]ous devons libérer notre subjectivité, notre rapport a nous-mêmes." "Foucault Examines Reason in Service of State Power," *Campus Report* 6, October 24, 1979, 5–6; republished as "Foucault étudie la rasion d'État," in *Dits et écrits, t. II*, 801–802.

13. "[l]a philosophie analytique de la politique." "Gendai no Kenryoku wo tou," *Asahi Jaanaru* (June 2, 1978), 28–35. In *Dits et écrits, t. II*, 534–551.

14. I am extremely grateful to Zachary Hale for his astute interpretations of this interview.

15. Foucault, "Discussion with John Searle," audio cassette available in the IMEC archive, Paris, France, Document C. 8.

16. Ibid.

17. Foucault, "Discussion at Stanford," audio cassette available in the IMEC archive, Paris, France, Document C. 9.

18. "l'âme, prison du corps." Foucault, *Discipline and Punish*, 38; this tight formulation was Foucault's way of saying that modern social-science discourses like psychology and psychiatry—discourses which posited a "soul" (or *psyche*) as their object—had, in fact, crafted in this concept an elaborate prison for real bodies. Heidrun Hesse has noted the jarring effect of Foucault's shift in attitude, writing of the late works: "Die gelassene Hinwendung zum Individuum, den unverwechselbaren Formen seiner Lebensführung und Möglichkeiten seiner Selbstgestaltung steht zumindest auf den ersten Blick in merkwürdigem Kontrast zu jene früheren Analysen Foucaults, die die Seele als Gefängnis des Körpers und die Figur der Subjektivität überhaupt als die zweifelhafte Produkt neuzeitlicher Disziplinar- und Biomacht erscheinen liessen." Heidrun Hesse, "'Ästhetik der Existenz': Foucaults Entdeckung des ethischen Selbstverhältnisses," in Axel Honneth and Martin Saar, eds., *Michel Foucault: Zwischenbilanz einer Rezeption* (Frankfurt am Main: Suhrkamp, 2003), 300.

19. Foucault, "Discussion with Philosophers," October 23, 1980; audio cassette available in the IMEC archive, Paris, France, Document C. 16.

20. Ibid.

21. Foucault, "Discussion at Stanford."

22. Remarkably, no work has yet appeared to provide the big picture on Foucault's interaction with the history and thought of the antique world. For a useful introduction to select portions of this engagement, see J. Joyce Schuld, *Foucault and Augustine* (Notre Dame: University of Notre Dame Press, 2003); Wolfgang Detel,

Macht, Moral, Wissen: Foucault und die klassische Antike (Frankfurt am Main: Suhrkamp, 1998); Frédéric Gros and Carlos Lévy, eds., *Foucault et la philosophie antique* (Paris: Kimé, 2003); Simon Goldhill, *Foucault's Virginity: Ancient Erotic Fiction and the History of Sexuality* (Cambridge, UK: Cambridge University Press, 1995).

23. Foucault, *Du gouvernement des vivants*, lecture of January 9, 1980.

24. "comment, dans notre civilisation, se sont mises en place les rapports entre le gouvernement des hommes, la manifestation de la vérité dans la forme de la subjectivité, et le salut pour tous et pour chacun." Foucault, *Du gouvernement des vivants*, lecture of January 30, 1980.

25. Foucault, *Du gouvernement des vivants*, lecture of January 9, 1980.

26. "de déplacer un peu les choses par rapport au thème maintenant usagé et rebattu du savoir–pouvoir." Ibid.

27. This account of the origins of power–knowledge has the merit, as Chapter 1 showed, of being far more faithful to the historical record than Foucault's average self-assessment.

28. "Or, le pouvoir n'est pas pris dans cette alternative: ou s'exercer en s'imposant par la violence, ou se cacher, se faire accepter en tenant le discours bavard de l'idéologie. En fait, tout point d'exercice d'un pouvoir est en même temps un lieu de formation, non pas d'idéologie, mais de savoir; et, en revanche, tout savoir établi permet et assure l'exercice d'un pouvoir." Foucault, *La société punitive. Cours au Collège de France: 1972–1973*. Unedited. Available in recorded form (13 cassettes), archives of Bibliothèque Générale du Collège de France, lecture of March 28, 1973.

29. For a fine and brief introduction to the Foucauldean notion of power–knowledge, see Joseph Rouse, "Power/Knowledge," in Gary Gutting, ed., *The Cambridge Companion to Foucault* (Cambridge, UK: Cambridge University Press, 1994), 92–114.

30. "Je dirait qu'il s'agit essentiellement"; "en passant de la notion *savoir–pouvoir* à la notion *gouvernement par la vérité* . . .de donner un contenu positif et différencié au terme . . . à ces deux termes de pouvoir et savoir." Foucault, *Du gouvernement des vivants*, lecture of January 9, 1980.

31. Foucault would declare in 1980 that his work was not so much about power as about the subject and truth.

32. "cette notion de gouvernement . . . me paraît être beaucoup plus opératoire que la notion de pouvoir." Foucault, *Du gouvernement des vivants*, lecture of January 9, 1980.

33. On Foucault's understanding of "government," see Graham Burchell, Colin Gordon, and Peter Miller, eds., *The Foucault Effect: Studies in Governmentality* (Chicago: University of Chicago Press, 1991). See also Mike Gane and Terry Johnson, eds.,

Foucault's New Domains (London: Routledge, 1993); and Thomas Keenan, "Foucault on Government," *Philosophy and Social Criticism* Summer 1982, 35–40, reprinted in Barry Smart, ed., *Michel Foucault: Critical Assessments*, vol. IV (London: Routledge, 1995), 422–426.

34. Hence Foucault's use of the expression "Gouvernement de soi et des autres" in the titles of his final two lecture courses.

35. "Pourquoi, sous quelle forme, dans une société comme la nôtre, existe-t-il un lien si profond entre l'exercice de pouvoir et l'obligation pour les individus de se faire eux-mêmes, dans les procédures de manifestation de vérité, . . . des acteurs essentiels? Quel relation entre le fait d'être sujet dans une relation de pouvoir, et sujet par lequel, pour lequel, et à propos duquel se manifeste la verité?" Foucault, *Du gouvernement des vivants*, lecture of January 30, 1980.

36. "point imaginaire fixé par le dispositif de sexualité, que chacun doit passer pour avoir accès à sa propre intelligibilité"; "à son identité." Foucault, *Histoire de la sexualité I: La volonté de savoir*. (Paris: Gallimard, 1976), 205–207.

37. Foucault, *Du gouvernement des vivants*, lecture of January 30, 1980.

38. "Ne me demandez pas qui je suis et ne me dites pas de rester le même." Foucault, *L'archéologie du savoir* (Paris: Gallimard, 1969), 28.

39. "Pour moi, le travail théorique ne consiste pas tellement à établir et fixer l'ensemble des positions sur lequel je me tiendrai et, dans le lien entre ces différentes positions supposées coherentes, formerai système. Mon problème, ou la seule possibilité de travail théorique que je me sent, ça serai de laisser, selon le dessein le plus intelligible possible, la trace des mouvements par lesquelles je ne suis plus à la place où j'étais toute à l'heure." Foucault, *Du gouvernement des vivants*, lecture of January 30, 1980. In a 1978 interview, Foucault declared, "Je suis un expérimenteur en ce sens que j'écris pour me changer moi-même et ne plus penser la même chose qu'auparavant." "Conversazione con Michel Foucault," *Il Contributo* 1, January–March 1980, 23–84; republished as "Entretien avec Michel Foucault" in *Dits et écrits, t. II*, 860–914.

40. "anarchéologie du savoir." Foucault, *Du gouvernement des vivants*, lecture of February 6, 1980. Foucault observed: "Après tout, il y a bien des théologies négatives. Disons que je suis un théoricien négative."

41. Hubert Dreyfus and Paul Rabinow, *Beyond Structuralism and Hermeneutics* (Chicago: University of Chicago Press, 1983), xi.

42. Quintus Septimius Florens Tertullian (c. 160 – c. 240), a Carthaginian, converted to Christianity around 198. One of the first great writers of the young religion, Tertullian defended his adopted faith against the charges of pagan opponents.

43. Foucault, *Du gouvernement des vivants*, lecture of February 13, 1980.

44. "aura évidemment une importance absolument décisive dans toute l'histoire de ce qu'on peut appeler la subjectivité, c'est-à-dire le rapport de soi à soi, l'exercice de soi sur soi, et la vérité que l'individu peut découvrir au fond de lui-même." Ibid.

45. "Le temps de l'ascèse est en train de se dégager du temps de l'illumination." Ibid.

46. "Le pêcheur doit pleurer ses fautes," Foucault, *Du gouvernement des vivants*, lecture of February 20, 1980.

47. "qu'est-ce qui se disait donc dans ce qui était dit?" Foucault, *L'archéologie du savoir*, 40.

48. Foucault, *The Order of Things* (New York: Random House, 1970), xi. In the 1970 foreword to the English edition, Foucault declares proudly, "I did not operate . . . at the level that is usually that of the historian of science—I should say at the two levels that are usually his. For, on the one hand, the history of science traces the progress of discovery, the formulation of problems, and the clash of controversy; it also analyzes theories in their internal economy; in short, it describes the processes and products of the scientific consciousness. . . . What I would like to do, however, is to reveal. . . . rules of formation, which were never formulated in their own right, but are to be found only in widely differing theories, concepts, and objects of study, that I have tried to reveal, by isolating, as their specific locus, a level that I have called, somewhat arbitrarily perhaps, archaeological."

49. "de telle manière qu'on essaie de retrouver par-delà les énoncés eux-mêmes l'intention du sujet parlant, son activité conscient, ce qu'il a voulu dire." Foucault, *L'archéologie du savoir*, 39.

50. "trop magique pour être bien analysé." Ibid., 32.

51. Foucault, *Du gouvernement des vivants*, lecture of January 30, 1980.

52. On this topic, see Ian Hacking, *The Social Construction of What?* (Cambridge, MA: Harvard University Press, 1999). Hacking looks specifically at the "biological vs. constructed" debate that swirled around madness. He also highlights the continuum that exists within what he calls construction-ism, advising that we rate thinkers on a scale of 1 to 5 depending on, for instance, how far they carry their nominalism.

53. Foucault, "Truth and Subjectivity," typescript available in the IMEC archive, Paris, France, document D. 2(1).

54. Foucault, "Discussion with Philosophers."

55. Peter Dews, "The Return of the Subject in Late Foucault," *Radical Philosophy* 51, Spring 1989, 37–41; reprinted in Barry Smart, ed., *Michel Foucault: Critical Assessments*, vol. VI (London: Routledge, 1994), 155.

CHAPTER FIVE. ARTS OF LIVING

1. "Des lors qu'il y a, dans une culture, un discours vrai sur le sujet, quelle expérience le sujet fait-il de lui-même?" Michel Foucault, *Subjectivité et vérité. Cours au Collège de France: 1980–1981*. Unedited. Available in recorded form (12 cassettes), archives of Bibliothèque Générale du Collège de France, lecture of January 7, 1981.

2. "Arts de vivre"; "genre mineur"; "conseils d'existence." Foucault, *Subjectivité et vérité*, lecture of January 14, 1981.

3. Foucault, *Subjectivité et vérité*, lecture of January 21, 1981.

4. Foucault, *Subjectivité et vérité*, lecture of February 7, 1981.

5. Foucault, *Histoire de la sexualité II: L'usage des plaisirs* (Paris: Gallimard, 1984), 18–19.

6. The terms "pratique de soi," "technique du soi," and "technologie du soi," appear nowhere in *The Government of the Living*, which concluded in March of 1980. While Foucault has clearly, by the end of the course, broached the themes that will later be discussed under these names, he has not as yet found the vocabulary for them. "Techniques of the self" first appears in Foucault's conceptual arsenal during a lecture given at Berkeley in October of 1980. See Foucault, "Subjectivity and Truth," typescript available in the IMEC archive, Paris, France, document D. 2(1).

7. Foucault, "L'éthique du souci de soi comme pratique de la liberté," *Concordia: Revista internacional de filosofia* 6, July–December 1984, 99, in *Dits et écrits, t. II*, 1528.

8. "[O]n a l'habitude de faire l'histoire de l'existence humaine à partir de ses conditions. . . . Mais il me semble aussi possible de faire l'histoire de l'existence comme art et comme style. L'existence est la matière première la plus fragile de l'art humain; mais c'est aussi sa donnée la plus immédiate." Foucault, "À propos de la généalogie de l'éthique: un aperçu du travail en cours," in *Dits et écrits, t. II*, 1448–1449. Officially, this document represents the transcript of a question-and-answer session conducted by Hubert Dreyfus and Paul Rabinow in April of 1983. As the original (and first-published) English edition of the interview reveals, however, this particular statement did not figure in the interview; it represents a subsequent modification on Foucault's part. For comparison, see "On the Genealogy of Ethics: An Overview of Work in Progress," in Hubert L. Dreyfus and Paul Rabinow, *Michel Foucault: Beyond Structuralism and Hermeneutics* (Chicago: University of Chicago Press, 1983), 250–251.

9. Friedrich Nietzsche, *The Gay Science* (New York: Vintage Books, 1974), 232. On Nietzsche's philosophical commitment to self-fashioning, see Alexander Nehamas, *Nietzsche: Life as Literature* (Cambridge, MA: Harvard University Press, 1985). With an eye to what he calls Nietzsche's "aestheticism," Nehamas argues that, "Nietzsche exemplifies through his own writings one way in which one individual may have succeeded in fashioning itself" (3–8). Nehamas has devoted an entire study to the notion of the art of living; see Nehamas, *The Art of Living* (Berkeley: University of

California Press, 1998). In treating Foucault, however, Nehamas is less concerned with the philosopher's use of formal arts of living than with his appropriation of the Socrates figure.

10. Dreyfus and Rabinow, "On the Genealogy of Ethics: An Overview of a Work in Progress," 237. Foucault, told in the course of the interview that his understanding of an art of living seemed to place him close to Nietzsche's view, agreed that this was the case.

11. Foucault, "What Is Enlightenment?" in Paul Rabinow, ed., *The Foucault Reader* (New York: Pantheon, 1984), 32–50.

12. See, for example, Maruzio Passerin d'Entrèves, *Critique and Enlightenment: Michel Foucault on "Was ist Aufklärung?"* (Manchester, UK: University of Manchester, 1996); and Raymond Geuss, "Kritik, Aufklärung, Genealogie," in Axel Honneth and Martin Saar, eds., *Michel Foucault: Zwischenbilanz einer Rezeption: Frankfurter Foucault-Konferenz 2001* (Frankfurt: Suhrkamp, 2003), 145–156.

13. See James Schmidt and Thomas E. Wartenberg, "Foucault's Enlightenment: Critique, Revolution, and the Fashioning of the Self," in Michael Kelly, ed., *Critique and Power: Recasting the Foucault/Habermas Debate* (Cambridge, MA: MIT Press, 1994).

14. The connections with Habermas's own project are apparent. While the tendency of recent scholarship has been to emphasize the antagonism inherent in the two thinkers' perspectives (see Kelly, ed., *Critique and Power: Recasting the Foucault/Habermas Debate*), Foucault in the 1980s seemed to feel that he was working on a parallel track to that of his Frankfurt School contemporary. He was suggesting as much when he said, in 1984, "Je m'intéresse bien à ce que fait Habermas, je sais qu'il n'est pas du tout d'accord avec ce que je dis—moi je suis un peu plus d'accord avec ce qu'il dit." "Face aux gouvernements, les droits de l'homme," *Libération* 967, June 30, 1984–July 1, 1984, 22; reprinted in *Dits et écrits, t. II*, 1545.

15. "des pratiques réfléchies et volontaires par lesquelles les hommes, non seulement se fixent des règles de conduite, mais cherchent à se transformer eux-mêmes, à se modifier dans leur être singulier, et à faire de leur vie une oeuvre qui porte certaines valeurs esthétiques et répondre à certains critères de style." Foucault, *Histoire de la sexualité II: L'usage des plaisirs*, 18.

16. "Il me semble qu'il était plus conforme aux domaines que je traitais et aux documents dont je disposais de penser cette morale dans le forme même où les contemporains l'avaient réfléchie, à savoir dans la forme d'un *art de l'existence*, disons plutôt d'une *technique de vie*." "Le souci de la vérité," *Magazine littéraire* 207, May 1984, 18–23; reprinted in *Dits et écrits, t. II*, 1490; italics mine.

17. "la formation et le développement d'une pratique de soi qui a pour objectif de se constituer soi-même comme l'ouvrier da la beauté de sa propre vie." Ibid.

18. Foucault, *Subjectivité et vérité*, lecture of January 14, 1981.

19. "technologies du soi"; Foucault's use of "technique" and "technologie" suggests that he considered them to be synonyms. Ibid.

20. "il raconte l'histoire singulière d'un choix sexuel qui, à l'intérieur d'une société donnée, a été mode de vie, culture et art de soi-même." See K. J. Dover, *Greek Homosexuality* (Cambridge, MA: Harvard University Press, 1978).

21. See Jacob Burckhardt, *The Civilization of the Renaissance in Italy* (Kitchner, ON: Batoche, 2001). Of particular relevance are the sections entitled, "Personality," 106–114, and "Education of the 'Cortigiano,'" 312–314.

22. Foucault, *Histoire de la sexualité II: L'usage des plaisirs*, 18–19. See Stephen J. Greenblatt, *Renaissance Self-Fashioning: From More to Shakespeare* (Chicago: University of Chicago Press, 1980).

23. Foucault, *Subjectivité et vérité*, lecture of January 14, 1981.

24. "L'art de vivre, c'est de tuer la psychologie, de créer avec soi-même et avec les autres des individualités, des êtres, des relations, des qualités qui sont innomés. Si on ne peut pas arriver à faire ça dans sa vie, elle ne mérite pas d'être vécue." "Conversation avec Werner Schroeter," in G. Courant, *Werner Schroeter* (Paris: Goethe Institute, 1982), 39–47; reprinted in *Dits et écrits, t. II*, 1075.

25. "alors que nous l'avons complètement oublié, surtout depuis la Renaissance." Ibid.

26. Foucault, *Les mots et les choses* (Paris: Gallimard, 1966), 338–339. Foucault writes, "La pensée moderne n'a jamais pu, à dire vrai, proposer une morale. . . . Pour la pensée moderne, il n'y a pas de morale possible; car depuis la XIXe siècle la pensée est déjà 'sortie' d'elle-même en son être propre, elle n'est plus théorie; dès qu'elle pense, elle blesse ou réconcilie, elle rapproche ou éloigne, elle rompt, elle dissocie, elle noue ou renoue; elle ne peut s'empêcher de libérer et d'asservir. Avant même de prescrire, d'esquisser un futur, de dire ce qu'il faut faire, avant même d'exhorter ou seulement d'alerter, la pensée, au ras de son existence, dès sa forme la plus matinale, est en elle-même une action,—un acte périlleux."

27. "la morale a cessé de'exister au cours du XXe siècle." "En intervju med Michel Foucault," in *Bonniers Litteräre Magasin* 3, March 1968, 203–211; republished as "Interview avec Michel Foucault," in *Dits et écrits, t. I*, 683–684.

28. Foucault, "Preface," in Gilles Deleuze and Félix Guattari, *Anti-Oedipus: Capitalism and Schizophrenia* (New York: Viking Press, 1977), xi–xiv; republished as "Préface," in *Dits et écrits, t. II*, 133–136.

29. Ibid., xiii (135); italics mine. Foucault here defines fascism as that thing "that causes us to love power, to desire the very thing that dominates and exploits us."

30. Francis de Sales, *L'introduction à la vie dévote* (Lyon: Frères Bruyset, 1712).

31. Foucault, *Subjectivité et vérité*, lecture of January 7, 1981. See also Foucault, "Usage des plaisirs et techniques de soi," *Le Débat* 27, November 1983, 46–72; reprinted in *Dits et écrits, t. II*, 1358–1380, in which Foucault once again deploys this same material.

32. The reasons why Foucault was in possession of the Francis de Sales material—yet did not make use of it prior to 1981—would make for an entire study in themselves. He notes in a 1983 interview, "I have more than a draft of a book about sexual ethics in the sixteenth century, in which also the problem of the techniques of the self, self-examination, the cure of souls is very important, both in the Protestant and Catholic churches. ("On the Genealogy of Ethics: An Overview of a Work in Progress," 231). From comments made during the interview and elsewhere, it seems likely that this draft was *Les Aveux de la chair*, which Foucault intended to publish as the second volume of *The History of Sexuality* (with *L'Usage des plaisirs* as the first). The content of the early lectures of Foucault's 1978 course at the Collège de France—*Territory, Security, Population*—show that Foucault had initiated research on confession and Christian sexuality almost immediately after the 1976 publication of *La volonté de savoir*. Yet this project proved abortive, as Foucault was sidetracked first by the investigation of reason of state, later by the study of liberalism, and finally by the acknowledgment that he would have to study the ancient world first in order to make sense of Christianity. One result was that de Sales's *Introduction* (1604) remained essentially in Foucault's back pocket until the philosopher was too ill to make proper use of the draft material. *Les Aveux de la chair* was never completed, and *Le Souci de soi*, which was never intended to form part of the *Sexuality* series—it has very little to do with sex—was published as its third volume. For additional background on the birthing pains of *The History of Sexuality*, see Arnold I. Davidson, "Ethics as ascetics: Foucault, the history of ideas, and ancient thought," in Gary Gutting, ed., *The Cambridge Companion to Foucault* (Cambridge, UK: Cambridge University Press, 1994), 117.

33. "un certain nombre de questions se posent à nous dans les termes mêmes où elles se posaient dans l'Antiquité. La recherche de styles d'existence aussi différents que possibles les uns des autres me paraît l'un des points par lesquels la recherche contemporaine a pu s'inaugurer autrefois dans des groupes singuliers." Foucault, "La retour de la morale," *Les nouvelles littéraires* 2937, June 28–July 5, 1984, 36; reprinted in *Dits et écrits, t. II*, 1525.

34. On Foucault's presentation of the aestheticization of existence in ancient Greece, see the informed discussion "Alcibiades Goes Wilde," in Timothy O'Leary, *Foucault and the Art of Ethics* (London: Continuum, 2002), 38–57.

35. "On the Genealogy of Ethics: An Overview of Work in Progress," 245.

36. "[p]lutôt de faire valoir que les individus ont des droits fondamentaux et naturels, nous devrions essayer d'imaginer et de créer un nouveau droit relationnel"; "institutions relationnellement appauvrissantes"; "il s'agit de créer des formes

culturelles." "The Social Triumph of the Sexual Will: A Conversation with Michel Foucault," *Christopher Street* 6, no. 4, May 1982, 36–41; republished as "Le triomphe social du plaisir sexuel: une conversation avec Michel Foucault," in *Dits et écrits, t. II*, 1128–1129.

37. "la création de nouvelles formes de vie, de rapports, d'amitiés, dans la société, l'art, la culture, de nouvelles formes qui s'instaureront à travers nos choix sexuels, éthiques et politiques." "Michel Foucault, an Interview: Sex, Power and the Politics of Identity," *The Advocate* 400, August 7, 1984, 26–30, 58; republished as "Michel Foucault, une interview: sexe, pouvoir et la politique de l'identité," in *Dits et écrits, t. II*, 1554–1565.

38. "Nous devons plutôt créer un mode de vie gay." Ibid.

39. "On the Genealogy of Ethics: An Overview of a Work in Progress," 236.

40. Ibid.

41. Ibid., 236–245.

42. On Foucault's Californian exploits, see James Miller, *The Passion of Michel Foucault* (New York: Anchor, 1994). Miller's journalistic account, while providing a wealth of background information, is, as David Halperin has ably shown, extremely suspect in its interpretive methodology (see David Halperin, *Saint Foucault: Towards a Gay Hagiography* (New York: Oxford University Press, 1995).

43. In the spring of 1975, Leo Bersani invited Foucault to Berkeley on behalf of the French Department. He gave two talks, "Discourse and Repression," and "Infantile Sexuality Before Freud," both of which continue to exist in unedited form. See "Chronologie," in *Dits et écrits, t. I*, 63.

44. Several of these discussions have been preserved. See "Discussion at Berkeley," audio cassette available in the IMEC archive, Paris, France, document C. 19; "Discussion with John Searle," document C. 8; "Discussion with Philosophers," document C. 16; and "Discussion with Philosophers 2," document C. 17.

45. In addition to Dreyfus and Rabinow's *Michel Foucault: Beyond Structuralism and Hermeneutics*, see "Discussion about Books," audio cassette available in the IMEC archive, Paris, France, document C. 18.

46. A transcription of this course is now available in an unedited and unauthorized English edition. See Joseph Pearson, ed., *Fearless Speech* (New York: Semiotexte, 2001).

47. See, for example, Foucault, *Subjectivité et vérité*, lecture of January 14, 1981, where Foucault explicitly acknowledges Brown's question to be his own: "Comment établir ce partage, comment faire la cartographie de ce partage des eaux, comme disait Peter Brown, entre ce qu'on appelle le Christianisme et ce qu'on appelle le paganisme?"

48. See Peter Brown, *The Making of Late Antiquity* (Cambridge, MA: Harvard University Press, 1978).

49. On *The Government of the Living*, see Chapter 5.

50. Brown, *The Making of Late Antiquity*, 58–59; it is also worth noting the image that Brown conjures in the concluding passages of the work. He writes: "The Christians looked to the earth alone. They claimed power from heaven; but they had made that heaven remote and they kept its power to themselves, to build up new separate institutions among upstart heroes on earth. . . . To these human institutions a new generation of Christians was prepared to transfer that sense of solemn delight which men of the old religion still sought in the clustering stars. The 'stars' that held the attention of a fourth-century Christian were the tombs of the martyrs, scattered like the Milky Way throughout the Mediterranean. The lives of human heroes, the spiritual struggles of the individual, and the fate of the traditions of doctrine passed from one human intermediary to the other in highly self-conscious, inward-looking institutions, came to hold the attention of men to the exclusion of those old problems whose solution had lain in placing man correctly against the overwhelming backdrop of the cosmos" (100). What is remarkable in the comparison that Brown establishes is not simply that it highlights (as would Foucault) the emergence of "the spiritual struggles of the individual." It is the fact that it contrasts Christian inwardness with a pagan exteriority *represented by man set against the stars*. It will be remembered from Chapter 4 that Foucault employed precisely this image—Septimus Severus in his starry chamber—to emphasize this difference.

51. "L'usage que je fais du 'style,' je l'emprunte en grande partie à Peter Brown." "La retour de la morale," 1517.

52. Ibid., 91–92; italics mine.

53. "ni helléniste ni latiniste." Foucault, *Histoire de la sexualité II: L'usage des plaisirs*, 14.

54. "une familiarité suffisante"; "d'un grand secours." "Usage des plaisirs et techniques de soi," 1361.

55. See Paul Veyne, *Le pain et le cirque: sociologie historique d'un pluralisme politique* (Paris: Éditions du Seuil, 1976); *Comment on écrit l'histoire* (Paris: Éditions du Seuil, 1971).

56. See, for instance, Foucault, *Subjectivité et vérité*, lecture of April. 1, 1981, in which social-historical background from Veyne's works provides the setup for the course's concluding section.

57. Daniel Defert, "Chronologie," 73.

58. "à comprendre que les choses ne sont que les objectivations de pratiques déterminées, dont il faut mettre au jour les déterminations." Paul Veyne, "Foucault

révolutionne l'histoire," in *Comment on écrit l'histoire suivi de Foucault révolutionne l'histoire* (Paris: Éditions du Seuil, 1978), 217.

59. Daniel Defert notes that, "[p]endant les deux années où [Foucault] traita de la gouvernementalité et de la raison politique libérale, le groupe de chercheurs qui intervenait à son séminaire se réunit régulièrement dans son bureau; c'est dans ce cadre que furent analysées les thèses nominalistes de Paul Veyne, développées dans 'Foucault révolutionne l'histoire.' "Chronologie," 73.

Veyne writes, "Tout tourne autour de ce paradoxe, qui est la thèse centrale de Foucault, et la plus originale: *ce qui est fait*, l'objet, s'explique par ce qu'a été le *faire* à chaque moment de l'histoire; c'est à tort que nous nous imaginons que le *faire*, la pratique, s'explique à partir de ce qui est fait. . . . Tout le malheur vient de l'illusion par laquelle nous 'réifions' les objectivations en un objet naturel: nous prenons l'aboutissement pour un but, nous prenons l'endroit où va de lui-même s'écraser un projectile pour une cible intentionnellement visée."

Compare, for instance, Foucault, *Subjectivité et vérité*, lecture of March 18, 1981, in which Foucault says the following about *discourse* as a practice: "si on interroge le discours dans son existence, non pas dans son fonction document, mais dans son existence, si vous voulez, de *monument*, dans le fait qu'il existe, dans le fait qu'il a effectivement été prononcé, si on s'interroge sûr le réel du discours, alors on ne peut pas se contenter de dire et d'affirmer que se sont les choses qui ont été dites qui peuvent rendre compte du fait qu'ils ont effectivement été dites. Il faut s'arrêter, il faut buter, si vous voulez, sur ce réel du discours, en levant le postulat que la fonction du discours est de répresenter le réel. Le réel ne contient pas en lui-même la raison d'être du discours. Je veux dire, le réel *dont* il est question dans le discours ne peut pas à lui seul rendre compte de l'existence du discours qui parle de lui."

60. "Son influence sur ces pages serait difficile à circonscrire." Foucault, "Usage de plaisirs et techniques de soi," 1362.

61. Pierre Hadot, *Philosophy as a Way of Life* (Oxford, UK: Blackwell, 1995), 206.

62. See endnote 7 above.

63. Arnold I. Davidson, "Introduction: Pierre Hadot and the Spiritual Phenomenon of Ancient Philosophy," in Hadot, *Philosophy as a Way of Life*, 1.

64. Ibid., 206–207.

65. See endnote 16 above.

66. "par une attitude et par une recherche qui *individualisent* son action, la modulent, et peuvent même lui donner un éclat singulier par la structure rationnelle et réfléchie qu'on lui prête." Foucault, *Histoire de la sexualite II: la volonté de savoir*, 84; italics mine.

67. Foucault, *L'herméneutique du sujet. Cours au Collège de France: 1981–1982* (Paris: Seuil/Gallimard, 2001), lecture of January 6, 1982, first hour, 4.

68. "On the Genealogy of Ethics: An Overview of a Work in Progress," 247.

69. Again, the affinities between Foucault's position and Habermas's contemporary account of the colonization of the life-world by "system" are manifest.

70. "On the Genealogy of Ethics: An Overview of a Work in Progress," 235.

71. "culture de soi." "Le style de l'histoire," in *Le Matin* 2168, February 21, 1984, 20–21; reprinted in *Dits et écrits, t. II*, 1472. Foucault noted, "Un monastère n'est pas une institution individualiste, et pourtant la vie intèrieure, l'attention à soi y sont extrêmement développées."

72. Foucault, *L'herméneutique du sujet*, lecture of March. 3, 1982, first hour, 333–334.

73. "On the Genealogy of Ethics: An Overview of a Work in Progress," 247; italics mine.

74. "le jour où le *bios* a cessé d'être ce qu'il avait été si longtemps pour la pensée grecque, à savoir le corrélatif d'une *tekhnê*; lorsque le bios (la vie) a cessé d'être le corrélatif d'une *tekhnê*, pour devenir la forme d'un épreuve de soi." Foucault, *L'herméneutique du sujet*, lecture of March 24, 1982, second hour, 466.

75. *Épreuve*, the critical term in this passage, holds a unique and important place in Foucault's vocabulary of concepts. Prior to its use in *The Hermeneutics of the Subject* and the two lecture courses that followed it, the word "épreuve"—which does not merit a listing in the terminological index of the *Dits et écrits*—had made only one significant appearance in twenty years. During the 1973 conference entitled "La vérité et les formes juridiques," Foucault argued that Western history could be characterized in terms of a limited number of "juridical forms." He labeled these forms inquest (*enquête*), examination (*examen*), and test (*épreuve*). While the first two were characteristic of successive stages of modernity, the last occurred variously in archaic Greece and in the Middle Ages.

The essence of the *épreuve*, and that which set it apart from the other two juridical forms, was that the truth emerged as the result of a challenge and a physical ordeal. There was no need for the patient mobilization of evidence, of witnesses, of a vast machinery intended to reconstruct the misdeed: to find truth in such a way was the province of the inquest, which demanded the resources of the administrative monarchies. The *épreuve*, in contrast, was a literal "trial" in which the truth was revealed. ("La vérité et les formes juridiques," *Dits et écrits, t. I*, 1424–1452).

The echo of this definition is still present in the term *épreuve* as Foucault uses it in 1982. Invoking Epictetus, he declaims: "'Philosopher, c'est se préparer'; philosopher, c'est donc par conséquent se mettre dans une disposition telle que l'on va considérer l'ensemble de la vie comme une épreuve. Et l'ascétique, l'ensemble des exercices qui sont à notre disposition, ont pour sens de nous permettre de nous préparer en permanence à cette vie qui ne sera jamais, et jusqu'au bout, qu'une vie d'épreuve, [au sens] où ce sera une vie qui sera une épreuve. . . . Je crois qu'on a là le moment où cette fameuse *epimeleia heautou*, ce souci de soi, qui apparaissait à l'intérieur du principe général, du thème général qu'on doit se donner une *tekhnê* (un art de vivre), a occupé en quelque sorte toute la place définie par la *tekhnê tou biou*. Ce que les Grecs cherchaient dans ces techniques de vie, sous des formes très différentes depuis tant de siècles, depuis le début de l'âge classique, cette *tekhnê tou biou*, elle est maintenant, dans ce genre-là de pensée, occupée entièrement par le principe qu'il faut se soucier de soi, que se soucier de soi, c'est s'équiper pour une série d'événements imprévus, mais pour lesquels on va pratiquer un certain nombre d'exercises qui les actualisent dans une nécessité inévitable, où on les dépouillera de tout ce qu'ils peuvent avoir de réalité imaginaire, pour les réduire au strict minimum de leur existence. Et ce sont dans ces exercises, c'est par le jeu de ces exercises que l'on pourra tout au long de sa vie vivre son existence comme une épreuve." (*L'herméneutique du sujet*, lecture of March 24, 1982, second hour, 464–465).

In this remarkably rich passage, Foucault suggests three things: firstly, that the period he has just examined—the second century C.E.—is the moment in which arts of living are overtaken from within by the care of the self; secondly, that from this period onward, life will be lived not *expressively* as art, but *reflexively* as *épreuve*; and thirdly, that this shift represents a radical diminution both of life's events ("on les dépouillera de tout ce qu'ils peuvent avoir de réalité imaginaire") and of life's substance (which will henceforth be lived "dans ces exercises . . . par le jeu de ces exercises"). (Ibid., 465) Life, now lived in and through a filtering set of discursive practices, is flattened down to the "true" words that one must perpetually speak about it.

It is through incomprehension of this use of *épreuve* that Thomas R. Flynn, whose studies of the late Foucault are otherwise so astute, veers astray in his analysis of the place of subjectivity. Flynn argues that, in Foucault's last lectures at the Collège de France, the philosopher, "drew a distinction between the Socrato-Platonic care of the soul (*epimeleia*), which was intellectualist and ontological, and the experience of life (*épreuve de la vie*), which was aesthetic and 'ethical' in his sense." (Thomas R. Flynn, "Truth and Subjectivation in the Later Foucault," *The Journal of Philosophy* 82, no. 10, October 1985, 537). As the previously cited texts show, Foucault's use of *épreuve* describes a phenomenon that is diametrically opposed to what Flynn holds him to mean: namely, the experience of life in all its richness. Flynn's commitment to the false opposites *epimeleia*/*épreuve* short-circuits the central historical conflict (*tekhnê*/*épreuve*) that Foucault seeks to establish. The damage to his interpretation of Foucauldean subjectivity is correspondingly great.

76. Foucault, *L'histoire de la sexualité I: La volonté de savoir*, 76–78.

77. "la vérité est extraite du plaisir lui-même"; "économie des corps et des plaisirs"; "austère monarchie du sexe"; "la tâche indéfinie de forcer son secret et d'extorquer à cette ombre les aveux les plus vrais." Ibid., 77, 211.

78. "On the Genealogy of Ethics: An Overview of a Work in Progress," 236.

79. Ibid., 235.

80. Peter Dews, "The Return of the Subject in late Foucault," in Barry Smart, ed., *Michel Foucault: Critical Assessments*, vol. VI (London: Routledge, 1995), 151.

81. "On the Genealogy of Ethics: An Overview of a Work in Progress," 245.

82. The relation of the individual to himself is, as was noted in the preceding chapter, the definition given by Foucault in 1980 to the term "subjectivity."

83. "On the Genealogy of Ethics: An Overview of a Work in Progress," 237.

84. Foucault, *Subjectivité et vérité*, lecture of January 7, 1981.

85. "jamais la folie, comme domaine d'expérience, ne s'épuisait dans la connaissance médicale ou para-médicale qu'on pouvait en prendre." Foucault, *Histoire de la folie à l'age classique* (Paris: Gallimard, 1972), 133.

86. "*M. Demonbynes*: . . . Puis-je vous demander dans quelle mesure, à votre avis, Nietzsche a eu l'expérience de la folie? . . . Ai-je bien compris? Car vous avez bel et bien parlé de cette expérience de la folie. Est-ce vraiment ce que vous avez voulu dire?/ *M. Foucault*: Oui./ *M. Demonbynes*: . . . Croyez-vouz vraiment qu'on puisse avoir. . . . que de grands esprits comme Nietzsche puisse avoir l'"expérience de la folie"?/ *M. Foucault*: Je vous dirai: oui, oui." "Nietzsche, Freud, Marx," *Cahiers de Royaumont*, t. VI (Paris: Éditions de Minuit, 1967), 183–200; reprinted in *Dits et écrits*, t. I, 607.

87. Foucault naturally continued to use it frequently in its colloquial sense. In 1971, for instance, speaking of the G.I.P.'s investigation into the living conditions of prisoners, he noted, "Il faut que l'information rebondisse; il faut transformer l'expérience individuelle en savoir collectif." ("Enquête sur les prisons: brisons les barreaux du silence," *Politique-Hebdo* 24, March 18, 1971, 4–6; reprinted in *Dits et écrits, t. I*, 1046.)

88. "D'une façon générale, l'*Histoire de la Folie* faisait une part beaucoup trop considérable, et d'ailleurs bien énigmatique, à ce qui s'y trouvait désigné comme une 'expérience', montrant par là combien on demeurait proche d'admettre un sujet anonyme et général de l'histoire." Foucault, *L'archéologie du savoir* (Paris: Gallimard, 1969), 26–27.

89. In a 1971 interview, Foucault described the project of *Madness and Civilization* in the language of his current archaeological concerns, claiming that what he had really been observing in that work were practices and discourse. "Et c'est cet ensemble 'pratiques et discours' qui a constitué ce que j'ai appelé l'expérience de la folie, mauvais mot d'ailleurs, car ce n'est pas en réalité une expérience." ("Un problème m'intéresse depuis longtemps, c'est celui du système pénal," *La Presse de Tunisie* August 12, 1971, 3; reprinted in *Dits et écrits, t. I*, 1075.)

Asked by an interviewer in 1974 why he always chose to express his philosophy through the study *of* something (rather than directly), Foucault lectured: "Il n'y a pas de discours philosophique sans objet. . . . L'être, l'espace, le temps, c'est-à-dire des objets fabriqués, de toute façon soigneusement conservés par la tradition philosophique, scolaire, universitaire. L'être, le temps, l'expérience sont des objets devenus si usés, quotidiens, familiers, c'est-à-dire transparents, que nous finissons par ne plus les considérer comme des objets." ("Carceri e manicomi nel congegno del potere," *Avanti* 53, March 3, 1974, 26–27; reprinted as "Prisons et asiles dans le mécanisme du pouvoir," *Dits et écrits, t. I*, 1390.)

90. See Foucault, "Introduction by Michel Foucault," in Georges Canguilhem, *On the Normal and the Pathological* (Boston: D. Reidel, 1978), ix–xx; also "Pour une morale de l'inconfort," *Le Nouvel Observateur* 754, April 23–29, 1979, 82; reprinted in *Dits et écrits, t. II*, 783–787; "Postface," in Michelle Perrot, ed., *L'impossible Prison: Recherches sur le système pénitentiáire au XIXe siècle* (Paris: Éditions du Seuil, 1980), 316–318; reprinted in *Dits et écrits, t. II*, 854–856; "Structuralism and Post-Structuralism," *Telos* XVI, no. 55, Spring 1983, 195–211; reprinted as "Structuralisme et poststructuralisme," in *Dits et écrits, t. II*, 1250–1276.

91. Foucault, "What Is Enlightenment?" 32.

92. Ibid., 41.

93. Ibid., 41–42.

94. Ibid., 42.

95. See Jürgen Habermas, "Taking Aim at the Heart of the Present," in Kelly, ed., *Critique and Power*, 149–156. "What Is Enlightenment?" should be read, however, not in parallel with Habermas's critique of Foucault from *The Philosophical Discourse of Modernity* (as it appears in *Critique and Power*), but rather in dialogue with his 1980 "Modernity: An Unfinished Project." The latter text, with its notion that the Enlightenment legacy must be retained or abandoned *in toto*, is directly targeted by Foucault.

96. It will be remembered that, when Foucault wrote the first volume of *The History of Sexuality*, there was as yet no legitimate basis upon which he might express a preference for the *ars erotica* over the *scientia sexualis*. The reader was left to surmise such a preference from context and language. This absence was among the first things noted by concerned liberal critics. See Nancy Fraser, "Foucault on Modern Power: Empirical Insights and Normative Confusions," *Praxis International* 1, 1981, 283; and Richard J. Bernstein, *The New Constellation: The Ethical-Political Horizons of Modernity/Postmodernity* (Cambridge, MA: MIT Press, 1992). See endnote 77 above.

97. Foucault, "What Is Enlightenment?" 47; italics mine.

98. Foucault, *Le Gouvernement de soi et des autres. Cours au Collège de France: 1982–1983.* Unedited. Available in recorded form (12 cassettes), archives of Bibliothèque Général du Collège de France, lecture of January 5, 1983, first and second hour.

99. "Je crois solidement à la liberté humaine." "Interview de Michel Foucault," *Actes: cahiers d'action juridique* 45–46, June 1984, 3–6; reprinted in *Dits et écrits, t. II*, 1512.

100. "La pensée, c'est la liberté par rapport à ce qu'on fait, le mouvement par lequel on s'en détache, on le constitue comme objet et on le réfléchit comme problème." "Polemics, Politics and Problematizations," in Rabinow, ed., *The Foucault Reader*, 381–390; reprinted as "Polémique, politique et problématisations," in *Dits et écrits, t. II*, 1416.

101. "pour voir comment la sexualité a été *manipulée, vécue et modifiée par un certain nombre d'acteurs.*" "Le retour de la morale," 1524; italics mine.

102. "à cette absence de morale répond, doit répondre une recherche qui est celle d'une esthétique de l'existence." "Une esthetique de l'existence," *Le Monde* July 15–16, 1984, xi; reprinted in *Dits et écrits, t. II*, 1551.

103. "Pour moi," he added, "la sexualité est une affaire de mode de vie, elle renvoie à la technique du soi." "Interview met Michel Foucault," *Krisis, Tijdschrift voor filosofie*, March 1984, 47–58; reprinted as "Interview de Michel Foucault," in *Dits et écrits, t. II*, 1482.

104. "Une esthétique de l'existence," 1551.

105. "[M]es livres sont, en un sens, des fragments d'autobiographie." "L'intellectuel et les pouvoirs," *La Revue nouvelle t. LXXX*, no. 10, October 1984, 338–343; reprinted in *Dits et écrits, t. II*, 1566.

106. "Interview de Michel Foucault," 1486.

CONCLUSION: FOUCAULT'S PENDULUM

1. "Stephen Riggins: Vous ne correspondez pas à l'image du Français raffiné qui pratique l'art du bien vivre. Vous êtes aussi le seul Français que je connaisse qui m'ait dit qu'il préférait la cuisine américaine./ Foucault: Oui, c'est vrai! Un bon club sandwich avec un Coca-Cola! Il n'y a rien de tel! C'est vrai. Avec une crème glacée, bien sûr." "Michel Foucault, An Interview with Stephen Riggins," *Ethos* 2, Fall 1983, 4–9; republished as "Une interview de Michel Foucault par Stephen Riggins," in *Dits et écrits, t. II*, 1352.

2. "Truth, Power, Self," in Luther H. Martin, Huck Gutman, and Patrick H. Hutton, eds., *Technologies of the Self: A Seminar with Michel Foucault* (Amherst, MA: University of Massachusetts Press, 1988), 12.

3. François Cusset, *French Theory: Foucault, Derrida, Deleuze & Cie et les mutations de la vie intellectuelle aux Etats-Unis* (Paris: Découverte, 2003). On this theme, see also the valuable collection of essays assembled in Sylvère Lotringer and Sande Cohen, eds., *French Theory in America* (London: Routledge, 2001).

4. Mark Lilla, "The Legitimacy of the Liberal Age," in Mark Lilla, ed., *New French Thought: Political Philosophy* (Princeton, NJ: Princeton University Press, 1994), 14–15.

5. Luc Ferry and Alain Renaut, *La pensée 68: Essai sur l'anti-humanisme contemporain* (Paris: Gallimard, 1985).

6. See, for instance, Pierre Manent, *La cité de l'homme* (Paris: Fauard, 1994); Marcel Gauchet, *La Révolution des droits de l'homme* (Paris: Gallimard, 1989); Pierre Rosanvallon, *Le moment Guizot* (Paris: Gallimard, 1985); Alain Renaut, *L'ère de l'individu: contribution à une histoire de la subjectivité* (Paris: Gallimard, 1989); Luc Ferry and Jean-Didier Vincent, *Qu'est-ce que l'homme?* (Paris: Odile Jacob, 2000).

7. "On conserve . . . dans leur intégralité, les positions antérieures, tout en bénéficiant d'un effet de langage qui, faisant apparaître le thème de la recherche de nouvelles subjectivités, permet de prendre en marche le mouvement de retour au sujet et de masquer ce qu'a de profondément suranné le discours que l'on tient." Ferry and Renaut, *La pensée 68: Essai sur l'anti-humanisme contemporain*, 152–153.

8. "une tentative désespérée pour masquer l'invraisemblable longueur de retard accumulée sur le devenir des idées et sur les moeurs." Ibid.

9. "L'anti-humanisme de la pensée 68 ouvre sur la 'barbarie,' non pas au sens où il conduirait à libérer on ne sait quels déchaînements de la violence, mais en tant que le procès intenté à la subjectivité détruit ici toute possibilité d'un véritable dialogue entre des consciences qui seraient susceptibles de penser leurs différences sur fond d'identité: lorsque ne subsiste que l'exacerbation des différences individuelles, l'autre devient pour chacun le 'tout autre,' le 'bar-bare.'"; "si ardemment cultivé l'inconséquence," Ibid., 163–164; italics mine.

10. Foucault, "Politics and Ethics: An Interview," in Paul Rabinow, ed., *The Foucault Reader* (New York: Pantheon Books, 1984), 373–374. See also "Interview met Michel Foucault," *Krisis Tijdschrift voor filosofie* March 1984, 47–58; republished as "Interview de Michel Foucault" in *Dits et écrits, t. II*, 1485–1486.

11. Gary Gutting, "Introduction: Michel Foucault: A User's Manual," in Gary Gutting, ed., *The Cambridge Companion to Foucault* (Cambridge, UK: Cambridge University Press, 1994), 2.

12. "Ce qui compte dans les choses dites par les hommes, ce n'est pas tellement ce qu'ils auraient pensé en deçà ou au-delà d'elles, mais *ce qui d'entrée de jeu les systématise.*" Foucault, *Naissance de la clinique* (Paris: Presses Universitaires de France, 2000), xv; italics mine.

13. It is not simply works like Habermas's *Philosophical Discourse of Modernity* (1985) that suggest that the theorization of power was the farthest that Foucault ever progressed on his path of thought. Treatments as recent as Sara Mills's 2003 *Foucault* continue to depict a Foucault for whom the genealogical perspective evidenced in

the first volume of *The History of Sexuality* is, in some sense, the final word. Sara Mills, *Foucault* (London: Routledge, 2003). See also Tilottama Rajan, *Deconstruction and the Remainders of Phenomenology: Sartre, Foucault, Derrida, Baudrillard* (Stanford, CA: Stanford University Press, 2002).

14. Foucault's first overt discussion of the significance of a Christian "pastoral power" came in February of 1978, in the context of his lecture course for that year, *Security, Territory, Population*. Foucault, *Sécurité, territoire, population. Cours au Collège de France: 1977–1978*. Unedited. Available in recorded form (10 cassettes), archives of Bibliothèque Générale du Collège de France, lecture of February 22, 1978.

15. "En se soulevant, les Iraniens se disaient—et c'est peut-être cela l'âme du soulèvement: il nous faut changer, bien sûr, de régime. . . . Mais surtout, *il nous faut changer nous-mêmes*. Il faut que notre manière d'être, notre rapport aux autres, aux choses, à l'éternité, à Dieu, etc., soient complètement changés, et *il n'y aura de révolution réelle qu'à condition de ce changement radical dans notre expérience*. Je crois que c'est là où l'islam a joué un rôle. . . . la religion était pour eux comme la promesse et la garantie de trouver de quoi *changer leur subjectivité*." Foucault, "L'esprit d'un monde sans esprit," in Pierre Blanchet and Claire Brière, *Iran: la révolution au nom de Dieu* (Paris, Éditions du Seuil, 1979), 227–241; reprinted in *Dits et écrits, t. II*, 749; italics mine.

16. Martin Jay, *Songs of Experience: Modern American and European Variations on a Universal Theme* (Berkeley, CA: University of California Press, 2005), 394–395. Jay cites the critique of Bataille put forth by Habermas in *The Philosophical Discourse of Modernity*: "the knowing subject would—paradoxically—have to surrender his own identity and yet retrieve those experiences to which he was exposed in ecstasy —to catch them like fish from the decentered ocean of emotions. In spite of this paradox, Bataille stubbornly makes a claim to objectivity of knowledge and impersonality of method—even for this science 'from within,' for the grasp of 'inner experience,'" 395.

17. Foucault's capacity to reinterpret his body of work in terms of his current preoccupations was boundless. At various times throughout the 1970s and early 1980s, the philosopher described his work as "toute une série d'analyses du pouvoir" ("Kenryoku to chi," *Umi* December 1977, 240–256; republished as "Pouvoir et Savoir" in *Dits et écrits, t. II*, 402); affirmed that, "mon problème, c'est de savoir comment les hommes se gouvernent (eux-mêmes et les autres) à travers la production de la vérité" ("Table ronde du 20 mai 1978," in Michelle Perrot, ed., *L'impossible Prison. Recherches sur le système pénitentiaire au XIXe siècle* [Paris: Editions du Seuil, 1980], 40–56; reprinted in *Dits et écrits, t. II*, 846); claimed that his guiding question had always been, "à quel prix le sujet peut-il dire la vérité sur lui-même?" ("Structuralism and Post-Structuralism," *Telos* 55, Spring 1983, 195–211; republished as "Structuralisme et poststructuralisme" in *Dits et écrits, t. II*, 1261); claimed that, "[l]a notion qui sert de forme commune aux études que j'ai

menées depuis l'*Histoire de la folie* est celle de la *problématisation*," ("La souci de la vérité," *Magazine littéraire* 207, May 1984, 18–23; reprinted in *Dits et écrits, t. II*, 1488); and said, of the subjectivity–truth axis, "En réalité, ce fut toujours mon problème, même si j'ai formulé d'une façon un peu différente le cadre de cette réflexion" ("L'éthique du souci de soi comme pratique de la liberté," *Concordia. Revista internacional de filosfia* 6, July–December 1984, 99–116; reprinted in *Dits et écrits, t. II*, 1527).

18. Friedrich Nietzsche, *Twilight of the Idols / The Anti-Christ* (London: Penguin Books, 1990), 184.

19. Michael Kelly, ed., *Critique and Power: Recasting the Foucault / Habermas Debate* (Cambridge, MA: MIT Press, 1994), 149–154.

Bibliography

Primary Sources

WORKS BY MICHEL FOUCAULT

Foucault, Michel. "Préface à la transgression." *Critique*, 195–196 (August–September 1963): 751–769. Reprinted in *Dits et écrits I, 1954–1975*, eds. Daniel Defert and François Ewald, 261–278. Paris: Gallimard, 1994; Paris: Gallimard, 2001.

——— "Distance, aspect, origine." *Critique* 198 (1963): 931–945. *Dits et écrits I, 1954–1975*, eds. Daniel Defert and François Ewald, 300–313. Paris: Gallimard, 1994; Paris: Gallimard, 2001.

——— *Naissance de la clinique*. Paris: Gallimard, 1963.

——— *Raymond Roussel*. Paris: Gallimard, 1963.

——— "Débat sur le roman." *Tel quel* 17 (1964): 12–54. Reprinted in *Dits et écrits I, 1954–1975*, eds. Daniel Defert and François Ewald, 366–418. Paris: Gallimard, 1994; Paris: Gallimard, 2001.

——— "Débat sur la poésie." *Tel quel* 17 (1964): 69–82. Reprinted in *Dits et écrits I, 1954–1975*, eds. Daniel Defert and François Ewald, 418–434. Paris: Gallimard, 1994; Paris: Gallimard, 2001.

——— "Le langage de l'espace." *Critique* 203 (April 1964): 378–382. Reprinted in *Dits et écrits I, 1954–1975*, eds. Daniel Defert and François Ewald, 435–440. Paris: Gallimard, 1994; Paris: Gallimard, 2001.

—— "Pourquoi réédite-t-on l'oeuvre de Raymond Roussel? Un précurseur de notre littérature moderne." *Le Monde* 6097 (22 August 1964): 9. Reprinted in *Dits et écrits I, 1954–1975*, eds. Daniel Defert and François Ewald, 449–452. Paris: Gallimard, 1994; Paris: Gallimard, 2001.

—— *Les mots et les choses.* Paris: Gallimard, 1966.

—— "L'arrière-fable." *L'Arc* 29 (May 1966): 5–12. Reprinted in *Dits et écrits I, 1954–1975*, eds. Daniel Defert and François Ewald, 534–541. Paris: Gallimard, 1994; Paris: Gallimard, 2001

—— "Entretien avec Madeleine Chapsal." Interview by Madeleine Chapsal. *La Quinzaine littéraire* 5 (16 May 1966): 14–15. Reprinted in *Dits et écrits I, 1954–1975*, eds. Daniel Defert and François Ewald, 541–46. Paris: Gallimard, 1994; Paris: Gallimard, 2001.

—— "L'homme est-il mort?" Interview by C. Bonnefoy. *Arts et Loisirs* 38 (15–21 June 1966): 8–9. Reprinted in *Dits et écrits I, 1954–1975*, eds. Daniel Defert and François Ewald, 568–572. Paris: Gallimard, 1994; Paris: Gallimard, 2001.

—— "Nietzsche, Freud, Marx." *Cahiers de Royaumont*, t. VI, 183–200. Paris: Éditions de Minuit, 1967. Reprinted in *Dits et écrits I, 1954–1975*, eds. Daniel Defert and François Ewald, 592–607. Paris: Gallimard, 1994; Paris: Gallimard, 2001.

—— "La philosophie structuraliste permet de diagnostiquer ce qu'est 'aujourd'hui.'" Interview by G. Fellous. *La Presse de Tunisie* (12 April 1967): 3. Reprinted in *Dits et écrits I, 1954–1975*, eds. Daniel Defert and François Ewald, 608–612. Paris: Gallimard, 1994; Paris: Gallimard, 2001.

—— "Sur les façons d'écrire l'histoire." Interview by R. Bellour. *Les Lettres françaises* 1187 (15–21 June 1967): 6–9. Reprinted in *Dits et écrits I, 1954–1975*, eds. Daniel Defert and François Ewald, 613–628. Paris: Gallimard, 1994; Paris: Gallimard, 2001.

—— "Che cos'è Lei Professor Foucault?" Interview by P. Caruso. *La Fiera letteraria* 39 (28 September 1967): 11–15. Reprinted as "Qui êtes-vous, professeur Foucault?" in *Dits et écrits I, 1954–1975*, eds. Daniel Defert and François Ewald, 629–648. Paris: Gallimard, 1994; Paris: Gallimard, 2001.

—— "En intervju med Michel Foucault." Interview by I. Lindung. *Bonniers Litteräre Magasin* March 1968, 203–211. Reprinted as "Interview avec Michel Foucault" in *Dits et écrits I, 1954–1975*, eds. Daniel Defert and François Ewald, 679–690. Paris: Gallimard, 1994; Paris: Gallimard, 2001.

———— "Foucault répond à Sartre." Interview by J.-P. Elkabbach. *La Quinzaine littéraire* 46 (1968): 20–22. Reprinted in *Dits et écrits I, 1954–1975*, eds. Daniel Defert and François Ewald, 690–696. Paris: Gallimard, 1994; Paris: Gallimard, 2001.

———— "Une mise au point de Michel Foucault." *La quinzaine littéraire* 47 (15–31 March 1968): 21. Reprinted in *Dits et écrits I, 1954–1975*, eds. Daniel Defert and François Ewald, 697–698. Paris: Gallimard, 1994; Paris: Gallimard, 2001.

———— "Réponse à une question." *Esprit* 371 (May 1968): 850–874. Reprinted in *Dits et écrits I, 1954–1975*, eds. Daniel Defert and François Ewald, 701–723. Paris: Gallimard, 1994; Paris: Gallimard, 2001.

———— "Sur l'archéologie des sciences. Réponse au Cercle d'épistémologie." *Cahiers pour l'analyse* 9 (Summer 1968): 9–40. Reprinted in *Dits et écrits I, 1954–1975*, eds. Daniel Defert and François Ewald, 724–759. Paris: Gallimard, 1994; Paris: Gallimard, 2001.

———— "Médecins, juges et sorciers au XVIIe siècle." *Médecine de France* 200 (1er trimestre 1969): 121–128. Reprinted in *Dits et écrits 1, 1954–1975*, eds. Daniel Defert and François Ewald, 781–794. Paris: Gallimard, 1994; Paris: Gallimard, 2001.

———— "Discussion à propos de l'Archéologie du savoir." Spring 1969. Unedited cassette, Document C. 120. Institut Mémoire de l'Édition Contemporaine (IMEC), Paris.

———— *L'archéologie du savoir*. Paris: Gallimard, 1969.

———— "Qu'est-ce qu'un auteur?" *Bulletin de la Société française de philosophie*, 63e année, no. 3 (July–September 1969): 73–104. Reprinted in *Dits et écrits I, 1954–1975*, eds. Daniel Defert and François Ewald, 817–849. Paris: Gallimard, 1994; Paris: Gallimard, 2001.

———— "Linguistique et sciences sociales." *Revue tunisienne de sciences sociales* 19 (December 1969): 248–255. Reprinted in *Dits et écrits I, 1954–1975*, eds. Daniel Defert and François Ewald, 849–870. Paris: Gallimard, 1994; Paris: Gallimard, 2001.

———— *The Order of Things*. New York: Random House, 1970.

———— "Le piège de Vincennes." Interview by P. Loriot. *Le Nouvel Observateur* 274 (9–15 February 1970): 33–35. Reprinted in *Dits et écrits I, 1954–1975*, eds. Daniel Defert and François Ewald, 935–941. Paris: Gallimard, 1994; Paris: Gallimard, 2001.

———— "Theatrum philosophicum." *Critique* 282 (November 1970): 885–908 Reprinted in *Dits et écrits I, 1954–1975*, eds. Daniel Defert and François Ewald, 943–967. Paris: Gallimard, 1994; Paris: Gallimard, 2001.

———— "Kyôki, bungaku, shakai." Interview with T. Shimizu and M. Watanabe. *Bungei* 12 (December 1970): 266–285. Reprinted as "Folie, literature, société," in *Dits et écrits I, 1954–1975*, eds. Daniel Defert and François Ewald, 972–996. Paris: Gallimard, 1994; Paris: Gallimard, 2001.

———— "Kyôki to shakai." *Misuzu* December 1970, 16–22. Reprinted as "La folie et la société," in *Dits et écrits I, 1954–1975*, eds. Daniel Defert and François Ewald, 996–1003. Paris: Gallimard, 1994; Paris: Gallimard, 2001.

———— "Nietzsche, la généalogie, l'histoire." In *Hommage à Jean Hyppolite*, Paris, P.U.F., coll. "Épiméthée," 1971, 145–172. Reprinted in *Dits et écrits I, 1954–1975*, eds. Daniel Defert and François Ewald, 1004–1024. Paris: Gallimard, 1994; Paris: Gallimard, 2001.

———— *La volonté de savoir*. Lecture course delivered at the Collège de France, Paris, 1970–1971. Unpublished text edited and prepared by Jacques Lagrange. Archives of the Bibliothèque Générale du Collège de France, Paris.

———— *L'ordre du discours*. Paris: Gallimard, 1971.

———— "Entrevista com Michel Foucault." Interview by J. G. Merquior and S. P. Rouanet. In *O Homen e o Discurso (A Arquelogia de Michel Foucault)*, eds. J. G. Merquior and S. P. Rouanet, 17–42. Rio de Janeiro: Tempo Brasileiro, 1971. Reprinted as "Entretien avec Michel Foucault," in *Dits et écrits I, 1954–1975*, eds. Daniel Defert and François Ewald, 1025–1042. Paris: Gallimard, 1994; Paris: Gallimard, 2001.

———— "Enquête sur les prisons: brisons les barreaux du silence." Interview by C. Angeli. *Politique-Hebdo* 24 (18 March 1971): 4–6. Reprinted in *Dits et écrits I, 1954–1975*, eds. Daniel Defert and François Ewald, 1044–1050. Paris: Gallimard, 1994; Paris: Gallimard, 2001.

———— "La prison partout." *Combat* 8335 (5 May 1971): 1. Reprinted in *Dits et écrits I, 1954–1975*, eds. Daniel Defert and François Ewald, 1061–1062. Paris: Gallimard, 1994; Paris: Gallimard, 2001.

———— Preface to *Enquête dans vingt prisons*. Paris, "Intolérable" collection, no. 1 (28 May 1971): 3–5. Reprinted in *Dits et écrits I, 1954–1975*, eds. Daniel Defert and François Ewald, 1063–1065. Paris: Gallimard, 1994; Paris: Gallimard, 2001.

———— "Un problème m'intéresse depuis longtemps, c'est celui du système penal." Interview by J. Hafsia. *La Presse de Tunisie* 12 August 1971, 3.

Reprinted in *Dits et écrits I, 1954–1975*, eds. Daniel Defert and François Ewald, 1075–1077. Paris: Gallimard, 1994; Paris: Gallimard, 2001.

——— "Monstrosities in Criticism." *Diacritics* 1 (Autumn 1971): 57–60. Reprinted as "Les monstruosités de la critique," in *Dits et écrits I, 1954–1975*, eds. Daniel Defert and François Ewald, 1082–1091. Paris: Gallimard, 1994; Paris: Gallimard, 2001.

——— "Par-delà le bien et le mal." Interview with high school students Alain, Frédéric, Jean-François, Jean-Pierre, and Serge. *Actuel* 14 (November 1971): 42–47. Reprinted in *Dits et écrits I, 1954–1975*, eds. Daniel Defert and François Ewald, 1091–1104. Paris: Gallimard, 1994; Paris: Gallimard, 2001.

——— "Foucault Responds." *Diacritics* 2 (Winter 1971): 60. Reprinted as "Foucault répond," in *Dits et écrits I, 1954–1975*, eds. Daniel Defert and François Ewald, 1107–1108. Paris: Gallimard, 1994; Paris: Gallimard, 2001.

——— "La volonté de savoir." *Annuaire du Collège de France, 71e année, Histoire des systèmes de pensée, année 1970–1971* (1971): 245–249. Reprinted in *Dits et écrits I, 1954–1975*, eds. Daniel Defert and François Ewald, 1108–1112. Paris: Gallimard, 1994; Paris: Gallimard, 2001.

——— *Histoire de la folie à l'age classique.* Paris: Gallimard, 1972.

——— "Michel Foucault Derrida e no kaino." *Paideia* 11 (1 February 1972): 131–147. Reprinted as "Réponse à Derrida," in *Dits et écrits I, 1954–1975*, eds. Daniel Defert and François Ewald, 1149–1163. Paris: Gallimard, 1994; Paris: Gallimard, 2001.

——— "Les intellectuels et le pouvoir." Interview by G. Deleuze (4 March 1972). *L'Arc* 49: *Gilles Deleuze* (2nd trimester 1972): 3–10. Reprinted in *Dits et écrits I, 1954–1975*, eds. Daniel Defert and François Ewald, 1174–1183. Paris: Gallimard, 1994; Paris: Gallimard, 2001.

——— "Sur la justice populaire: Débat avec les maos." Interview with Gilles and Victor (5 February 1972). *Les Temps Modernes* 310 *bis* (June 1972): 355–366. Reprinted in *Dits et écrits I, 1954–1975*, eds. Daniel Defert and François Ewald, 1208–1237. Paris: Gallimard, 1994; Paris: Gallimard, 2001.

——— "Théories et institutions pénales." *Annuaire du Collège de France 1971–1972*, 283–386. Reprinted in *Dits et écrits I, 1954–1975*, eds. Daniel Defert and François Ewald, 1257–1261. Paris: Gallimard, 1994; Paris: Gallimard, 2001.

―――― *La société punitive*. Lecture course delivered at the Collège de France, Paris, 1972–1973. Unpublished text edited and prepared by Jacques Lagrange. Archives of the Bibliothèque Générale du Collège de France, Paris.

―――― *La société punitive*. Lecture course delivered at the Collège de France, Paris, 1972–1973. Thirteen unedited cassettes. Archives of Bibliothèque Générale du Collège de France, Paris.

―――― "Carceri e manicomi nel congegno del potere." Interview by M. D'Eramo. *Avanti* 53 (3 March 1974): 26–27. Reprinted as "Prisons et asiles dans le mécanisme du pouvoir," in *Dits et écrits I, 1954–1975*, eds. Daniel Defert and François Ewald, 1389–1393. Paris: Gallimard, 1994; Paris: Gallimard, 2001.

―――― "La vérité et les formes juridiques." *Cadernos da P.U.C.* 16 (June 1974): 5–133. Reprinted in *Dits et écrits I, 1954–1975*, eds. Daniel Defert and François Ewald, 1406–1514. Paris: Gallimard, 1994; Paris: Gallimard, 2001.

―――― "Loucura, uma questão de poder." *Jornal do Brasil* 12 November 1974: 8. Reprinted as "Folie, une question de pouvoir," in *Dits et écrits I, 1954–1975*, eds. Daniel Defert and François Ewald, 1528–1532. Paris: Gallimard, 1994; Paris: Gallimard, 2001.

―――― *Surveiller et punir*. Paris: Gallimard, 1975.

―――― "Sur la sellette." Interview by J.-L. Ezine. *Les Nouvelles littéraires* 2477 (17–23 March 1975): 3. Reprinted in *Dits et écrits I, 1954–1975*, eds. Daniel Defert and François Ewald, 1588–1593. Paris: Gallimard, 1994; Paris: Gallimard, 2001.

―――― "Pouvoir et corps." *Quel corps?* 2 (September–October 1975): 2–5. Reprinted in *Dits et écrits I, 1954–1975*, eds. Daniel Defert and François Ewald, 1622–1628. Paris: Gallimard, 1994; Paris: Gallimard, 2001.

―――― "Hospicios. Sexualidade. Prisoẽs." *Revista Versus* 1 (October 1975): 30–33. Reprinted as "Asiles. Sexualité. Prisons," in *Dits et écrits I, 1954–1975*, eds. Daniel Defert and François Ewald, 1639–1650. Paris: Gallimard, 1994; Paris: Gallimard, 2001.

―――― *Histoire de la sexualité I: La volonté de savoir*. Paris: Gallimard, 1976.

―――― "Hanzai tosite no chishiki." Interview by S. Terayama. *Jyôkyô* April 1976, 43–50. Reprinted as "Le savoir comme crime," in *Dits et écrits II, 1976–1988*, eds. Daniel Defert and François Ewald, 79–86. Paris: Gallimard, 1994; Paris: Gallimard, 2001.

—— "Preface." In *Anti-Oedipus: Capitalism and Schizophrenia*, Gilles Deleuze and Félix Guattari, xi–xiv. New York: Viking Press, 1977. Reprinted as "Préface," in *Dits et écrits II, 1976–1988*, eds. Daniel Defert and François Ewald, 133–136. Paris: Gallimard, 1994; Paris: Gallimard, 2001.

—— "L'oeil du pouvoir." Interview with J.-P. Barou and M. Perrot. In *Le Panoptique*, ed. J. Bentham, 9–31. Paris: Belfond, 1977. Reprinted in *Dits et écrits II, 1976–1988*, eds. Daniel Defert and François Ewald, 190–207. Paris: Gallimard, 1994; Paris: Gallimard, 2001.

—— "Non au sexe roi." Interview by B.-H. Lévy. *Le Nouvel Observateur* 644 (12–21 March 1977): 92–130. Reprinted in *Dits et écrits II, 1976–1988*, eds. Daniel Defert and François Ewald, 256–269. Paris: Gallimard, 1994; Paris: Gallimard, 2001.

—— "La grande colère des faits." *Le Nouvel Observateur* 652 (May 9–15, 1977): 84–86. Reprinted in *Dits et écrits II, 1976–1988*, eds. Daniel Defert and François Ewald, 277–281. Paris: Gallimard, 1994; Paris: Gallimard, 2001.

—— "El poder, una bestia magnifica." Interview by M. Osorio. *Quadernos para el dialogo* 238 (19–25 November 1977). Reprinted as "Le pouvoir, une bête magnifique," in *Dits et écrits II, 1976–1988*, eds. Daniel Defert and François Ewald, 368–382. Paris: Gallimard, 1994; Paris: Gallimard, 2001.

—— "Die Folter, das ist die Vernunft." Interview by K. Boesers. *Literaturmagazin* 8 (December 1977): 60–68. Reprinted as "La torture, c'est la raison," in *Dits et écrits II, 1976–1988*, eds. Daniel Defert and François Ewald, 390–398. Paris: Gallimard, 1994; Paris: Gallimard, 2001.

—— "Kenryoku to chi." Interview by S. Hasumi (Paris, 13 October, 1977). *Umi* December 1977, 240–256. Reprinted as "Pouvoir et savoir," *Dits et écrits II, 1976–1988*, eds. Daniel Defert and François Ewald, 399–414. Paris: Gallimard, 1994; Paris: Gallimard, 2001.

—— *Securité, territoire, population*. Lecture course delivered at the Collège de France, Paris, 1977–1978. Ten unedited cassettes. Archives of the Bibliothèque Générale du Collège de France, Paris.

—— *Naissance de la biopolitique*. Lecture course delivered at the Collège de France, Paris, 1978–1979. Twelve unedited cassettes. Archives of the Bibliothèque Générale du Collège de France, Paris.

—— "Introduction." *Herculine Barbin, dite Alexina B.* Paris: Gallimard, 1978.

—— "Introduction by Michel Foucault." In *On the Normal and the Pathological*, Georges Canguilhem, ix–xx. Boston: D. Reidel, 1978.

—— "Dialogue on Power." Interview with Los Angeles students. In *Chez Foucault*, ed. S. Wade, 4–22. Los Angeles: Circabook, 1978. Reprinted as "Dialogue sur le pouvoir," in *Dits et écrits II, 1976–1988*, eds. Daniel Defert and François Ewald, 464–477. Paris: Gallimard, 1994; Paris: Gallimard, 2001.

—— "Une érudition étourdissante." *Le Matin* 278 (20 January 1978): 25. Reprinted in *Dits et écrits II, 1976–1988*, eds. Daniel Defert and François Ewald, 503–505. Paris: Gallimard, 1994; Paris: Gallimard, 2001.

—— "Incorporación del hospital en la tecnología moderna." *Revista centroamericana de Ciencias de la Salud* 10 (May–August 1978): 93–104. Reprinted as "L'incorporation de l'hôpital dans la technologie moderne," in *Dits et écrits II, 1976–1988*, eds. Daniel Defert and François Ewald, 508–521. Paris: Gallimard, 1994; Paris: Gallimard, 2001.

—— "Gendai no Kenryoku wo tou." *Asahi Jaanaru* (2 June 1978): 28–35. Reprinted as "La philosophie analytique de la politique," in *Dits et écrits II, 1976–1988*, eds. Daniel Defert and François Ewald, 534–551. Paris: Gallimard, 1994; Paris: Gallimard, 2001.

—— "L'esercito, quando la terra trema." *Corriera della sera* 103, no. 228 (28 September 1978): 1–2. Reprinted as "L'armée, quand la terre tremble" in *Dits et écrits II, 1976–1988*, eds. Daniel Defert and François Ewald, 662–669. Paris: Gallimard, 1994; Paris: Gallimard, 2001.

—— "La scia ha cento anni di ritardo." *Corriera della sera* 103, no. 230 (1 October 1978): 1. Reprinted as "Le chah a cent ans de retard," in *Dits et écrits II, 1976–1988*, eds. Daniel Defert and François Ewald, 679–683. Paris: Gallimard, 1994; Paris: Gallimard, 2001.

—— "À quoi rêvent les Iraniens?" *Le Nouvel Observateur* 727 (16–22 October 1978): 48–49. Reprinted in *Dits et écrits II, 1976–1988*, eds. Daniel Defert and François Ewald, 688–694. Paris: Gallimard, 1994; Paris: Gallimard, 2001.

—— "Una rivolta con le mani nude." *Corriere della sera* 103, no. 261 (5 November 1978: 1–2. Reprinted as "Une révolte à mains nues," in *Dits et écrits II, 1976–1988*, eds. Daniel Defert and François Ewald, 701–704. Paris: Gallimard, 1994; Paris: Gallimard, 2001.

—— "I 'reportages' di idee." *Corriere della sera* 103, no. 267 (12 November 1978): 1. Reprinted as "Les 'reportages' d'idées," in *Dits et écrits II, 1976–1988*, eds. Daniel Defert and François Ewald, 706–707. Paris: Gallimard, 1994; Paris: Gallimard, 2001.

———— "Il mitico capo della rivolta dell'Iran." *Corriera della sera* 103, no. 279 (26 November 1978): 1–2. Reprinted as "Le chef mythique de la révolte de l'Iran," in *Dits et écrits II, 1976–1988*, eds. Daniel Defert and François Ewald, 713–716. Paris: Gallimard, 1994; Paris: Gallimard, 2001.

———— "L'esprit d'un monde sans esprit." Interview with P. Blanchet and C. Brière. In *Iran: la révolution au nom de Dieu*, Pierre Blanchet and Claire Brière, 227–241. Paris: Editions du Seuil, 1979. Reprinted in *Dits et écrits II, 1976–1988*, eds. Daniel Defert and François Ewald, 743–755. Paris: Gallimard, 1994; Paris: Gallimard, 2001.

———— *Du Gouvernement des vivants*. Lecture course delivered at the Collège de France, Paris, 1979–1980. Twelve unedited cassettes. Archives of the Bibliothèque Générale du Collège de France, Paris.

———— "Un plaisir si simple." *Le Gai Pied* 1 (1 April 1979): 10. Reprinted in *Dits et écrits II, 1976–1988*, eds. Daniel Defert and François Ewald, 777–779. Paris: Gallimard, 1994; Paris: Gallimard, 2001.

———— "Lettre ouverte à Mehdi Bazargan." *Le Nouvel Observateur* 753 (14–20 April 1979): 46. Reprinted in *Dits et écrits II, 1976–1988*, eds. Daniel Defert and François Ewald, 780–782. Paris: Gallimard, 1994; Paris: Gallimard, 2001.

———— "Pour une morale de l'inconfort." *Le Nouvel Observateur* 754, (23–29 April 1979): 82–83. Reprinted in *Dits et écrits II, 1976–1988*, eds. Daniel Defert and François Ewald, 783–787. Paris: Gallimard, 1994; Paris: Gallimard, 2001.

———— "Inutile de se soulever?" *Le Monde* 11–12 May 1979: 1–2. Reprinted in *Dits et écrits II, 1976–1988*, eds. Daniel Defert and François Ewald, 790–794. Paris: Gallimard, 1994; Paris: Gallimard, 2001.

———— "Discussion at Stanford." 11 October 1979. Unedited cassette, Document C. 9. Institut Mémoire de l'Édition Contemporaine (IMEC), Paris.

———— "Discussion with John Searle." 23 October 1979. Unedited cassette, Document C. 8. Institut Mémoire de l'Édition Contemporaine (IMEC), Paris.

———— "Foucault Examines Reason in Service of State Power." Interview by M. Dillon. *Campus Report* 6 (24 October 1979): 5–6. Reprinted as "Foucault étudie la rasion d'État," in *Dits et écrits II, 1976–1988*, eds. Daniel Defert and François Ewald, 801–805. Paris: Gallimard, 1994; Paris: Gallimard, 2001.

———— "Postface." In *L'impossible Prison: Recherches sur le système pénitentiaire au xixe siècle*, ed. Michelle Perrot, 316–318. Paris: Éditions du Seuil, 1980.

Reprinted in *Dits et écrits II, 1976–1988*, eds. Daniel Defert and François Ewald, 854–856. Paris: Gallimard, 1994; Paris: Gallimard, 2001.

———— "Conversazione con Michel Foucault." Interview by D. Trombadori (Paris, 1978). *Il Contributo*, January–March 1980, 23–84. Reprinted as "Entretien avec Michel Foucault," in *Dits et écrits II, 1976–1988*, eds. Daniel Defert and François Ewald, 860–914. Paris: Gallimard, 1994; Paris: Gallimard, 2001.

———— "Truth and Subjectivity." Howison Lecture delivered at Berkeley, CA, 20 October 1980. Unedited transcription, Documents D. 1 and D. 2. Institut Mémoire de l'Édition Contemporaine (IMEC), Paris, France.

———— "Discussion with Philosophers." 23 October 1980. Unedited cassette, Document C. 16. Institut Mémoire de l'Édition Contemporaine (IMEC), Paris.

———— "Discussion with Philosophers 2." 23 October 1980. Unedited cassette, Document C. 17. Institut Mémoire de l'Édition Contemporaine (IMEC), Paris.

———— "Discussion about Books." 24 October 1980. Unedited cassette, Document C. 18. Institut Mémoire de l'Édition Contemporaine (IMEC), Paris.

———— "Discussion at Berkeley." 24 October 1980. Unedited cassette, Document C. 19. Institut Mémoire de l'Édition Contemporaine (IMEC), Paris.

———— *Subjectivité et vérité*. Lecture course delivered at the Collège de France, Paris, 1980–1981. Twelve unedited cassettes. Archives of the Bibliothèque Générale du Collège de France, Paris.

———— "Conversation avec Werner Schroeter." Interview with G. Courant and W. Schroeter (3 December 1981). In *Werner Schroeter*, ed. G. Courant, 39–47. Paris: Goethe Institute, 1982. Reprinted in *Dits et écrits II, 1976–1988*, eds. Daniel Defert and François Ewald, 1070–1079. Paris: Gallimard, 1994; Paris: Gallimard, 2001.

———— *L'herméneutique du sujet: Cours au Collège de France (1981–1982)*. Paris: Gallimard Seuil, 2001.

———— "The Social Triumph of the Sexual Will: A Conversation with Michel Foucault." Interview by G. Barbedette. *Christopher Street* 6, no. 4 (May 1982): 36–41. Reprinted as "Le triomphe social du plaisir sexuel: une conversation avec Michel Foucault," in *Dits et écrits II, 1976–1988*, eds. Daniel Defert and François Ewald, 1127–1133. Paris: Gallimard, 1994; Paris: Gallimard, 2001.

——— *Le Gouvernment de soi et des autres*. Lecture course delivered at the Collège de France, Paris, 1982–1983. Twelve unedited cassettes. Archives of the Bibliothèque Général du Collège de France, Paris.

——— "Structuralism and Post-Structuralism." *Telos* 55 (Spring 1983): 195–211. Reprinted as "Structuralisme et poststructuralisme" in *Dits et écrits II, 1976–1988*, eds. Daniel Defert and François Ewald, 1250–1276. Paris: Gallimard, 1994; Paris: Gallimard, 2001.

——— "On the Genealogy of Ethics: An Overview of Work in Progress." Interview with Paul Rabinow and Hubert Dreyfus (Berkeley, CA, April 1983). In *The Foucault Reader*, ed. Paul Rabinow, 340–372. New York: Pantheon, 1984.

——— "Politics and Ethics: An Interview." Interview with Paul Rabinow, Charles Taylor, Martin Jay, Richard Rorty, and Leo Lowenthal (Berkeley, CA, April 1983). In *The Foucault Reader*, ed. Paul Rabinow, 373–380. New York: Pantheon Books, 1984.

——— "Michel Foucault, An Interview with Stephen Riggins." *Ethos* 2 (Fall 1983): 4–9. Reprinted as "Une interview de Michel Foucault par Stephen Riggins," in *Dits et écrits II, 1976–1988*, eds. Daniel Defert and François Ewald, 1344–1357. Paris: Gallimard, 1994; Paris: Gallimard, 2001.

——— "Usage des plaisirs et techniques de soi." *Le Débat* 27 (November 1983): 46–72. Reprinted in *Dits et écrits II, 1976–1988*, eds. Daniel Defert and François Ewald, 1358–1380. Paris: Gallimard, 1994; Paris: Gallimard, 2001.

——— *Histoire de la sexualité II: L'usage des plaisirs*. Paris: Gallimard, 1984.

——— "What Is Enlightenment?" In *The Foucault Reader*, ed. Paul Rabinow, 32–50. New York: Pantheon, 1984.

——— "On the Genealogy of Ethics: An Overview of Work in Progress." Interview with H. Dreyfus and P. Rabinow. In *Michel Foucault: un parcours philosophique*, eds. H. Dreyfus and P. Rabinow, 322–346. Paris: Gallimard, 1984. Reprinted as "À propos de la généalogie de l'éthique: un aperçu du travail en cours," in *Dits et écrits II, 1976–1988*, eds. Daniel Defert and François Ewald, 1428–1450. Paris: Gallimard, 1994; Paris: Gallimard, 2001.

——— "Le style de l'histoire." Interview with A. Farge, F. Dumont, and J.-P. Iommi-Amunategui. *Le Matin* 2168 (21 February 1984): 20–21. Reprinted in *Dits et écrits II, 1976–1988*, eds. Daniel Defert and François Ewald, 1468–1474. Paris: Gallimard, 1994; Paris: Gallimard, 2001.

———— "Interview met Michel Foucault." Interview by J. François and J. de Wit. *Krisis, Tijdschrift voor filosofie* March 1984, 47–58. Reprinted as "Interview de Michel Foucault," in *Dits et écrits II, 1976–1988*, eds. Daniel Defert and François Ewald, 1475–1486. Paris: Gallimard, 1994; Paris: Gallimard, 2001.

———— "Le souci de la vérité." Interview by F. Ewald. *Magazine littéraire* 207 (May 1984): 18–23. Reprinted in *Dits et écrits II, 1976–1988*, eds. Daniel Defert and François Ewald, 1487–1497. Paris: Gallimard, 1994; Paris: Gallimard, 2001.

———— "Polemics, Politics and Problematics: An Interview with Michel Foucault." Interview by Paul Rabinow (May 1984). In *The Foucault Reader*, ed. Paul Rabinow, 381–390. New York: Pantheon, 1984. Reprinted as "Polémique, politique et problématisations," in *Dits et écrits II, 1976–1988*, eds. Daniel Defert and François Ewald, 1410–1417. Paris: Gallimard, 1994; Paris: Gallimard, 2001.

———— "Interview de Michel Foucault." Interview by C. Baker. *Actes: cahiers d'action juridique* 45–46 (June 1984): 3–6. Reprinted in *Dits et écrits II, 1976–1988*, eds. Daniel Defert and François Ewald, 1507–1515. Paris: Gallimard, 1994; Paris: Gallimard, 2001.

———— "La retour de la morale." *Les nouvelles littéraires* 2937 (28 June–5 July 1984): 36. Reprinted in *Dits et écrits II, 1976–1988*, eds. Daniel Defert and François Ewald, 1515–1526. Paris: Gallimard, 1994; Paris: Gallimard, 2001.

———— "Face aux gouvernements, les droits de l'homme." *Libération* 967 (30 June–1 July 1984): 22. Reprinted in *Dits et écrits II, 1976–1988*, eds. Daniel Defert and François Ewald, 1526–1527. Paris: Gallimard, 1994; Paris: Gallimard, 2001.

———— "L'éthique du souci de soi comme pratique de la liberté." Interview with H. Becker, R. Fornet-Betancourt, and A. Gomez-Müller. *Concordia: Revista internacional de filosofia* 6 (July–December 1984): 99–116. Reprinted in *Dits et écrits II, 1976–1988*, eds. Daniel Defert and François Ewald, 1527–1548. Paris: Gallimard, 1994; Paris: Gallimard, 2001.

———— "Une esthétique de l'existence." *Le Monde* 15–16 July 1984, xi. Reprinted in *Dits et écrits II, 1976–1988*, eds. Daniel Defert and François Ewald, 1549–1554. Paris: Gallimard, 1994; Paris: Gallimard, 2001.

———— "Michel Foucault, an Interview: Sex, Power and the Politics of Identity." Interview with B. Gallagher and A. Wilson (Toronto, June 1982). *The Advocate* 400 (7 August 1984): 26–30, 58. Reprinted as "Michel Foucault, une interview: sexe, pouvoir et la politique de l'identité," in *Dits et écrits II, 1976–1988*, eds. Daniel Defert and François Ewald, 1554–1565. Paris: Gallimard, 1994; Paris: Gallimard, 2001.

———— "L'intellectuel et les pouvoirs." Interview with C. Panier and P. Watté. *La Revue nouvelle* t. LXXX, no. 10 (October 1984): 338–343. Reprinted in *Dits et écrits II, 1976–1988*, eds. Daniel Defert and François Ewald, 1566–1571. Paris: Gallimard, 1994; Paris: Gallimard, 2001.

———— "Maurice Blanchot: The Thought from Outside." In *Foucault Blanchot*, translated by Brian Massumi, 7–58. New York: Zone Books, 1990.

———— "Truth, Power, Self." In *Technologies of the Self: A Seminar with Michel Foucault*, eds. Luther H. Martin, Huck Gutman, and Patrick H. Hutton, 9–15. Amherst, MA: University of Massachusetts Press, 1988.

———— *"Il faut défendre la société": Cours au Collège de France (1975–1976)*. Paris: Gallimard Seuil, 1997.

———— *Les anormaux: Cours au Collège de France (1974–1975)*. Paris: Gallimard Seuil, 1999.

———— *Dits et écrits I, 1954–1975*. Edited by Daniel Defert and François Ewald. Paris: Gallimard, 1994; Paris: Gallimard, 2001.

———— *Dits et écrits II, 1976–1988*. Edited by Daniel Defert and François Ewald. Paris: Gallimard, 1994; Paris; Gallimard, 2001.

———— *Fearless Speech*. Edited by Joseph Pearson. New York: Semiotexte, 2001.

———— *Naissance de la clinique*. Reprint, Paris: Presses Universitaires de France, 2000.

———— *Le pouvoir psychiatrique: Cours au Collège de France (1973–1974)*. Paris: Gallimard Seuil, 2003.

Foucault, Michel, ed., *I, Pierre Rivière, having slaughtered my mother, my sister, and my brother . . .* Translated by Frank Jellinek. Paris: Gallimard, 1973; Lincoln, NE: University of Nebraska Press, 1982.

WORKS BY OTHER AUTHORS

Amiot, Michel. "Le relativisme culturaliste de Michel Foucault." *Les Temps Modernes* 248 (January 1967): 1285–1298.

Aubral, Xavier and François Delcourt. *Contre la nouvelle philosophie*. Paris: Gallimard, 1977.

Barbin, Herculine. *Herculine Barbin: Being the Recently Discovered Memoirs of a Nine-teenth-Century French Hermaphrodite*. Translated by Richard McDougall. With an introduction by Michel Foucault. Paris: Gallimard, 1978; New York: Pantheon, 1980.

Barthes, Roland. "Savoir et folie." *Critique* 174 (1961): 915–922. Reprinted as "De part et d'autre," in *Essais Critiques*, 167–174. Paris: Éditions du Seuil, 1964.

——— "Eléments de sémiologie." *Communications* 4 (1964): 91–135.

——— *Système de la mode*. Paris: Éditions du Seuil, 1967.

Baudrillard, Jean. *Le système des objets*. Paris: Gallimard, 1968.

——— *Oublier Foucault*. Paris: Éditions Galilée, 1977.

Blanchot, Maurice. *Le Très-Haut*. Paris: Gallimard, 1948.

——— *Thomas L'Obscur*. Paris: Gallimard, 1950.

——— *The Space of Literature*. Translated by Ann Smock. Paris: Gallimard, 1955; Lincoln, NE: University of Nebraska Press, 1982.

——— "L'Oubli, la déraison." *Nouvelle Revue Française* October 1961, 679–686.

Borges, Jorge Luis. "El idioma analítico de John Wilkins." *La Nación* (February 8, 1942). Reprinted as "John Wilkins' Analytical Language" in *Selected Non-Fictions*, ed. and trans., by Eliot Weinberger, 229–232. New York: Viking, 1999.

Brown, Peter. *The Making of Late Antiquity*. Cambridge, MA: Harvard University Press, 1978.

Canguilhem, Georges. *On the Normal and the Pathological*. Boston: D. Reidel, 1978.

Castel, Robert. *Le Psychanalysme*. Paris: François Maspero, 1973.

Castoriadis, Cornelius. "Les divertisseurs." *Le Nouvel Observateur* 20 June 1977, 50–51.

Courant, Gérard. *Werner Schroeter*. Paris: Goethe Institute, 1982.

Daniel, Jean. "Etre un intellectuel journaliste." *L'Arc* 70 (December 1977): 84–86.

de Sales, Francis. *L'introduction à la vie devote*. Lyon: Frères Bruyset, 1712.

Deleuze, Gilles. *Logique du Sens*. Paris: Éditions de Minuit, 1969.

——— "Ecrivain non: un nouveau cartographe." *Critique* 343 (December 1975): 1207–1227.

———— "A propos des nouveaux philosophes et d'un problème plus general." *Minuit* 24 (June 1977): n.p.

———— "Faille et feux locaux." In *L'île déserte et autres texts*. Paris: Éditions de Minuit, 2002.

Deleuze, Gilles, and Félix Guattari. *Anti-Oedipus: Capitalism and Schizophrenia*. Translated by Robert Hurley, Mark Seem, and Helen R. Lane. Paris: Éditions de Minuit, 1975; Minneapolis: University of Minnesota Press, 1983.

Devade, Marc. "Chromatic Painting: Theorem Written Through Painting." In *The Tel Quel Reader*, eds. Patrick ffrench and Roland-François Lack, 181–197. London: Routledge, 1998.

Domenach, Jean-Marie. "Le système et la personne." *Esprit* 360 (May 1967): 771–780.

Dover, K. J. *Greek Homosexuality*. Cambridge, MA: Harvard University Press, 1978.

Dreyfus, Hubert L. and Paul Rabinow. *Michel Foucault: Beyond Structuralism and Hermeneutics*, 2nd ed. Chicago: University of Chicago Press, 1983.

ffrench, Patrick, and Roland-François Lack, eds. *The Tel Quel Reader*. London: Routledge, 1998.

Fraser, Nancy. "Foucault on Modern Power: Empirical Insights and Normative Confusions." *Praxis International* 1, no. 3 (October 1981): 272–287.

Glucksmann, André. *La cuisinière et le mangeur d'hommes*. Paris: Seuil, 1975.

———— "Réponses." *Tel quel* 64 (Winter 1975): 67–73.

———— *Les maîtres penseurs*. Paris: Grasset, 1977.

Greenblatt, Stephen J. *Renaissance Self-Fashioning: From More to Shakespeare*. Chicago: University of Chicago Press, 1980.

Habermas, Jürgen. "Modernity: An Unfinished Project." In *Habermas and the Unfinished Project of Modernity: Critical Essays on the* Philosophical Discourse of Modernity, eds. Maurizio Passerin d'Entrevès and Seyla Benhabib, 38–58. Cambridge, MA: MIT Press, 1997.

Hadot, Pierre. *Exercices spirituals et philosophie antique*. Paris: Études Augustiniennes, 1981.

Jambet, Christian, and Guy Lardreau. *L'ange*. Paris: Grasset, 1976.

———— "L'ange entre Mao et Jésus." *Magazine littéraire* 112–113 (May 1976): 54–57.

Lacroix, Jean. "La fin de l'humanisme." *Le Monde* (9 June 1966). Quoted in Didier Eribon, *Michel Foucault*, 159–160. Cambridge, MA: Harvard University Press, 1991.

Le Bon, Sylvie. "Un positiviste désesperé: Michel Foucault." *Les Temps Modernes* 248 (January 1967): 1299–1319.

Lévi-Strauss, Claude. *Tristes Tropiques*. Paris: Librairie Plon, 1955.

Levinas, Emmanuel. "There Is: Existence without Existents." *Deucalion* 1 (1946): 141–154. Reprinted in *The Levinas Reader*, ed. Seán Hand, 29–36. Oxford, UK: Blackwell, 1989; Oxford: Blackwell, 1992.

Lyotard, Jean-François. *Des dispositifs pulsionnels*. Paris: Union Générale d'Editions, 1973.

Nietzsche, Friedrich. *Beyond Good and Evil*. Translated by Walter Kaufmann. New York: Random House, 1966; New York: Vintage, 1989.

——— *On the Genealogy of Morals* and *Ecce Homo*. Translated by Walter Kaufmann and R. J. Hollingdale. New York: Random House, 1967; New York: Vintage, 1989.

——— *Twilight of the Idols* and *The Anti-Christ*. Translated by R. J. Hollingdale. London: Penguin, 1968; 1990.

——— *The Gay Science*. Translated by Walter Kaufmann. New York: Vintage, 1974.

——— *The Birth of Tragedy*. Translated by Shaun Whiteside. London: Penguin, 1993.

Perrot, Michelle, ed. *L'impossible Prison: Recherches sur le système pénitentiaire au xixe siècle*. Paris: Editions du Seuil, 1980.

Rabinow, Paul, ed. *The Foucault Reader*. New York: Pantheon Books, 1984.

Ricoeur, Paul. "La structure, le mot, l'événement." *Esprit* 360 (May 1967): 801–821.

Sartre, Jean-Paul. *Nausea*. Translated by Lloyd Alexander. Paris: Gallimard, 1938; New York: New Directions, 1964.

——— *L'homme et les choses*. Paris: Seghers, 1947.

——— *Critique of Dialectical Reason*. Translated by Alan Sheridan-Smith. Vol. 1. Paris: Gallimard, 1960; New York: Verso, 2004.

——— *Search for a Method*. Translated by Hazel E. Barnes. Paris: Gallimard, 1960; New York: Vintage, 1968.

—— *Les Mots*. Paris: Gallimard, 1964.

—— "Jean-Paul Sartre répond." Interview by Bernard Pingaud. *L'Arc* 30 (October 1966): 87–96.

Sollers, Philippe. *Le Parc*. Paris: Éditions du Seuil, 1961.

—— "Logicus Solus." *Tel quel* 14 (Summer 1963): 46–50.

—— *Nombres*. Paris: Éditions du Seuil, 1968.

—— "Lois." *Tel quel* 46. (Summer 1971): 3–9.

—— "La révolution impossible." *Le Monde* (13 May 1977):

Steiner, George. "The Mandarin of the Hour: Michel Foucault." *The New York Times Book Review* (28 February 1971): 23–31.

Touraine, Alain. "Intellectuels d'en haut et intellectuels d'en bas." *L'Arc* 70 (December 1977): 87–91.

Veyne, Paul. *Comment on écrit l'histoire*. Paris: Éditions du Seuil, 1971.

—— *Le pain et le cirque: sociologie historique d'un pluralisme politique*. Paris: Éditions du Seuil, 1976.

—— *Leçon Inaugurale*. Nogent-le-Rotrou: Daupeley-Gouverneur, 1976.

—— *Comment on écrit l'histoire suivi de Foucault révolutionne l'histoire*. Paris: Éditions du Seuil, 1978.

Vincent, Jean-Marie. "Du Goulag à l'Abbaye de Vézelay." *Rouge* (6 July 1977): n.p.

Wade, S. *Chez Foucault*. Los Angeles: Circabook, 1978.

SECONDARY SOURCES

Afary, Janet, and Kevin B. Anderson. *Foucault and the Iranian Revolution*. Chicago: University of Chicago Press, 2005.

Alves da Fonseca, Marcio. *Michel Foucault e o Direito*. São Paulo: Editora Max Limonad, 2002.

Arnal, André-Pierre, et al. *Supports/Surfaces: 1966–1974*. Saint-Etienne: Musée d'art moderne Saint-Etienne, 1991.

Barker, Philip. *Michel Foucault: Subversions of the Subject*. London: Harvester Wheatsheaf, 1993.

—— *Michel Foucault: An Introduction*. Edinburgh: Edinburgh University Press, 1998.

Bernauer, James, and David Rasmussen, eds. *The Final Foucault*. Cambridge, MA: MIT Press, 1988.

Bernauer, James, and Jeremy Carrette, eds. *Michel Foucault and Theology: The Politics of Religious Experience*. Burlington, VT: Ashgate, 2004.

Bernstein, Richard J. *The New Constellation: The Ethical/Political Horizons of Modernity/Postmodernity*. Cambridge, MA: MIT Press, 1992.

Blanchet, Pierre, and Claire Brière. *Iran: la révolution au nom de Dieu*. Paris: Éditions du Seuil, 1979.

Blanchot, Maurice. "Michel Foucault as I Imagine Him." In *Foucault Blanchot*, translated by Jeffrey Mehlman, 61–109. New York: Zone Books, 1990.

Bois, Yve-Alain. "Les années supports/surfaces." *Artforum International* 37, issue 4 (December 1998): 119–120.

Bonnafous-Boucher, Maria. *Un liberalisme sans liberté: Pour une introduction du terme de 'libéralisme' dans la pensée de Michel Foucault*. Paris: L'Harmattan, 2001.

Brown, B., and M. Cousins. "The Linguistic Fault: The Case of Foucault's Archaeology." In *Michel Foucault: Critical Assessments*, vol. II, ed. Barry Smart, 186–208. London: Routledge, 1994.

Burchell, Graham, Colin Gordon, and Peter Miller, eds. *The Foucault Effect: Studies in Governmentality*. Chicago: University of Chicago Press, 1991.

Burckhardt, Jacob. *The Civilization of the Renaissance in Italy*. Translated by S. G. C. Middlemore. Kitchner, ONT: Batoche, 2001.

Carroll, David. *Paraesthetics: Foucault, Lyotard, Derrida*. New York: Methuen, 1987.

Colebrook, Claire. *Gilles Deleuze*. London: Routledge, 2002.

Cronin, Joseph. *Foucault's Antihumanist Historiography*. Lewiston, NY: The Edwin Mellen Press, 2001.

Cusset, François. *French Theory: Foucault, Derrida, Deleuze & Cie et les mutations de la vie intellectuelle aux Etats-Unis*. Paris: Découverte, 2003.

Davidson, Arnold I. "Ethics as Ascetics: Foucault, The History of Ideas, and Ancient Thought." In *The Cambridge Companion to Foucault*, ed. Gary Gutting, 115–140. Cambridge: Cambridge University Press, 1994.

———. "Introduction: Pierre Hadot and the Spiritual Phenomenon of Ancient Philosophy." In *Philosophy as a Way of Life*, ed. Pierre Hadot, 1–20. Oxford: Blackwell, 1995.

———— "Structures and Strategies of Discourse: Remarks Towards a History of Foucault's Philosophy of Language." In *Foucault and His Interlocutors*, ed. A. Davidson, 1–20. Chicago: University of Chicago Press, 1997.

Defert, Daniel. "Chronologie." In Michel Foucault, *Dits et écrits*, t. I.

Deleuze, Gilles. *Foucault.* Translated by Séan Hand. Paris: Éditions de Minuit, 1986; Minneapolis: University of Minnesota Press, 1988.

———— "Foucault and the Prison." *History of the Present*, vol. 2 (1986): 1, 2, 20–21. Reprinted in *Michel Foucault: Critical Assessments*, vol. III, ed. Barry Smart, 266–271. London: Routledge, 1994.

Detel, Wolfgang. *Macht, Moral, Wissen: Foucault und die klassische Antike.* Frankfurt am Main: Suhrkamp, 1998.

Dews, Peter. "The Return of the Subject in Late Foucault." *Radical Philosophy* 51 (Spring 1989): 37–41. Reprinted in *Michel Foucault: Critical Assessments*, vol. VI, ed. Barry Smart, 148–156. London: Routledge, 1994.

Dosse, François. *History of Structuralism*, vols. I, II. Minneapolis: University of Minnesota Press, 1997.

Elden, Stuart. *Mapping the Present: Heidegger, Foucault, and the Project of a Spatial History.* London: Continuum, 2001.

Eribon, Didier. *Michel Foucault.* Translated by Betsy Wing. Paris: Flammarion, 1989; Cambridge, MA: Harvard University Press, 1991.

Evrard, Franck. *Michel Foucault et l'histoire du sujet en Occident.* Paris: Bertrand-Lacoste, 1995.

Ewald, François. "A power without an exterior." In *Michel Foucault, Philosopher*, ed. Timothy J. Armstrong, 169–175. New York: Routledge, 1992.

Ferry, Luc, and Alain Renaut. *La pensée 68: Essai sur l'anti-humanisme contemporain.* Paris: Gallimard, 1985.

Ferry, Luc, and Jean-Didier Vincent. *Qu'est-ce que l'homme?* Paris: Odile Jacob, 2000.

ffrench, Patrick. *The Time of Theory: A History of Tel Quel (1960–1983).* Oxford, UK: Clarendon Press, 1995.

Flynn, Thomas R. "Truth and Subjectivation in the Later Foucault." *The Journal of Philosophy* 82, no. 10 (October 1985): 531–540.

———— *Sartre, Foucault, and Historical Reason.* Chicago: University of Chicago Press, 1997.

Forrest, Philippe. *Histoire de Tel quel: 1960–1982.* Paris: Editions du Seuil, 1995.

Frank, Manfred. *What Is Neo-Structuralism?* Minneapolis: University of Minnesota Press, 1989.

Furet, François. "Faut-il brûler Marx?" In *Un itinéraire intellectuel.* Paris: Calmann-Lévy, 1999.

Gane, Mike, and Terry Johnson, eds. *Foucault's New Domains.* London: Routledge, 1993.

Gauchet, Marcel. *La Révolution des droits de l'homme.* Paris: Gallimard, 1989.

Geuss, Raymond. "Kritik, Aufklärung, Genealogie." In *Michel Foucault: Zwischenbilanz einer Rezeption: Frankfurter Foucault-Konferenz 2001,* eds. Axel Honneth and Martin Saar, 145–156. Frankfurt: Suhrkamp, 2003.

Goldhill, Simon. *Foucault's Virginity: Ancient Erotic Fiction and the History of Sexuality.* Cambridge, UK: Cambridge University Press, 1995.

Gros, Frédéric, and Carlos Lévy, eds. *Foucault et la philosophie antique.* Paris: Kimé, 2003.

Gutting, Gary. *Michel Foucault's Archaeology of Scientific Reason.* Cambridge, UK: Cambridge University Press, 1989.

——— "Introduction: Michel Foucault: A User's Manual." In *The Cambridge Companion to Foucault,* ed. G. Gutting, 1–27. Cambridge, UK: Cambridge University Press, 1994.

Gutting, Gary, ed. *The Cambridge Companion to Foucault.* Cambridge, UK: Cambridge University Press, 1994.

Habermas, Jürgen. *The Philosophical Discourse of Modernity.* Translated by Frederick G. Lawrence. Frankfurt am Main: Suhrkamp, 1985; Cambridge, MA: MIT Press, 1992.

——— "Taking Aim at the Heart of the Present." In *Critique and Power,* ed. Michael Kelly, 149–156. Cambridge, MA: MIT Press, 1994.

Hacking, Ian. *The Social Construction of What?* Cambridge, MA: Harvard University Press, 1999.

——— *Historical Ontology.* Cambridge, MA: Harvard University Press, 2002.

Hadot, Pierre. *Philosophy as a Way of Life.* Oxford, UK: Blackwell, 1995.

Halperin, David. *Saint Foucault: Towards a Gay Hagiography.* New York: Oxford University Press, 1995.

Han, Béatrice. *Foucault's Critical Project: Between the Transcendental and the Historical.* Stanford, CA: Stanford University Press, 2002.

Hanssen, Beatrice. *Critique of Violence: Between Poststructuralism and Critical Theory.* London: Routledge, 2000.

Hawkes, Terence. *Structuralism and Semiotics.* London: Routledge, 1997.

Heidegger, Martin. *Being and Time.* Translated by Joan Stambaugh. Tubingen: Max Niemeyer Verlag, 1953; Albany: State University of New York Press, 1996.

Hesse, Heidrun. "'Ästhetik der Existenz': Foucaults Entdeckung des ethischen Selbstverhältnisses." In *Michel Foucault: Zwischenbilanz einer Rezeption; Frankfurter Foucault-Konferenz 2001,* eds. Axel Honneth and Martin Saar, 300–308. Frankfurt am Main: Suhrkamp, 2003.

Honneth, Axel, and Martin Saar, eds. *Michel Foucault: Zwischenbilanz einer Rezeption.* Frankfurt am Main: Suhrkamp, 2003.

Jay, Martin. *Downcast Eyes: The Denigration of Vision in Twentieth-Century French Thought.* Berkeley, CA: University of California Press, 1994.

—— *Songs of Experience: Modern American and European Variations on a Universal Theme.* Berkeley, CA: University of California Press, 2005.

Keenan, Thomas. "Foucault on Government." *Philosophy and Social Criticism* (Summer 1982), 35–40. Reprinted in *Michel Foucault: Critical Assessments,* vol. IV, ed. Barry Smart, 422–426. London: Routledge, 1995.

Kelly, Michael, ed. *Critique and Power: Recasting the Foucault/Habermas Debate.* Cambridge, MA: MIT Press, 1994.

Kendall, Gavin, and Gary Wickham. *Using Foucault's Methods.* Thousand Oaks, CA: Sage, 1999.

Kurzweil, Edith. *The Age of Structuralism: Lévi-Strauss to Foucault.* New York: Columbia University Press, 1980.

Lecourt, Dominique. *Les piètres penseurs.* Paris: Flammarion, 1999.

Leezenberg, Michiel. "Foucault on the Islamic Revolution in Iran." In *Michel Foucault and Theology: The Politics of Religious Experience,* eds. James Bernauer and Jeremy Carrette, 99–115. Burlington, VT: Ashgate, 2004.

Lévy, Bernard-Henri. "Les nouveaux philosophes." *Les nouvelles littéraires* 2536 (10 June 1976): 15–16.

—— *Barbarism with a Human Face.* Translated by George Holoch. Paris: B. Grasset, 1977; New York: Harper & Row, 1979.

Levy, Neil. *Being Up-to-Date*. New York: Peter Lang, 2001.

Lilla, Mark. "The Legitimacy of the Liberal Age." In *New French Thought: Political Philosophy*, ed. Mark Lilla, 3–34. Princeton, NJ: Princeton University Press, 1994.

――― *The Reckless Mind: Intellectuals in Politics*. New York: New York Review Books, 2001.

Lotringer, Sylvère, and Sande Cohen, eds. *French Theory in America*. London: Routledge, 2001.

Macey, David. *The Lives of Michel Foucault*. New York: Pantheon, 1993; New York: Vintage, 1995.

Mahon, Michael. *Foucault's Nietzschean Genealogy: Truth, Power, and the Subject*. Albany, NY: State University of New York Press, 1992.

Manent, Pierre. *La cité de l'homme*. Paris: Fauard, 1994.

Marx-Scouras, Danielle. "Requiem for the Postwar Years: The Rise of *Tel Quel*." *The French Review* 64, no. 3 (February 1991): 407–416.

――― *The Cultural Politics of* Tel Quel. College Park, PA: Pennsylvania State University Press, 1996.

Mauriac, Claude. *Le rire des pères dans les yeux des enfants*. Paris: Grasset, 1981.

――― *Le Temps immobile 3: Et comme l'espérance est violente*. Paris: Grasset, 1976. Quoted in Daniel Defert, "Chronologie," in *Dits et écrits I, 1954–1975*, eds. Daniel Defert and François Ewald, 13–90. Paris: Gallimard, 1994; Paris: Gallimard, 2001.

May, Todd. *Between Genealogy and Epistemology*. University Park: Pennsylvania State University Press, 1993.

Megill, Alan. *Prophets of Extremity: Nietzsche, Heidegger, Foucault, Derrida*. Berkeley, CA: University of California Press, 1985.

Milchman, Alan and Alan Rosenberg, eds. *Foucault and Heidegger: Critical Encounters*. Minneapolis: University of Minnesota Press, 2003.

Miller, James. *The Passion of Michel Foucault*. New York: Anchor, 1994.

Mills, Sara. *Michel Foucault*. Routledge Critical Thinkers. London: Routledge, 2003.

Nehamas, Alexander. *Nietzsche: Life as Literature*. Cambridge, MA: Harvard University Press, 1985.

———— *The Art of Living*. Berkeley, CA: University of California Press, 1998.

Nola, Robert, ed. *Foucault*. Portland, OR: Frank Cass, 1998.

O'Leary, Timothy. *Foucault and the Art of Ethics*. London: Continuum, 2002.

Passerin d'Entrèves, Maruzio. *Critique and Enlightenment: Michel Foucault on 'Was ist Aufklärung?'* Manchester, UK: University of Manchester, 1996.

Payne, Michael. *Reading Knowledge: An Introduction to Barthes, Foucault, and Althusser*. Malden, MA: Blackwell, 1997.

Pleynet, Marcelin. *Le plus court chemin:* De Tel *quel à* L'Infini. Paris: Gallimard, 1997.

Prado, C. G. *Starting with Foucault: An Introduction to Genealogy*. Boulder, CO: Westview Press, 1995.

Rajan, Tilottama. *Deconstruction and the Remainders of Phenomenology: Sartre, Derrida, Foucault, Baudrillard*. Stanford, CA: Stanford University Press, 2002.

Renaut, Alain. *L'ère de l'individu: contribution à une histoire de la subjectivité*. Paris: Gallimard, 1989.

Riza, Salah. *Michel Foucault: De l'archiviste au militant*. Paris: Josette Lyon, 1997.

Rosanvallon, Pierre. *Le moment Guizot*. Paris: Gallimard, 1985.

Rouse, Joseph. "Power/Knowledge." In *The Cambridge Companion to Foucault*, ed. Gary Gutting, 92–114. Cambridge, UK: Cambridge University Press, 1994.

Schmidt, James, and Thomas E. Wartenberg. "Foucault's Enlightenments: Critique, Revolution, and the Fashioning of the Self." In *Critique and Power: Recasting the Foucault/Habermas Debate*, ed. Michael Kelly, 283–314. Cambridge, MA: MIT Press, 1994.

Schuld, J. Joyce. *Foucault and Augustine*. Notre Dame, IN: University of Notre Dame Press, 2003.

Sériot, Patrick. *Structure et totalité: les origines intellectuelles du structuralisme en Europe centrale et orientale*. Paris: Presses Universitaires de France, 1999.

Shapiro, Gary. *Archaeologies of Vision: Foucault and Nietzsche on Seeing and Saying*. Chicago: University of Chicago Press, 2003.

Shumway, David R. "Genealogies of Knowledges." In *Critical Essays on Michel Foucault*, ed. Karlis Racevskis, 82–100. New York: G. K. Hall & Co, 1999.

Smart, Barry, ed. *Michel Foucault: Critical Assessments.* Vols. I–VII. London: Routledge, 1994–1995.

Starr, Peter. *Logics of Failed Revolt: French Theory after May '68.* Stanford, CA: Stanford University Press, 1995.

Stauth, Georg. "Revolution in Spiritless Times: An Essay on Michel Foucault's Enquiries into the Iranian Revolution." In *Michel Foucault: Critical Assessments,* vol. III, ed. Barry Smart, 379–401. London: Routledge, 1994.

Sturrock, John, ed. *Structuralism and Since.* Oxford, UK: Oxford University Press, 1979.

Taylor, Charles. *Sources of the Self: The Making of the Modern Identity.* Cambridge, MA: Harvard University Press, 1989.

Thibaudeau, Jean. *Mes années* Tel quel: *mémoire.* Paris: Ecriture, 1994.

Turner, Bryan S. "The Disciplines." In *Michel Foucault: Critical Assessments,* vol. IV, ed. Barry Smart, 372–387. London: Routledge, 1995.

Visker, Rudi. *Michel Foucault: Genealogy as Critique.* Translated by Chris Turner. Meppel: Boom, 1990; New York: Verso, 1995.

Index

DATE DUE			
GAYLORD			PRINTED IN U.S.A.